LIVING ENE

The Patterns & Techn

EmoTrance™

Vol. 2

Silvia Hartmann, PhD

First Edition 2004

ISBN 1 873483 74 0

Published By

Dragon Rising

Living Energy

The Patterns & Techniques Of EmoTrance Volume 2

© Silvia Hartmann, PhD 2004

ISBN 1 873483 74 0

First Edition 2004

Published by
Dragon Rising
18 Marlow Avenue
Eastbourne
East Sussex BN22 8SJ
United Kingdom
http://DragonRising.com

Printed and bound by Antony Rowe Ltd, Eastbourne

Other titles by this author:

Adventures In EFT
The Advanced Patterns Of EFT
EFT & NLP
Oceans of Energy: The Patterns & Techniques Of EmoTrance, Volume 1
Project Sanctuary
The Story Teller
Energy Healing For Animals
In Serein
For You, A Star

TABLE OF CONTENTS

Editorial Notes

In compiling this first edition of "Living Energy – The Patterns & Techniques of EmoTrance, Volume 2" it has been attempted to preserve as much of Dr Silvia Hartmann's unique style of presentation as possible. The main body of material is a direct transcript which remains essentially unedited as well as uncensored; only direct product references have been replaced.

During the lectures, occasions arose where Dr Hartmann delivered hypnotic inductions for the audience. These have been line broken so that a reader may recognise these events.

We hope that in the production of this edition we have succeeded in allowing Dr Silvia Hartmann's voice and energy to carry across from the spoken word to the written pages, so that the contact between the author and the reader is preserved.

The Editorial Team,

Dragon Rising Publishing

January 2004

Acknowledgements

We thank the following for their support in developing this material.

The primary research team:

Nicola Quinn

Derek McCarthy

Steve Collins

Also acknowledged are:

Alex Kent

Ananga Sivyer

The Heros Team

The Users, Practitioners & Trainers of EmoTrance

& The Contributors From The MindMillion Group

Welcome To "Living Energy" By Silvia Hartmann

Dear reader,

I would like to welcome you personally to "Living Energy – The Patterns of EmoTrance, Volume 2".

This is by no means an academic, "last word on the subject" kind of book, but instead, a diary of events of what has happened with the energy system called EmoTrance since we first began working in this way with human experiences 18 months ago.

Really, and of course, my own personal research and odyssey has been going on for much longer than this. EmoTrance is a vehicle which allows me to unify and present some of my findings and results, and much more than that, it **is in and of itself** a research tool, firstly and fore mostly.

It is in the using of EmoTrance and its principles, and the reality feedback we derive, the understandings we glean and the experiences we have that we learn new things about the world, about ourselves and how things work - **ONE PERSON AT A TIME**.

There is no bus scheduled to go to the Holy Land.

Each one of us has to find their own way, and that is absolutely my experience. But that does NOT mean we have to do it all alone, or that there can't be help – only this help has to be **ABSOLUTELY systemic** in all ways.

It has to be based on each individual's experiences, their own truths, their own observations, their own life, else it is totally meaningless.

What I am trying to do with my work is to resolve things for **myself** and in doing that, **role modelling a single individual's quest for human actualisation.**

This may be in and of itself more useful than trying to tell other people what to do or how to solve their problems, but either way, it offers the opportunity for others to watch what I do with interest and then, **compare** my ideas to their own experiences.

We are all of a basic model and have things in common; I call this the Venn diagram, when problems or solutions match or are similar, not just between a bunch of Westerners, but also have resonances across the ages too and regardless of whether it was a problem written up by William Shakespeare, or an attempted solution by a Chinese meridian specialist 6000 years ago, or the words of a prophet.

Chances are therefore that some of the things that I have been thinking about, working with, experimenting with, trying out and generally tinkering with have a resonance for you also, but the proof is in our own experiences, one person at a time, one life at a time.

Trails Of Techniques

This book therefore contains, in a non-linear fashion, some of the exercises, techniques and developments from the Universe from which EmoTrance originated.

Now, what you must understand is that I do this all the time, and I literally do nothing else – I am indeed attempting to be **living energy** and the principles all the time and without omission.

I am doing this not whilst sitting on a mountain top or in a monastery – it is just too easy to do that, step out of the world that men have created and thus attain an illusion of enlightenment which is worth **nothing** at the end of the day. Anyone can be enlightened when there aren't any challenges at all and only perfect sunsets and sunrises to soothe the soul!

I am living as a typical Westerner with family, in a real house, in a real street and in a real town; I have credit cards, mortgages, taxes to pay and I am trying to do all of that **from the living energy principles**. That is not easy but at the end of the day, it is more exciting than just sitting around in a beautiful place, and it is one hell of a lot more **real**.

It offers so many opportunities and challenges with their requisite learnings that a traditional monk would go green with envy and I believe it is important that the greater Universe should be merged with the people created world, rather than having to choose one, or the other.

This is the deal.

There really is a greater truth.

There really is a creative order to things, and we humans really are a part of it.

This creative order has the answer to all our problems – and not just the answer to esoteric ones, but even to problems such as how to pay the bills, what to do about a love affair that is driving you insane, or how to decorate your sitting room.

From the sublime to the ridiculous, from a decent physics theory via a sound maths equation and to everlasting life, it is **all there in the creative order** and **totally available to each one of us** – that is my belief, that is my personal truth, and I'm using my life to prove this.

You could say, I'm staking my incarnation on it.

My money, my health, my family, my children and my karma – everything.

I'm no guru. I'm no genius and I'm no great teacher. No angel came down and gave me some sort of holy mission. I'm only a middle aged woman in a little house, but I am **trying**.

If I can at least try, so can you. So can anyone who wants to make a difference for themselves.

The patterns, ideas, thoughts, techniques and so forth in this book are just the tip of my own iceberg – what I am hoping this will do for you is to stimulate and encourage you to get on with **YOUR** incarnation and resolve **YOUR** own challenges, to **YOUR** satisfaction.

Essays & Transcripts

So much has happened over the past 18 months, it would be impossible for me to write it all down. You start working with flow and in a Universe of living energy, and understandings and insights simply start to cascade!

For this reason I have decided to give a special two day lecture about the main aspects of our discoveries and use a transcript of this lecture as the basis of this book.

This transcript is supported by a number of essays and articles I wrote in that 18 month period interval between EmoTrance 1 (which is outlined in the manual, Oceans Of Energy) and this new material up until this point.

I really want you to understand that this book is not about the techniques or patterns, but about **the world from which they came** – that place of living energy which once we open up to it, literally blows us away with ideas, possibilities, options and represents **an opening to new ways of being** on every level.

Before I go, I would like to say something about the title of the book.

Living Energy means two things. The first meaning is obvious – we are living in a Universe of living energy, where everything, but absolutely everything is alive and in constant flow. We forget this with our human made structures of limitations sometimes, but it is true. The world – your world and mine! – is **vibrantly alive and it is dancing**. It is so incredible, so rich and so beautiful that words fail entirely and no matter what, if we tune into **that** ever so slightly, how could we ever be angry, or sad?

But more importantly, Living Energy is about – LIVING the principles of the real, true Universe.

Every day.

All the time.

While we work, sleep, play, make love – always and without exceptions.

Contrary to public opinion, the principles of the one true Universe and the creative order are **not** incompatible with "Constructville" or in other words, the societies, worlds, illusions and lives that **people** have constructed for themselves (badly) through the ages.

Indeed, the principles of living energy, once they are understood, are the **solutions** to every conceivable problem and make **living in Constructville easier** just as well as they make everything else more easy, more joyous and more right – because they **are right** and true.

They work.

It is as simple as that.

Living Energy really means that "getting into the flow", "contacting the creative order" and "being your true self" **DOES NOT STOP WHEN YOU GO BACK TO WORK**.

IT MUST NOT BE CONTAINED TO WEEKEND WORKSHOPS AND SPECIAL TIMES OF MEDITATION.

It has to be with us all the time to be able to work its magic, for us to live in creative flow and in harmony with ourselves and all things.

All the time. Even when you are talking to an accountant or a bank manager!

That is the message, that is what I have learned in the past 18 months, and this has truly changed my life. I am sincerely hoping that some who will read this book will be inspired and try it for themselves. Perhaps to begin with, in a small way – little experiments to get their feet wet in the real, true living Universe to help convince themselves of what is right for THEM.

Should that be the case, I will be delighted and know that I've done my bit to bring about true change.

And so ...

I would like to begin with an article that bridges between EmoTrance 1 and the new material, namely a report on a practitioner training I gave in September 2003 in Germany.

Then we will go into the transcript of the Eastbourne EmoTrance Level 2 & 3 presentations; and the rest of the book consists of supporting articles and essays, as well as a round up of the techniques discussed.

I sincerely hope you enjoy the ideas expressed here; I encourage you with all your heart to try out at least some of the exercises and wish you the very best on your own journey, on your own explorations.

Silvia Hartmann

January 2004

Preface: A Special EmoTrance Practitioner Training

The morning dawned happily and I made my way to teach what was actually my first ever personal practitioner training for EmoTrance, in German to a group of 32 people who ranged from those who hadn't even really heard of EFT, or TFT for that matter (!) to some who had specially come in for this training and were pretty up to date with energy therapies already.

But after what had happened on the preceding days and people's responses to my ideas and presentations, I was really looking forward to letting the participants interact with EmoTrance - that would tell its own story much, much better than anything I'd be talking about ever could.

I am entirely aware that you can't talk about ET and ever begin to understand it, you really do have to do it, FEEL IT, really experience what it does and how it affects you and your partners in the exercises in order to have some idea of what an interesting and expanding techniques set this actually is.

I am also aware that working as directly and as intensively with energy and the body as ET does is experienced as really quite exhausting by the participants. A key element of ET trainings are the experiential exercises and the fact is, when someone has just directly worked with some thing in their energy system which has been causing them major grief for many, many years and the whole thing re-organised itself on all these different levels, they are NOT then afterwards in any state to be assimilating long lectures, statistics or anything really that I would want them to remember after the training was over. That's a light challenge for the trainers of course, but you just have to know it and account for it, by giving people plenty of time after the exercises to go into a break, get a drink, walk in the gardens (if any) and generally, come back to themselves BEFORE we start with more theory and explanations.

So, an ET practitioner training is a very, very practical thing, very experiential, and all the exercises are set up to directly teach the participants something that they will then know, totally integrate and always remember, because they have done it and now KNOW it rather than just to have heard about it and know ABOUT it.

As the translation of the practitioner manual was - a little strange to my eyes, shall we say, and as I had not thought to bring an English practitioner manual or, for that matter, a proper trainer's manual with me, the bizarre occasion arose that I had actually no idea what I had originally designed for this training. That was over a year ago and the Lord alone knows why I didn't think to bring a trainer's manual - at any rate, I didn't and so just decided to teach the group as it would come naturally to me, and in response to their experiences, letting us as a unit set the progression of the training in a very free-flowing format.

That was a neat thing indeed and it led directly to me coming up with a whole new set of exercises for this group and a different order and sequence than normal.

The very first exercise in my original set-up (although not all ET trainers follow this for their own various reasons) is to play the "Insult Game" with a practice partner.

Hereby, one of the partners gets to choose an insult which has been a source of annoyance or pain for them and which is guaranteed to produce a strong physiological response. Let's say as an example that for this person it would be, "You're a fat pig!", an unfortunate left-over from long gone school days and an "energetic injury" which has never been properly healed.

The person then coaches their partner in just how to throw that insult at them; the partner does this, the kinaesthetic response is triggered and the most basic of all ET protocols then runs its course, and as this is happening, both partners are learning about the pathways, the softening and flowing, the "it's only an energy" directive, and most importantly, they both get to learn what exactly happens when it all flows smoothly and the flip into the "energised end state" has occurred - when the former insult just creates a rush of energised, bright sensation and the person is laughing, clapping their hands and dancing with joy.

This is a simple and basic exercise which covers so many things and this group really went for it; insulting folk is actually quite good fun in and of itself and everyone gave it a good old go.

In a way, this group was great because they were so very innocent in working with the energy body directly; most of these people really didn't ever do much work with this kind of thing before and they were simply delighted how easy it was, and how good it felt.

Lots of people commented on how revolutionary a concept it was that one should feel so good and so alive afterwards; like most others, they were just used to looking for a cessation of pain into just "peace" or such and had not experienced that other dimension when it actually flips into the "My God, I can fell GREAT!!" scale which exists on the other side of peace.

After this first exercise, they were really up for things and rearing to go. Some of them were a little over-eager and wanted to do and know EVERYTHING there and then, resented the long breaks and such - but that's ok, it was only 11am by now and we still had HOURS to go before the first training day concluded at 6pm.

And a lot more to learn.

In the question and answer session after the first exercise, shields came up very strongly and rather than deferring this to a later date, I decided to go straight into shields because they were there with us, and set a whole new shields exercise which came to me on the spur of the moment.

Rather than trying to guess for something or hoping shields would come up on some topic naturally for everyone, I decided to simply go for something that each participant already KNEW they lacked connection to - just some topic, idea, thing, person, anything at all they felt as though there was a barrier between them and it.

Their practise partner would just stand by and help out as and when required as they together explored what shielding existed between the active partner and their topic of choice; I suggested they might try something like computers if they felt they had little or no connection to those, just as an example of what I meant by this.

This was a totally fascinating exercise for me in every way imaginable; I'd never done this or even seen it done before, and to be able to walk amongst these practice groups and to observe what they were doing with it was just - blissfully interesting, is all I can say.

One lady had decided she wanted to overcome her disconnection from "maps".

I couldn't help but raise both eyebrows at this and asked to explain it a little further, and she said that she just couldn't make any sense of maps - all kinds of maps, road maps for one thing, but also operating instructions when you have to build a cupboard or such, or even further, instructions for an exercise.

"Aha," I said, putting on my NLP hat for a moment, "so you mean **maps in their widest possible metaphorical sense**?"

She nodded seriously and so her set began. She said there was a shield between her and the "map" - full body size, at least three hand spans thick and it made it impossible to read the symbols on the other side! (I couldn't help but think "dyslexia" ??? most strongly at that point - the energetic shield wavered and distorted what was behind it so it could not be **seen clearly**.).

When she had gone through the routine of letting a little energy in to find injuries and disturbances which need to be repaired before a shield can be dissolved (and a considerable erea of injury had been found and restored near the centre of her body), she gave the command to dissolve the entire shield and just shouted out aloud, "Oh my, oh my, it's like roads, roads streaming into me! Blue roads!!!" and at the same time, I had the feeling I myself was standing under an electric shower, the shift was so strong and noticeable. At the very same time and before she had even shouted about the roads, three or four people from other groups were turning around and looking over to her curiously - these people had felt HER energy shift all across the room! It was way, way cool and we hugged briefly (couldn't help it, it was just - called for!) and we both agreed that we didn't need to know what the "roads" were about but that it was just simply wonderful. I sent her off to walk in the garden and think her own thing for a while and went to observe further.

One practice team really, really made me laugh. The active partner felt very disconnected from their clients and had immediately seen that there was a big wall straight in front of them (a big shield) with the clients on the other side.

What was funny about this was that the helper was standing directly opposite them - and THEY were thus on the other side of that self same huge shield, and strangely (!!) were thus "not getting through" to their partner. I made them move and stand shoulder to shoulder with the active partner and boy, did that make a difference! First comment from the active partner, the owner of the shield was, "Oh I feel as though I have some support from someone else at last!" The helper could now understand the nature of the shield and help to dissolve it after the injuries had been repaired, and I thought how neat that was, and further, how often people are in such situations and not just in therapy. Perhaps just standing shoulder-to-shoulder with someone rather than facing them squarely on and running right into their existing shields can be a useful manoeuvre, whether you're an EmoTrance practitioner or not ...

Someone used the exercise to "drop shields" to a relative, another used it to re-connect themselves to the subject of numbers and mathematics and a truly fine and exciting time was had by all.

And of course, the basics of shield work had thoroughly been learned without anyone actually noticing this because they were way too caught up inside the unfoldment of the actual experiences.

Going back to that "dyslexia" idea with the lady who couldn't see the symbols of her maps properly because of the distortion of the shield, it was really noticeable in this large group that people did say over and over again some key things. Now these people were very different in age, background, nationality and experience, yet they used the same phrases time and time again. In this shields exercise for example, they said that "the colours became brighter", "everything was more clearly defined", "things became more 3 dimensional", and later on in the training, people commented that it was as though "people themselves became more real somehow".

It was truly exciting to me to see this in action and I really couldn't help but muse and wonder about disassociation in general, about people in particular feeling lonely behind their shields and being unable to connect to each other, simply because there are these shields in the way.

One further interesting note on the shields front. One participant did not have a classic StarTrek shield of a certain thickness and consistency but instead, the entire space in which his consciousness and the "other" existed was filled with mist, thick white mist which made it virtually impossible to make out any details about the other or to relate to it. This participant also talked about being lost a lot, and being confused which this state of energetic occurrence would naturally engender. When this mist was cleared and they could "see clearly" again, a relationship with the other sprang into being quite naturally and this was an amazing moment to witness and to feel for me.

It is an extraordinary thing, in a way. Here I am inventing this stuff, I write it up and mostly forget about it then and move onto the next challenge. But to actually be there and EXPERIENCE people's responses to the various EmoTrance exercises was profoundly moving, and newly so each time I was witness to this.

After the shields exercises and some more feedback and a little gentle reminder and wrap up session, there was a break and then it was time for abreaction city.

The fun thing is that we do the insults first and the **positive statements** much later in ET trainings because it is NOT the insults which cause people to burst out into tears on the spot, but actually when you tell them they are beautiful, or that they have a right to be here on this planet, or that you love them.

It is extraordinary but absolutely true that it is those kinds of statements, energies and the words which carry these energies which an individual has desperately longed to hear ALL their lives (but never did) show up the worst ereas of injuries and devastation in the energy body. New ET Trainers are given to arguing that it surely would be better to start with the positives and work round to the nasty negatives a bit later but anyone who has ever actually done this with clients or groups KNOWS that it is a very global thing indeed - a general occurrence and event for at least the 1st World Westerners we have in our trainings.

Love brings them to their knees like nothing else can.

Some brief glimpses of what happened during this exercise and which have staid with me.

I always instruct people in trainings to find a new and different practice partner each time, and to deliberately choose someone they might not normally be wanting to deal with, to extend their flexibility and to understand how very STRUCTURAL EmoTrance actually is. That it really doesn't matter if your partner is a small African lady or a big grim looking older man, as long as they're human and they really want to play, EmoTrance will work.

One lady therefore chose deliberately to pair herself up for this exercise with a second lady she didn't know, but who had deeply annoyed her earlier in the morning by her conduct in the restaurant. This second lady had not even noticed her there because she had been "bitching at the checkout person" for some considerable time and the first was just behind her in the queue.

So imagine her surprise when the second lady, the one who had bitched in the cafeteria, expressed her desire for her practice partner to say to her, "You are a really likeable person!"

It was not until AFTER the work was completed that the practice partner revealed herself and her reasons for her choice of practice partner, and they got on really well and between them made some superb magic on that day. Ah, energy, synchronicity, being in the right place at the right time - it's wonderful, really, when you just sit back and look at it!

I saw a pair working on having a lady accept "You are the most attractive woman I have ever seen!" and once again, shivers went all through me as I watched and felt them do it.

A gentleman who had asked for, "You are a good teacher." ended up curled up on the floor and had to be lovingly helped by two partners to straighten out his energy system. Following the intervention he had finally some colour to his face - he had looked like a ghost, pale and drawn, all the time before and it was wonderful to observe the change.

This reminds me of something else I noted time and time again - namely that people actually and literally "came to life" during these exercises. Before, they stood pale and still, rigid throughout, and after, there was high colour in their faces, and there was MOVEMENT in their bodies, necks, feet, faces - wonderful! And highly noticeable, of course, to everyone who was watching. We didn't have to "trust our intuition" or hope for the best, you could really SEE and FEEL how increased energy flow throughout the energy body really wakes folk up, gives them a spark, gives them new energy and makes them so much more lively and alive. And that is infectious. Even I couldn't help but do little dances and hug people now and then, and that is saying something about me ...

We did a couple more exercises and people had now begun to get the hang of it. They were no longer talking about heart chakras or trying to re-phrase or lead the interventions; they were beginning to do this new thing rather than what they had come with and that was great as well to see as the day progressed. It was an indication to me that they were beginning to trust the underlying processes.

I had already decided that I was going to massively diverge from the standard practitioner programme with this group and basically, conclude all the ET1 level stuff by lunchtime the next day at the latest, so that I would have time to have them play with some of the new material.

This was partially because they were working so hard and were so extremely easy to teach; I had more time than with previous groups and of course, basic EmoTrance isn't exactly brain surgery and very easy to learn once you have decided that you actually want to learn it. But it was also because I had the thought in the back of my mind that they would not have access to the general English speaking resources of the websites, add on protocols and SFI group and might not have another chance at an ET training for the foreseeable future.

So with a very happy group and a blown-away presenter, we went into the evening fun activities before the second and last day of this extraordinary training.

EmoTrance Training - Day Two

The morning of the second day, I had decided to make a point of the fact that in ET, **everything** is really and truly, **JUST AN ENERGY**. That I'm not joking when I say this; that when I talk about emotional energies being simply injuries in the energy body this actually encompasses all and everything under the topic, no matter how horrendous, how old, how hard or how painful it was or still is.

For this purpose, I chose two exercises, namely "The Deepest, Darkest Secret" and "The Oldest Burden".

The EmoTrance Confession

EmoTrance can be run with "content unknown".

This means that the partner, helper or practitioner need not know what the topic of the intervention or problem is; imagine this as the equivalent of someone coming to the doctor's with a big hole in their stomach, and it is not really relevant how that got to be there, or who actually took a chunk out of this person, or whether it was the person's own fault that they now have this injury and so on and so forth - what I tend to say is that, "We're dealing with these energetic injuries like you would deal with a hole in a sock. Look, there's a sock. It's got a hole in it. We mend it. End of story."

This is a very, very essential component of EmoTrance and what that does is to take both the practitioner and the owner of the injury into this other mindspace where things are clear and logical and incredibly easy to resolve, because you just don't get involved with what it means, whether it is a karma thing, what the lessons are, whose fault it is, how horrible it all is and so on and so forth which kept people in therapy for a lifetime.

So, and to demonstrate these three components, namely:

1. No-one ever needs to know where the injury came from or "what it means" (content unknown) and the problem can be perfectly well resolved in all ways;

2. We don't need to talk **about the problem** in order to resolve the problem (clear mind space of simple structural repair work); and

3. It doesn't matter how "bad" something is or how old, it is **ONLY AN ENERGY** and energy can be moved with consciousness in quantum time, easily, and just for the asking, ...

... I chose the "Deepest, Darkest Secret".

On the Heart Healing HypnoDreams album, there is a journey/process in which one gives things one doesn't need to carry any longer to the universal ocean, and the words are:

"The ocean is enormous,

and it will with gladness take all you have to give -

even your deepest, darkest secrets,

those things you thought could never be revealed,

you could not tell another or yourself,

and which pressed the breath from your lungs,

and the bright star of hope from your eyes."

(excerpt from Ocean Wood - Heart Healing HypnoDreams 2)

In EmoTrance, we really do return things to the ubiquitous universal "oceans of energy" and they are indeed enormous, and carrying secrets in the energy body is one of those things I've noted which can and do cause the most horrendous disturbances; to release these is a huge, huge relief all around.

When the group came back from this exercise, they were different.

Quieter, much more thoughtful. I think what happened was that they were beginning to appreciate the depth and power of working with energy in this way; the day before we did have a lot of good fun and there, it seems to be this easy, happy little thing, but this exercise and the one to follow, "The Oldest Burden", really do show up how very structural ET is and that there is, in short, **no problem at all that is too hard, too heavy or immune** to this way of working. I understand that this makes one rather thoughtful as a great many ideas one might have had about healing and even about oneself and what it takes to heal or to make changes has been so very practically challenged.

For the "oldest burden" exercise I have a story which really did amaze me. The day before, one of the participants asked if they could have a word with me and they told me the following (all details have been changed for confidentiality).

This gentleman had a son who had died of AIDS some two years previously. The son had been 21 years old when this happened, and the gentleman in question, let's call him Tony, was in a process of systemic collapse. His energy system was folding in on itself; that's the best I can describe it; and the symptoms and occurrences he told me about reminded me strongly of what has been observed in "The Dying Process", a paper written by a hospice nurse[1] to explain what happens in very regular and systemic stages when a person is in a hospice and dying. In his quest to help his son, Tony had gone, like so many, to the end of the available allopathic remedies and treatments, and then in desperation turned to the holistic and esoteric fields of human healing because there was nothing else left to do.

This is why he was at this energy therapies conference; this is why he now was sitting in a cafe with me and telling me these things, how he couldn't sleep anymore, had no energy left for his wife, his other children, his clients at work, and how he had these terrible stabbing pains in the area of his testicles which would spread all through his abdomen and were so excruciating that he was then literally on the floor, crying out in pain.

---

[1] The Dying Process is available from http://sidereus.org

Needless to say, the doctors couldn't find "anything wrong" physically and had now referred him to a psychiatrist; he told me that he knew full well that it wasn't physical, but he had to go through the motions for his wife's sake who was of course terribly upset too and after losing the son, was terrified she was going to lose him as well. He further told me that he thought the son had died "on his behalf", that he had died for his father, in his place.

I did what I could for him in the cafe and now, back in the training, the participants are doing "The Oldest Burden" exercise and there is Tony, as I'm making the rounds, and his two practice partners, a very young lady and a nice older lady, both kinesiologists with little or no psychology experience, working on his abdominal area.

"Bloody hell," I thought, "He's really done it - he's really given them THAT for this exercise! Wow!" and so I went over to the group and asked the older lady who was the "observer" in the team at that time, "Well, how's it going?"

The lady looked up from her notepad, smiled brightly and said all cheerfully, "Oooh, that was a bit of a tricky one, but it's getting there - halfway up the stomach now, it's starting to flow!"

And I thought, "And you have NO IDEA of the severity of what that was, what that was about, and thank the Lord you didn't because if you did, you would have been - well, probably petrified would be a good word for it!"

I made a point of having a quick word with Tony in the next available break, and what he said was this: "Something unlocked today, something - unhooked and it has changed. I feel hope for the first time - oh, since long before my son died. Hope that there is some reason for being here, and hope that I can now turn this around. Do something useful so that he didn't die for nothing."

Personally I am not given to making any predictions or promises of healing; I don't even allow myself to consider that, not in my work nor with myself, but if there was any hope at all for Tony to make it to 80 years of age then I would have thought that working this directly with the energy body, resolving these things from the energy body up like we do, is about the most gentle and best bet we have at this time, and that was worth a lot to me.

Re-Defining Psychosomatic Disease

As a result of this, I also told the group when we came back from these exercises and the much needed breaks afterwards, that I would like to officially announce that I am no longer going to use the phrase or concept of psychosomatic or neurosomatic illness, but that I consider these to be simply emotions now, and that would bring those kind of "physical pains without a seemingly physical origin" right into the brief of EmoTrance treatments.

I believe that this re-definition of psychosomatics as being simply the highest end class of emotions will not just help those who are treating these to have a much clearer idea of what they are dealing with, and HOW to deal with these, at that, but also that people who are experiencing the pain of these high end emotions can then understand THEMSELVES better and no longer need to feel that they are mad, or having some sort of aberration going on there.

This is particularly important to me. Feeling intense and disabling pain in the absence of a physical cause is thereby strictly systemic, normal and absolutely what one would expect with the highest end injuries in the energy system and how these warning signals progress if left untreated.

Size and State Of The Human Energy System

I would like to return now briefly to my observation about Tony and that his energy system was "collapsing in on itself" as well as my noting that his processes were remarkably similar, if not the same, as what had been observed by the hospice nurse in "The Dying Process".

A set of exercise which are amongst my favourites in EmoTrance revolve around the concept as how you can turn those miserable things I've never liked, namely "affirmations", into a powerful "evocation" of that form of energy or change which is required (Zaubersprueche!).

Very simply put, if someone believes themselves to be unlovable, and they look into a mirror and say, "I am lovable", they're not doing themselves any good but instead, experience emotional pain AGAIN - because the reason they thought that they were unlovable in the first place is most likely a blockage or energetic injury somewhere in their systems and when something of the right frequency (such as an affirmation!) hits that injury, IT HURTS SOME MORE and really, doesn't do any good at all. Very rarely and entirely by accident, SOME affirmations work but the majority of them don't, or at least not until and unless some serious other work has been done somehow else; rest of the time, it causes even more pain and depression. I'd been observing this for 20 years and more and got the point where when someone said, "Affirmation" I would spit fire in response, instantly.

Shamanic Energy Evocations

With EmoTrance what you do is to say or evoke the energy form you want, for example, "I am a superb lover." Then you note where that HURTS when you say it aloud or even think it; you heal that, and then you when you say it again and those energies rush through and out clearly, you really get a sense of what it was that you were trying to evoke and you FEEL the shift, feel the difference the evocation has created with you and for you.

This group decided mostly to do animals for this exercise - shamanic energy evocation of the ESSENCE of an eagle, a tiger, an elephant, a dolphin and so forth.

This is a little unusual for this exercise; I think someone started with animals and then everyone else thought, yeah that's cool, I always wanted to evoke "the stallion within" and did the same; but I was really glad it happened because there was a very, very interesting aspect to this I became aware of after the third person said exactly the same thing.

They all reported that their sense of their energy field **expanded massively** when they tuned into being these animals.

For example:

"I decided to evoke being an eagle. I had a blockage in my throat and then found another near the top of my stomach. When that dissolved, my vision became sharper and I could feel myself expanding hugely, I had this sense of being so big and so high, so very powerful."

Or this one:

"I used, I am an elephant. I was really surprised, I always thought elephants were kind of lumbering and slow. But wow, when I had cleared a blockage in my head and neck, I felt this amazing sense of expansion, and physical power - I felt so strong and so alive!"

Now, eagles are considerably SMALLER than human beings, so why would the experience of an eagle's energy system lead a person to feel their energy field expanding?

Unless - people's energy systems are drawn in unnaturally?

Unless - and this was indeed a very frightening thought! - they are in that process of collapse that I had observed in Tony?!

Not as fast or catastrophic as in his case, but actually and practically, doing the "dying process" over a longer period of time? Might that lead to the proverbial "grey men, leading lives of quiet desperation"?

I was most intrigued by that thought and what it also did was to bring to the fore once more how IMPORTANT working with the energy system directly might be for long term health and longevity even, if you want.

It may well be so that even we who are working with the human energy systems every day are still really seriously underestimating the importance of it as the very BASIS FOR HUMAN LIFE altogether. That we still may live in the old construct entrainments where there never was such a thing as an energy system, or that playing around with that said energy system is something you do "after all else has failed", if you have nothing better to do or if you're bored at the weekend.

It is certainly a fascinating supposition and one that would behoove us all to take a good long look at; and especially in the context of what one might DO in order to reverse this slow collapse and put things to rights.

Living Energy

And now, to a personal highlight of this training for me - very personal and very, very important indeed.

Following Richard Bandler's failed court cases to try and claim ownership of NLP back (which he indeed had invented!) I was advised when I invented EmoTrance to make sure that everyone I train signs a document which clearly states that they didn't invent it, and that I was not passing over the name into their ownership but just renting it out for the duration of the practitioner/trainer's license.

This is a legal document of some two pages and it has caused havoc ever since we had it during EmoTrance trainings because people simply freak out when faced with such a thing, refuse to sign it, demand to know what every paragraph means and generally go into a cataclysm of fear, distrust and God alone knows what kinds of "psychological reversal".

Well, so here I'm doing this training and it is going so beautifully, flowing so beautifully, the whole group bonding lovingly and people really connecting with each other, and in the lunch break of the second day, these documents come out for the group to sign, and the usual freakouts occur on the spot.

Only this time, I'm standing there and I'm seeing this thing energetically. And what I'm seeing is the pleasant blue green flow of the ET training, and the legal documents are like a sharp, nasty black evilness with spikes coming out of it - *they don't belong here.*

I remember thinking this very clearly, "They don't belong here."

So, and as I indeed am the inventor and owner of EmoTrance, I held up my hand and said to the group, "Right. That does it. I've had all I can take of this nonsense.

"These stupid legal documents do NOT belong into one of my trainings. They are energetically incompatible and are producing a disturbance in the flow that is entirely unnecessary.

"Either I believe in energy, or I don't.

"I cannot stand here and tell you people about EmoTrance and energy and the Even Flow, and then hand out this energetic shrapnel, not for one moment longer.

"From this day forth, we're going to do without these. I'm going to instruct The Sidereus Foundation accordingly and have all the trainers informed as soon as I'm back home tomorrow, that's the end of it, once and for all.

"So if you please, ladies and gentlemen, rip up those contracts, right now, and throw them away.

"I cannot be preaching energy, I must be living energy. I can't do anything else, and I won't."

After this impassioned outburst, the group was a little speechless at first. Then they took the contracts, ripped them up and spontaneously burst out into applause which turned into a standing ovation - LOL! A wonderful moment actually, and a conscious watershed for me.

Unlike a great many people I've met, I am LIVING what I learn and what I teach at every way. It is entirely REAL to me and energy does not stop for "the real world" with legal documents and such.

If some idiot comes along and "steals" the name (or attempts this) then I'll make something else, find an ENERGETICALLY CORRECT solution for the problem. Seriously, court cases over "ownership" of a term are for constructs and I won't have anything to do with that. Other than feeling sorry for people who consider themselves so entirely resourceless that they have to steal other people's work and try and pretend it's their own. Perhaps they did an ET evocation on "I'm a mangy half starved coyote" or such. Who can know.

But I believe in energy work absolutely and it was quite wonderful for me personally to really have to opportunity to understand this, and to make a stand for myself and in myself for energy work and my belief in it.

Magical, that was, and very healing and re-aligning.

The Rainbow Connection Exercise

So, and in the terms of the training, as I'd said, by lunchtime we were finished with the ET practitioner programme and now it was time to play a little with the new techniques, with the stuff that is basically outside the skin barrier and thereby, perceived differently.

For a basic and first introduction to working with ereas outside the physical body, I choose the Rainbow Connection, an energetic polarity/parts integration device that has simply wonderfully noticeable effects on people's physicalities, their states and their conscious awareness/thought; and as the Level 2 equivalent of the "Oldest Burden" carried inside the body, "The Shadow" exercise.

Hereby what we do is to take a "something" that exists in the energy field and of which its owner has been entirely aware for a long time, possibly their entire conscious lives, and which is functionally a major disturbance in the wider energy field, hence the name, "The Shadow". Following the usual precepts of EmoTrance, this is then systemically explored and released and Even Flow is being brought to those ereas of the energy body which are linked into that particular wider system.

One lady I observed had a life-long problem with something that turned out to be a permission issue - it was as though there were parts in her energy system where she was not allowed to go, or know about, or have contact with. This was a most profoundly interesting experience and the lady in question was literally (and very physically!) reeling as she needed to find a whole new balance all around. When she did, I can only say that I was most impressed with the changes, indeed.

I also gave the group as a bonus and gift from me to them for all their honest attention and hard work over the two days a short overview of Project Energy[2], a true multi-purpose energetic alignment device for use in business, family therapy and other systems where more than one component needs to be working and function within a "group flow system". They enjoyed this quite a bit, as I did talking about this - it's one of my favourite patterns of 2003 (so far :-) and very, very magical.

I also made a quick mention of Thought Flow, and then invited the group to join me for a Heart Healing session.

This was very interesting. As you probably know, I'm a General Semanticist and also a long term NLPer and hypnotist, so as soon as I started on the words to the basic Heart Healing invocation in German I became aware that I wasn't doing this right to be speaking it TO them; what would have happened was that they would have gone away thinking that **I** was healing their hearts!

This of course leads to the totally wrong conclusions and also, "Guru disturbances" of which I am acutely aware and highly allergic to; so I stopped everything immediately and explained that the core, very deepest core of what I do is to bring people online so they get to step into THEIR OWN HEALING POWERS and use those to grow stronger

---

[2] Project Energy is a development from the MindMillion project, and is available as a special training from http://starfields.org

from within THEMSELVES, rather than leaving this to another outside of themselves.

So, instead, what I did was to speak a single line, and then having the group repeat the single line in the Heart Healing posture[3], much like you would do on an oath or pledge of allegiance. That gave me the time to phrase it right and to make sure that the right ENERGY AND INTENTION was present.

I don't remember the exact words and of course, they were in German, but it went something like this.

These are MY healing hands.

(Group repeats gestures and words - These are MY healing hands.)

I place MY OWN healing hands on MY OWN dear heart.

With all my love, it is my full intention

to make right what once went wrong,

to make whole what once was broken,

with all my love and all my power,

I nourish and awaken

my dear beloved heart.

That was absolutely amazing, absolutely magical as the group spoke these words and the energy in the room was just totally wonderful, is all I can say. Holy, even, and in this format it was right - all these people there and each was an individual, adding their own individuality to the time and place, and knew they were.

I was most satisfied with this and so, we finished up with a Q&A session, and the training was indeed, complete.

---

[3] See "Heart Healing" in Addendum 2, Articles (p284)

Thoughts and Further Developments

Personally, I had not actually conducted an ET training since the first one in Kensington last year and had had no plans whatsoever to ever do that again - this was and is the reason I only do a limited amount of trainer's trainings once in a while, so that I don't have to go over the basics over and over again and keep my time free for going forward.

I was very stressed at the inaugural Kensington training for various reasons and don't actually remember much at all of what went on there; I do know there was a participant who wanted their money back half way through the first day because I was "too old and ugly" which rather cemented my views that the general public is best avoided at all cost and the only reason I chose to do this German training was in order to show some solidarity to the publishing company which was sponsoring the conference and to thank them for having faith in this new system.

However, it turned out to be one of the most extraordinary experiences of my training career and one could say, reconciled me with the whole EmoTrance system in a big way.

It is a superb system from every angle, and really, I should have done much, much more to publicise it and to make sure that folk would know about it. It is gentle and a whole new experience for practitioners and therapists alike, and allows one to tackle the very worst disturbances swiftly and with confidence, even if one has no training in existing therapy forms at all. It fits like a glove with just about every imaginable form of therapy and counselling, from kinesiology to massage and psychology and can be as easy as saying a few words; as the therapist, you can't go wrong and you learn stacks about people as you're paying attention to each client's unfoldments in total safety because the client is totally in control all the way through.

For clients, it is finally a way to deal with things one has been afraid of and suffering from for such a long time; things one might have thought could never possibly be resolved, or would have to hurt as much again if one was to turn one's attention there; and for people like me who have been severely abused the idea of retaining full control over the processes yet to be supported by another in this totally respectful and gentle manner is nothing short of a Godsend. I can't just lie there and let people prod my energy system to their heart's content, all of me goes simply on flat out red alert and so I have avoided this scenario all my life. With this way of working, I'm in control and can call halt to things if I'm getting scared and I get not only to decide exactly what we're working on and in which order, but also the ONLY feedback mechanism are MY feelings and experiences and what I say - no-one is telling me any more what's wrong with me, nor how THEY are going to put this right by a quick prod here and a quick prod there.

Further, for the very worst stuff I don't have to tell anyone at all what it was and where it came from and put myself back through the mill yet again, but can simply point and say where it hurts - and I am the one whose attention in the end, moves and restores these energy blockages, gives permission and the instruction for healing to be executed, it is all **my** choice, **my** doing.

Lastly, as I am doing this, the very fact that my various bizarre emotions, thoughts and behaviours are simply structural and systemic responses to a deeply disturbed and injured energy body beneath, and NOT signs of madness, that God doesn't love me or that I've deserved any of this is simply a cooling rain to a fire of pain which has smouldered for 40 years or more.

Those are my own responses to EmoTrance exercises when I take part in person.

Those types of responses are mirrored by the other participants and indeed, in this case so very powerfully so that I have to conclude it is not only me who finds this way of working with old problems incredibly relieving from both angles - that of the practitioner, and that of the therapist. I actually had **wanted** to hug some of the participants, and I don't touch nor hug unless the cavalry is standing by and I've basically given birth myself to the person in question! Others there said that their practice partners "came to life before their eyes", that they felt the others in the room "became so much more real" and some remarked that they had "never before felt so connected to a client" as they had done during these exercises.

THAT is perhaps the most truly amazing and profound effect of this whole deal and where as far as I am concerned, the greatest hope for further healing and resolution resides for those amongst us who, like myself, have lost it somewhere with the human race, have crept off in pain and defeat to hide behind their shields just so they might survive another day without going completely insane and have remained there, disconnected, lonely and slowly "starving for love amidst the oceans of energy".

What I also did see and experience so profoundly that I think I've finally learned is that working with the energy body in this way and entirely honouring the PHYSIOLOGICAL responses of the body is perhaps the master key to a true re-connection of consciousness, energy body and physicality in the end.

I've had a very brief personal experience of what happens when that happens, when all of you comes into sync just for a flash of a moment - it is a sense of lucidity and presence, of connection and incredible clarity of mind which encompasses all that IS indeed just like an enlightenment state, an epiphany, a numinous experience. I had this brief experience during this training, and you could say that it has re-set my goal posts as to what it is that I'm trying to achieve, what I'm actually after, and what can be done if we get this right.

This has also re-set my ideas as to what has to be done next with EmoTrance, and where it needs to go.

I'm going to presenting these new directions in a one off training in November 2003 (for details please see http://emotrance.com); before, I thought I knew where we were going - the wider energy body, energetic realities, putting things right on those wider levels and in those planes, and of course the Triad system of the HEROS.

That is still perfectly correct and needs to be done, but there has emerged another aspect most strongly, and that would be the body itself, and the body/energy body injuries on all these levels and layers which have not been treated correctly and never been dealt with correctly.

What I saw and experienced for myself in Germany was that we need to bring the physicality directly into this game, combining physical stimulation and touch with the basic EmoTrance system and thereby working with **physicality AND the energy system** at the same time. This is a very long story and those who would like to find out more about the physical EmoTrance connections and exercises will be able to find articles on this later on http://EmoTrance.com and most likely, I will be writing interim reports about this extraordinary topic for http://starfields-group.com

In the meantime, I am going to conclude this series of articles on the "German Energy Experiences" with saying that I am most deeply grateful to have been given the opportunity to work with a system which is custom made for people like myself; that however this came to be, it is truly the most extraordinary gift and it deserves my attention.

Thank you for listening and have a gentle day and night,

Silvia Hartmann

Creator, The EmoTrance System

http://EmoTrance.com

PART 1 - THE HEROS SYSTEM

Energy Re-Unifies The Universe

Well, here we are, and how delightful to see you here! There are so many of you I recognise from other places and some of you have been taking this trip for quite some years. Thank you for being here and giving me your precious time and attention.

We are all EmoTrance practitioners here, right? So what I am going to do this morning is to very, very briefly back up on the whole Universe from which EmoTrance has come, which is quite different from many other Universes you may have visited, or stayed within, over the years.

- **EmoTrance comes from a Universe in which energy is not just an idea, but an actuality.**

Energy is the one concept which reunifies personal human experience with what is actually happening around us, what we can see, what we can perceive, what we can hear, and how we respond to the Universe as people on the larger scale – the sunsets and the sunrises, supernovas, the stars in the sky, the really, really big stuff.

The concept of there being REAL energy in the Universe we may not be able to see as yet with the eyes and the vision we are using, that is what reunifies the Universe for human beings, and it makes this world a place which is LOGICAL, which is REASONABLE, and most of all, a place which we were **designed to navigate**, that we were designed to understand, that we were designed to appreciate in every way.

Now that is a message of hope which I have never heard before, not even from the world religions, but at the basis of this lies a massive attempt at **REUNIFICATION.**

People's consciousness has spent a long time cutting the Universe into bits.

There have been a lot of programmes on British TV at the moment about string theory and the scientists are now thinking how it wasn't such a good idea to accelerate an atom for seven miles and smashing it into another atom to learn about atoms. We have a joke at the StarFields Network about accelerating a frog for seven miles and smashing into other frogs in order to find out what a frog is.

This whole idea of pulling things apart in order to learn how they work is sweet but ultimately misguided and it cannot give us the answers we are looking for – why am I here, who am I? Is there a Creator!

Of course there is!

Good God!

I saw a movie in the cinema not long ago and there was this woman who stood in the 14th century in one of their rather drab cathedrals and she looked up at this stained glass window and she sighed, "The only bit of colour in an otherwise grey and dreary world ..."

I actually jumped out of my chair and I screamed, "You STUPID BITCH! Didn't they have fucking sunsets in the 14th century?"

Didn't they?

Sunrises?

Moons and storm clouds?

Oceans, blue?

Infinite skies, every morning, every night, every time you raise your eyes – well there it is, the beauty of creation.

But perhaps they invented that in the early 20th century, they didn't have it in the 14th. That's why they had to use stained glass windows to give their grey, drab and dreary worlds a little bit of colour.

Now this reunification process has to start somewhere for us people, and something that I was particularly interested in was that the world religion always leave a bit out.

Do you know about my totality concept? If you haven't heard my version of the totality concept, let me know and I'll explain it.

Now as you can't – well you can but there's no point in it – accelerate a frog to light speed and smash it into another frog and then study the bits that are left over to learn about the nature of frogdom, what a frog does, what its for, what its karma is and so on, much the same is true for people.

You can't split people into mind-body-spirits and all this business. The world religions have an unfortunate habit of trying to bring you to salvation but leaving out a major component.

Now, some religions don't like the physicality. When I use that term what I mean by that is our bodies. If you would be so kind as to briefly touch yourself somewhere, on your skin, just to remind ourselves what that feels like, what that is, what our physicality represents.

It is purely an organic, Creator-designed vehicle that works absolutely amazingly for a hundred and fifty years or more, at least, unless we fuck with it too badly, in which case it wears out sooner.

Now there are a lot of religions which will try and get you to the promised land – but you cannot take your physicality. Your body is bad, sex is bad, meditate until your legs fall off. I heard this story about an Indian saint and his claim to fame was sitting in front of a brick wall for 30 years until his legs fell off. Wheyhey, what an achievement ...

I'm sure the Creator is delighted with that one.

"I gave the bloody guy some legs ..."

The thing most religions like to leave at the door of the promised land, which is what I have personally had a lot of fun with, is the conscious mind.

Now, the conscious mind is what we're sitting here with, talking to each other and listening with. There is a lot to it. Has anyone here ever tried to switch off their conscious mind? Through meditation, flagellation, hanging themselves by their nipples from various trees, while young acolytes beat you with thorny sticks, drugs, alcohol?

There's lots and lots of ways of trying to switch your conscious mind off – but you know what, the bugger keeps coming back!

When I went at this whole thing of making a map of the Universe that works for me, one of the things I did was this. People always call me arrogant, opinionated and that kind of thing. And that's true, I'll argue the toss with anyone and everything that will come along. However, the one thing I will never, ever argue with is the Creative.

I do NOT argue with the Creative.

I will quite happily stand there in front of a scientist and say, "You sad little weasel! The only reason you're not getting anywhere is because **you're not thinking!**"

However, I never say this when I am faced with a sunset. A cloud or something like that. A tree, a small leaf, an ant. I look at it and go, "Wow! I could never, ever make anything as amazing at that. Never. I wouldn't even want to try. This is completely beyond my reach. Whoever did that, wow."

I won't be arguing with that, I don't argue with THAT.

I would, for example, never say something like, "I know better than the Creative. The Creative may have given women a clitoris, but I will know better and I will cut it out."

Now, there are a great many "religious" people who argue this. And they call themselves religious and god-fearing, but my definition of god-fearing is slightly different. It is to take a look at what's going on and take the Creative as an inspiration and as a **directive device** to steer our own personal endeavours as human beings.

The Creator gave me a conscious mind.

Are you telling me, they made a mistake?!

Is there anybody here who wants to stand up and say, "Ah well, God's just stupid. God's just like one of us, just a slob like one of us."

Anybody would like to come up and argue that point?

Any priests like to step up, right now, and argue that point **with me**?

They would be welcome.

So, the Creator's given me consciousness. So I'm supposed to switch it off, trample on it, beat the crap out of myself?

How about we just presume that the clitoris has a function, and conscious mind does, in the greater scheme of things?

How about that for a change?

Rather than beating up on our consciousness in the same way the poor physicality has been beaten up across the ages, give the poor bugger a break, back up and say, "Ok, what does the consciousness do? What is it good for? How does it work **as a functioning part of the totality** of a human being?"

Next.

We have the so-called unconscious mind.

44

Now according to Freud and a whole lot of other people, this is a slimy pit of evil, disgustingness with writhing monsters and atrocities of all kinds, and under no circumstances must the unconscious mind be factored into anything. The scientists, particularly, are so afraid of it. And I know why, but never mind.

I have re-phrased the unconscious mind and I'm going to use the term, **the energy mind**, because I consider the unconscious mind to be a part of the energy matrix which processes energetically derived data, which is an **intensely information rich stream** of incoming information from the environment, which is happening all the time and which the conscious mind does not have the computing power to actually process.

Previously known as the artist, this is the **energy mind**.

I would like you to keep in mind as I am writing these terms on the board that I consider in order to get to the promised land, the garden of Eden, personal development, enlightenment, holy grail, immortality, whatever people call this thing that they want to be and they know they could, but they're not, the idea was that we should put everything back together into a working frog and see if it'll jump into the pond.

The energy mind is a part of this deal.

Now mercifully I don't have to convince anyone here that we also have an energy body. Hallelujah. I'm very pleased I don't have to do that, so let's add the **energy body** to this list.

So we have some bits here of our frog that I have picked up off the floor of humanity after they smashed the frogs into each other for the last ten thousand years:

- **Physicality**
- **Conscious Mind**
- **Energy Mind**
- **Energy Body**

Now the fact is that we actually don't know very much about any of them, in spite of the mountains of dusty tomes you can find that make up the "pyramid of learning". There truly is not a lot known about any of these by themselves, and never mind how they **actually work when you put them all together**. And this is where things are becoming really interesting, because this is the foundation and the underlying principle for this thing we have called as a label, EmoTrance.

Now, EmoTrance is simple. It is embarrassingly simple. I've spent years trying to see if anyone else had come up with that but they hadn't. A simple little thing – where do you feel this in your body? A pressure in your chest? Oh look, there is no foot on your chest, what's causing it?

Ah it's just the conscious mind being stupid. You're just being neuro-somatic. You haven't got enough willpower?

What kind of an answer is **that**?!

It is not a scientific answer, is it ... ts, ts, ts.

Science is a religion in my books. I class science simply as another religion, just right next to Catholicism, Lutheranism, all the other religions. Science is only another religion – full of lies, misinformation, priests who pretend they know what they are doing, and very little truth at the end of the day.

Beyond Remediality

When I started working with the energy body, the very first thing I noticed that I was not at all happy with the maps of the energy body.

Something I never like is when something is over ten thousand years old.

Chinese whispers!

I studied hypnotherapy a little bit, and you would be amazed what has been lost since 1908! What people nowadays think of as hypnosis bears no resemblance to what the originators in that field were actually doing. They were doing extremely powerful things with this stuff. Snap! Operate on a guy and take his liver out. Snap! Heal. Snap. No blood loss. Snap. You can't remember who you ever were. Like that.

Just barely 80 years later, with Internet and with reading and writing, that field has lost so much! It is hardly a vague resemblance of what there once used to be.

8,000 years and more?

Don't make me laugh.

We can't trust **that** anymore.

EmoTrance is to me, and has always been, a **tool for discovering more about the energy body**. By practically asking any person off the street – old, young, man, woman, religions, races, backgrounds, injuries, regardless – where do you feel that in your body, what happens when you let it go, and those of you who use EmoTrance a lot will know that this shows you some very interesting things about the human energy body.

Every client you deal with, every person you do this with, you learn something about the energy body. And yes, there are channels that resemble what we are taught about the "meridian channels" but there are also things going where there **are no channels** painted on the model, and going to very strange places. And there are things happening outside of us, too.

Cracking The Egg

One thing that is very important about EmoTrance is this.

You know that image that is often produced, here is our enlightened guy sitting in cross-legged position, you've seen this, right, with the chakras stacked like dinner plates, in this egg.

And the problem is, that's blatantly an egg. And I would **love** to see what happens when the guy comes out of it. When that shell cracks open and this embryo we have been given **as the end result** of a developed energy system was to actually unfold and come out ...

Wouldn't that be something?

Would you like to do that?

Would you like to **be that**?

Give it your jolly best shot?

Well then you are my people here because I want to know as well!

Just because its never been done doesn't mean that we can't do it! Quite in the opposite! It is so – fruit machine. People who study fruit machines know that after a certain time, it **has** to pay out. It really has to pay out –

it can't not. So what people do is they wait until everyone's put a whole lot of money in, then they sneak around and put just ten pence in.

The "human misinformation fruit machine" has been going for so long, we don't have a big deal to do here, just literally put our 10p in and it all comes out, because it is so balanced on the verge of this forward movement, it **wants** to happen, it really does – else I wouldn't have found it as easily as this.

So, EmoTrance for me is very much not about remediality, only in so far that let's say I wanted to go for a walk to this mountain over there because I want to see what's on that mountain – but my feet hurt. That makes me think it's not going to be a pleasant journey or easy to get there unless I do something about it. So the only way in which I look at EmoTrance as a "healing" modality is to get the feet fixed quick so I can get to the mountain.

This is NOT just about healing. Healing is **only the beginning** to get us back to an even keel, a platform from which we actually start to go **forward**.

Forward to the New.

States of health that none of you have ever had.

States of joy and happiness that we don't even know exist.

Ourselves, each one of us, actually **doing things** for which there have been no role models – **ever**.

Now that is exciting, and this is what EmoTrance is really about.

ET Level 1, the practitioner level, deals with things as they are right now.

People are hurt, people are desperate, people are a mess. They are unhappy, they are not functioning properly, they don't know what's wrong with themselves, their conscious minds are not talking to their energy minds, their energy minds can't make sense of contact lenses or what the hell is going on; as far as they are concerned, they never had an energy body so just anyone can go and distort it, say weird things to them, and all those maladies ...

So the core, EmoTrance Level 1, is to **get people ready** to a point where they are thinking pro-actively, rather than remedially, and this is what we're here for.

We'll do some more remedial stuff but this weekend is about pro-activity.

Luckily, EmoTrance is also a nice tool for pro-activity, because when you do are thinking about doing things you have never done before, chances are you are going to be scared, right?

And how are you going to deal with that fear?

Or you might have doubts.

How are you going to deal with those doubts?

And here comes EmoTrance as life's happy companion ...

I personally went out and faced the ghosts of my past, the biggest ghosts of my past, by booking a trip and presenting at a conference in Germany.

Now people, you have no idea. That was like going back to the concentration camp. It was horrendous. I would not have even dared to be there without EmoTrance. EFT is good, but it doesn't help you **in the moment**. In the moment, when you are actually faced with something that just brings up ... vooom! the worst moments of your life. And I got through it.

I got through it.

And I even think that the people who were down there even noticed that there was anything wrong with me at all. That's powerful stuff. It allowed me personally to do something – and **doing** is the word! It is not about thinking about it, tap, tap, tap, do it, run back into your hole. For me this was five days straight into the situation, constant, constant, keep moving forward, in, through, and out the other side – and bloody hell, am I proud of myself.

Now that's another feeling I didn't have much of before this.

See look if you are too frightened to challenge yourself because of the energetic injuries in your body and all the stuff we've been exposed to, then you don't get to a point where you **can challenge yourself**, get through to the other side and then become proud of yourself. That is a hugely lifting, powerfully motivating emotion and once you've done it a few times, you'd be surprised of what you can do.

I would just like to make a note of how inordinately proud I am of Nicola for doing yesterday's training. That was absolutely brilliant and the same kind of thing as what I did in Germany.

She had never taught a group of people before, would not have conceived of it, but she did it, got through it and I am incredibly proud of you. Yeah, really.

And what I'm hoping, for every one of you, I don't know what your own personal challenges are, what areas they are in, if they have aspects of, like me going to Germany, that was a trip into the past. Facing the demons of the past. Physically, personally, not in therapy. Getting on a plane, facing those houses and those flowerboxes. Seriously, don't laugh. Triggers, trauma has triggers. I had a nervous breakdown at a large garden gnome and I'm not kidding. It was just ... <shudders>

But what **your own personal challenges** are, where they are, what you want to do, and go into that, and even if you just do it the once and you've done it, and you can be proud of yourself and you **know** that you can do it now, that is so extraordinary.

If I have one prayer for you guys is that you get to do that because it clears the path for the future and towards the New. We've all done so much cleaning of the past, therapy and tapping, and worrying about it, and now we want to go **into the future**.

We haven't go much time, people. None of us are spring chickens anymore and it's a big Universe, a lot to see and a lot of discover, we've got to get started, all of us do.

EmoTrance and the Energy Body

What I would like to talk to you this morning whilst you're bright and fresh and engaged – not that you're not going to be even brighter, fresher and even more engaged later on! – is the concept of the trinity and the HEROS.

Without the HEROS, none of us would be here today, Nicola wouldn't have been here yesterday and I would not have been in Germany.

That is to me one of the greatest wonderful things I learned about the energy system, simply by **using** EmoTrance a lot, and seeing and feeling and noting the channels where things were happening with people.

One of the things I noticed was that the conscious mind is overheating like hell in a lot of people.

It is going round and round in circles, trying to find solutions for problems, old, new, current, and it really is literally overheating.

Ananga Sivyer, who is a real meridian expert and ayurvedic specialist, tells me that this causes **massive** imbalances in the rest of the energy system when that happens. When the conscious mind's systems are overheating, the imbalances created are so bad that certain energy pathways get shut down to stop you from complete overload.

So I thought, we have a conscious mind, and its produce, if you will, thought, needs to go somewhere. What I noticed for myself when I was having one of those "Aaargh!" moments and asked myself, where does this energy wants to go? And where it wanted to go was over my head and down the back, getting it away from me.

I found this inordinately relieving.

This is Thought Flow[4].

---

[4] For diagrams, see "Thought Flow" in Addendum 2, Articles.

Thought Flow

Have you all done this?

<Audience member>: I've seen it but never done it.

Never done it? Why not?

<Audience member>: I wasn't sure if I would do it right.

Ok, just for fun, take one of your own worst repetitive thoughts, project it out and forward, sweep it up with your hands and throw it up and over down your back.

What do you notice as you are doing it?

<Audience members>: Silence, stillness, peace.

Yes, that's right, there is a moment of stillness.

Whoa, where did it go?

Now this moment of stillness **may** not seem such a lot, because you can soon go back into the old loop if you try, especially if you have a number of anchors and reminders on your person and in your environment, on the wall or post it notes on your forehead, but:

- This moment of stillness gives **you the opportunity** to <u>**think of something else**</u>.

This moment of stillness is for many people the first experience and opportunity they've ever had to take control of their conscious thoughts and direct the thoughts **to something else**.

It is an extremely important moment.

The Moment Of Stillness

Thought Flow is such a simple little thing, and as you are thinking something, to catch it in your hands and just sweep it away, put it away in order to create this momentary moment of stillness. A lot of psychological and behavioural interventions have the idea of a pattern interrupt, when someone is freaking out and you tip a bucket of water over them, or you make a shrill noise, clap your hands, distract them somehow.

All these devices are designed to create this moment of stillness.

To break that linked one-to-the-other-and-the-next "train of thought", because you need that moment of stillness to **insert a new thought**, give the whole train a new direction; without it, it runs on like the train on a track, and you know what that's like, it doesn't have an exit point and it goes from one thing to another.

Sometimes, it's a complicated track that goes over the daughter, and the son, and their baby, and your health, and the house and the money, and the daughter and the son, and their baby ... Complicated and with sub loops, but a track nonetheless.

So don't underestimate the power of that one moment of stillness.

When you are doing this with clients, have them appreciate that.

If they can experience that second of stillness, then that means that they have a real chance to **take control of their conscious minds** and just imagine what could happen if you had control of your conscious mind ...

Leverage Points

See, really dramatic things, breakthrough things need not be a piano falling on your head.

That second of stillness on the Thought Flow process is something **to pay attention to** because these are **leverage points**.

It's like there are moments in our lives when we can apply a tiny bit of leverage, and it will have enormous inference on the rest of our lives. And there are other times when we can struggle and fight, and even engage armies of other people to help us out, and nothing valuable happens at all.

Now one of the real clues to universal magic is to **become aware** of these leverage points, like the moment of stillness, where you can actually make with one little thought a whole cascade of events to occur.

But in order to do that, we have to **pay attention** and that's another very nice thing about the conscious mind.

Paying Attention

Someone told me the other day that they would have liked to have more of this stillness, and if I had any good ideas that would make it so that they could experience more of these moments of stillness.

I gave this some thought and then it occurred to me that the conscious mind isn't actually designed to shut up.

It is not designed to shut up.

It is designed to work **all the time** - which is what it does, and that is correct.

The conscious mind is supposed to do **something all the time**.

It's like your heart is supposed to beat all the time. It's not supposed to stop for two hours at a time to give you a near death experience.

But what can the conscious mind **do** other than trying to figure out things it can't figure out, and drive itself crazy and start to overheat?

Well one thing the conscious mind **can do** is to **pay attention**.

This is an **active** thing for the conscious mind to do, to pay attention. To gather more data. That's one of the things it's supposed to do, to gather more data. And when we're gathering more data, then we're not thinking the same old rubbish again that got us into the mess we are in today.

That's a very profound thing to do, to pay attention. And not to just one thing, either. To lots of things. Lots and lots and lots of things – to **everything**!

In fact, if you're "thinking too much" a great remedy is the Betty Erickson hypnosis induction. Useful if you can't get to sleep, too. You're instructed to pay attention to **everything** – in turn, five noises, five smells, five sights, five feelings, five energy body shifts, five noises ...

Very meditative, very trancey. And you learn something about the environment which is always useful.

The Energy "System"

I look at the energy system at a very simplistic level as **a system** that works – with input and output.

Electricity in, light bulb on, that kind of thing. Nice and simple. Not complicated.

And one of the things I asked myself was, where do these thoughts in the Thought Flow technique **go**?

Where do they go?

You think them, you take them, you put them there ... then what?

Do you end up with a large sack of thoughts on your back that grows ever heavier as you're dragging yourself to life?

My sensation when I did this and the thoughts sort of slithered down my back was that I could track an energy shift up until the middle of my shoulder blades, but then it got fainter and fainter and then I lost it. I tell Ananga Sivyer this and she goes, "Oh my God it's the Shushumna Nadi!" That's not a joke, it's actually called that and apparently, some ancient guy reckons it connects the energy system to the higher energy system, one that you can't feel anymore because it doesn't have a direct connection in that sense to the physical body, and I thought that was amusing, and interesting to think that the thoughts went **somewhere**.

I didn't actually think on it much further, I was just happy to have something for the moment. That's really only all I ever ask for, to have something for the moment. But what happened was that a couple of the things I shoved down the old nadi – I **got answers to**!

This is what happened! And one of those was a "meaning of life" kind of deals, I can't even remember what it was all about now, it would be written on my wall at home somewhere, but it was something I'd been worrying and worrying and worrying about, it came up all the time and I kept pushing it over, again and again.

Then one day I'm just wandering about at home and – boom! I'm having some sort of major insight and then I got it, it was the answer! Oh my God, I got **an answer**!

I never expected that. Good God! You mean you can ask questions **and you get an answer**?!

And not just "an" answer, but a **meaningful** answer, an answer that is both so simple and so complex you just couldn't believe **that** was the answer – you know, one of **them**, a totally blinding insight!

And I went, "Wow! THAT could be useful!"

And we've been using this happily ever since. It is a great deal of fun all the way around.

Not only do you get a moment of stillness where you get a chance to take your own thought and direct it in any direction you want to direct it to; not only do you get to learn to pay attention – but also, you sometimes get answers!

And the kind of answers that you get are of a **different order and quality** than the kind of answers the conscious mind normally provides.

They are much richer, much more information dense, much more global and much more profound.

When these answers turn up, there is further no conscious objection or conscious rejection at all, and this is interesting and important both.

Say, I ask someone a question. "Why don't I have a love life?" Depending who they are, they'll give me an answer such as, "You're buying that whole Freudian crap." And I'll immediately argue back, "No, no, no, that's not why ..."

Yet with those answers that come as the result of the Thought Flow process, there **is no argument**. It is immediately clear and understood that this answer **is correct for me**. I can't believe that I should have someone talk to me, and give me an answer, and I'm not arguing. It is unheard of, people, really.

Has anyone here used this and received one of these answers I have talked of?

Yes.

And their quality is amazing, isn't it?

<Audience member> They are profound.

Profound – just a different order of being.

However, it doesn't come churning out like a machine. I think it would be unfair to promise you that if you start to do Thought Flow, you'll get the answers instantly. What's the meaning of life? Booom!

Firstly, these channels haven't been used in a while, and secondly, it is not just about giving the question but you also need some space to receive the answer – which is why it is so important to **train the conscious mind** to pay attention. Energetically, this is actually an energy reversal. Instead of going out actively, trying to figure it out, pushing and prodding, in paying attention you are **reversing the information flow** – information is **flowing to you**.

In order to get the answers, we need to pay attention.

The Energy Mind

The next question we must surely have is, "WHO is computing these answers?!"

Now I always thought that my "unconscious mind" does this for me, because my unconscious mind is pretty good. I love it dearly, I wouldn't be here without it. We have a great relationship, we really do. Earlier I made a mention that I re-named the unconscious mind to the energy mind, just so we can get away from all that prejudice. I also don't think it's "unconscious".

Anyone ever done any deep meditation or lucid dreaming, and your conscious mind is there, and your unconscious mind **is there as well**?

It isn't actually "un"conscious at all, one just has to get to a state of lucidity where the two merge.

Now we have the energy mind, and this is where it's getting interesting, and it is interesting, this is.

So, we think something, we shove it down this nadi thing, and **something** happens to it – it gets changed somehow, it gets processed because if we get an answer, the data-stream is different, else we would be getting the exact same question back ad infinitum.

How does this system work?

Walt Disney to the rescue! I'm pondering these things all day, every day, and someone's got the TV on and there's this movie playing, I think it was Anastasia, and I hear this voice saying, "So, you've come for the ransom of my daughter?" and the other voice says, "No, I've come to bring your daughter back and ask for her hand in marriage instead."

Father says, all astonished, "What, have you changed your mind?"

The other answers, "No. I had a change of heart."

And Silvia went, caboom! All circuits alight! The energy system! The heart!

Now let's forget **everything** about the heart centre, about the lotuses, or the chakras, or the fluffy bunny rabbits dancing in circles – let's forget all of that and let's think clearly and logically for a moment.

This heart centre is **only** an energy system. It doesn't mean you're gay if you have one.

So, this is what we've got so far. Thought goes somewhere where it is changed, it goes to the heartsystem, and when THAT speaks, a heroin addict will crawl out of the gutter, STOP using and be saved – just like that.

When THAT speaks, a father of seven will pack up and leave for the monastery, no matter the wailing or the crying of his loved ones.

When THAT speaks, every human problem can be overcome, and you are not left alone, not left with willpower, and there's nothing to choose and nothing to decide – you obey.

No matter how ridiculous, no matter how dangerous, no matter how inexplicable something is – when the heart speaks, you obey.

I just went, oh, of course!

People talk about "who's driving the bus".

Making up your mind, changing your **mind** – how often have I done that, and it doesn't change a bloody thing. It does NOTHING. Willpower lasts so long and then it runs out. You can't run an entire incarnation on willpower, and good God do they try, those poor bastards who die of Parkinson's.

You can't run an incarnation on willpower, but the heart, there, THAT energy system, when THAT gives a command, the conscious mind obeys.

And you can see that is the beginning of a circuit.

There is an input and an output happening. Now what?

There is something missing.

There is a transmission system missing between the energy mind and the heart, and that really is the funniest thing. I tried to work out different things, but nothing really fitted, until one morning, as I was boiling eggs for breakfast – true story! – and I just went, "Fuck me, it's the soul!"

Oh my God, that **is** the connector, that missing piece, between the energy mind and the heart.

This is an energy system that does **not have a counterpart** in the physical body.

An energy system that is immortal.

An energy system that **does not rely upon the physical body to keep functioning**.

The immortal soul.

And that component, ladies and gentlemen, completed my triad.

I took one look at that and I knew it was right, and it actually works.

It works practically.

The Triad

Although represented here as three balls, they are of course not balls but in fact, a single system; however it helps at the moment to conceptualise this better.

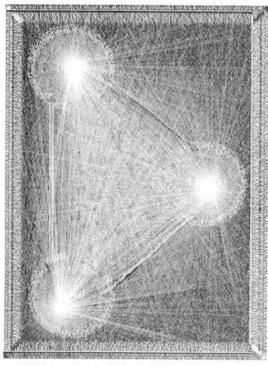

- **The Heart Of Energy**
- **The Mind Of Energy**
- **The Immortal Soul**

Not only does this work perfectly, in fact the human energy **doesn't work at all** without this system being there.

The human energy system doesn't work unless it has a soul as a transmission device in it.

As you can see, and as many religions have quite rightfully posited, the conscious mind does create a problem, because if it wasn't there, this would actually work so perfectly.

But there it is.

Ladies and gentlemen, welcome to Eastbourne and let me tell you, you **have an immortal soul**.

Has honestly anyone ever told you that?

Meaningfully, personally?

That you have the potential to be truly immortal?

Your very own immortal soul?

Immortality.

Not **physical** immortality. But **practical immortality**.

Is that a book title?

"Practical immortality for everyday 21st century humans".

The triad is one big, enormously complicated system. ONE system. I have put it like this to have something logical for the conscious mind to follow. See, our soul doesn't need any help. Our heart of energy doesn't need any help. Our energy mind doesn't need any help.

But by God, our conscious mind needs all the help we can give it so that it can catch up.

We are all here because I want our conscious minds to catch up with the programme of the Creator, because if it doesn't, it creates havoc.

It is my personal contention that unless this energy system is actually a part of your incarnation, a functional part of your incarnation, that when you die, there is **nothing recorded** and you might as well have never existed at all.

It is my contention that this energy system needs to be **consciously activated** and that it needs to be a **conscious part of our existence** for it to store the data from this incarnation. I see the immortal soul as a massive hard drive that isn't connected to the computer – there's **nothing** on it. One or two scratches, one or two notepad files, that is not enough.

This needs to be a part of our daily life.

It needs to be present to record our life for that immortality deal.

So you're not just saved by somebody waving a wand, that's not enough.

The conscious mind is stopping the information energy, the data, to go **into this triad system** and this information energy is required to **activate** and actualise the soul, to **record YOU**, not just some other thing but **your experiences, your feelings, your dealings**.

Your life.

<Audience Member>: You talked about the soul imprinting things, is that where the Akashic records come from?

Well I wasn't going to go there just yet but whilst we're on the topic ...

My metaphor for a soul is a star.

My metaphor for a whole bunch of soul stars is "StarFields" and they are in a standing resonant connection with one another. It is a quantum thing so no division in time or space, everyone knows what everyone else knows. You can call that Indra's web or the Akashic records, as well.

The HEROS

So, here we have the HEROS. That stands for higher existing reality energetic operating systems and it abbreviates to HEROS because by God, do we need some heroes!

One of the things which blew me away the most when I first started understanding some of this was that all these things I'd considered to be low self esteem or problems that needed to be personally developed away, were **all absolutely true**!

The definition of "I" as just the conscious mind operating sort of not quite at ease with the physicality, which is the definition of "I" which most 21st century Westerners operate under, namely a conscious mind, an unconscious mind with that weird shit in it and a physicality that does these things that we don't want it to most of the time and isn't good enough to some standard or the other, that definition of "I" is really perfectly correct in thinking that it can't do "it" by themselves.

That it isn't enough.

That it isn't good enough.

That it can't face the challenges of life.

That it needs to find others to help it through the day.

That it **needs help**.

When I understood that, I understood that it was correct and all these things that people enter therapy for, and those who don't enter therapy will still think it, I'm not good enough, there's something missing, there's **something wrong** with me, this isn't right, what is this madness that surrounds me?

And there's nothing I can do. I'm not strong enough. I'm not intelligent enough. I'm not fast enough, I'm not powerful enough to make it through.

And I am afraid.

And I don't know what happens when I die.

And I'm so afraid of pain.

And I am NOT ENOUGH to cope with all of this.

These thoughts, these fears ...

... they are **completely and utterly correct** as an assessment **of the reality of the situation.**

The conscious mind and the physicality **can't** do it by themselves.

They need their heroes, they need their own HEROS.

They need their lionheart.

They need their own immortal soul.

And by God do they need their energy mind!

This is why I very much liked the abbreviation of HEROS.

Now, people look for their soul mate.

Only, they're not really looking for their soul **mate**, they are looking **for their own soul**.

When you hear people talking about looking for "the one who will make it all alright", "the one" who will be with you, who will protect you, who will love you, no matter what, will never let you down, will always be by your side ... If I can just find **that one** then I'll be alright.

Now, no human can be THAT for you.

And deep down, we know this. We've tried many human beings in our endless quest for "the one who will make it all alright" and that never worked.

Some people then turn to God for being "the one who will make it all alright".

But God is – big, you know. It doesn't cuddle up with you in bed at night. And you might even think that when you're in the middle of pain, or despair, or depression that there is no God at all, because there's just you.

Just you, being in pain.

Again.

And there's no angel coming down from heaven, just you.

Suffering.

Again.

The thing is this.

If you have access to your own HEROS, then **you are NOT alone**.

You are – WE.

And WE are **incredibly powerful**.

Incredibly powerful.

Lionheart & Heart Healing

When I first came up with this, I came up with this "healing prayer" called Heart Healing, which is the dedication to one of the HypnoDreams albums.

I wrote the poem in response to a lady who had been terribly abused and couldn't cope with life at all, she really couldn't. Just getting out of bed in the mornings without killing herself was a true feat of such courage, that King Arthur himself would be on his knees and applauding her, if only she knew.

But anyway, she was really depressed and sought help and the best thing I could come up with was the Heart Healing prayer. Words failed me so I turned to poetry as I do, and that is an example of that.

So the Heart Healing prayer made the rounds, and the gentlemen all thought, that wasn't for them. Ah, it's ok. Hearts are alright for women.

They are emotional and they sob a lot. We don't need a heart. It just makes us weak, and feeble.

And in response to one of those comments I just saw it – of course, the **lionheart**.

Richard The Lionheart. Big strong men. Inspired such devotion that tens of thousands of people followed him into battle. Courage. Enormous conviction.

The Heart of Energy is what I would call the **"nuclear reactor at the very core of our energy system"**, the thing that powers all else.

And it's not just a reactor that provides energy for the **entire energy system**, it is also Victoria Station Central of the energy system, where all and everything meets. From there, you can go anywhere, any level and every layer, right down to physicality.

I don't want to begin to go into all the research that has been done on the effects of energy work on the heart level on people's actual hearts, to stop people from having heart attacks, which is that fear over a long period of time, so much so that people can't handle it anymore.

The Heart As The Ultimate Defence System

One other thing with that "heart of energy" is that it also serves as a **defence mechanism**.

When that works as it should, you do not need shields anymore.

Think of some evil thing flying close to a sun, what happens to it?

It just burns up, of course – it can't do a thing to the sun. And the radiation of that heart of energy keeps the entire energy system clean. All these rubbish bits, like the evil CDs, that haunt **us**, and that mess up our energy systems can't survive in the solar storms when the heart is really working as it should.

So I thought to revitalise our energy systems from the **inside out**, we might start with Heart Healing.

I can highly recommend this to you and your clients as just one of the simplest things and I was wondering if you'd like to do it now, as a family, because it is such a nice thing. I invite the staff to join us too, for they too are human ... although in their efforts you may think that they were super-human ...

Ok, so what we do is to put our hands in the centre of our chests. This is one of the oldest of all prayer positions for human beings, you can see this on so many old tombstones through the ages.

What I would like you to do is to repeat the words that I speak, because if you say it to me, you'll be doing things for my heart and I'd like you to focus on your own.

I place my own healing hands

on my own dear heart

with all my love

and all my intention

to give my dear heart

everything

I have to give.

Isn't that nice?

That's a wonderful anchor for moments of crisis.

It is a wonderful anchor for moments of despair.

It is a wonderful anchor for moments when you're not quite sure what the problem is or you are too distressed. It is a wonderful self healing prayer.

And just the gesture in itself is nice.

It is a conscious thing – this is what I said earlier, all of this would work just fine if it wasn't for the poor conscious mind throwing a spanner in the works. All of it would just work in perfection.

The HEROS Journey

Now, the healing, or re-education, or re-unification that we have been talking about and that you talk about with your own clients, and the people you love and want to help, funnily enough doesn't really centre around the energy system at all, but instead it centres around the conscious mind.

- **The conscious mind is who has to say YES to all of this**.

The conscious mind is the one who has to come home to this.

You can't bring the heart of energy, the immortal soul and the energy mind into the conscious mind. There isn't enough room.

The conscious mind has to go back to the HEROS.

And you could call that a HEROS journey, if you will; the one and only HEROS journey, to find the holy grail, the philosopher's stone, whatever metaphor you want to give the immortal soul.

And how do we do that?

We pay attention.

Attention is the sword that Archangel Michael is holding; conscious attention is one of the most powerful and extraordinary forces in the Universe.

Conscious attention, which has been trapped inside the poor conscious mind.

One of the things that is a hallmark of this system, whether you want to call it EmoTrance or something else, is that every part of it, **every part** of it, plays a part and every part needs our **absolute and unconditional compassion**.

Every self destructive thought you've ever had, every thing about yourself you never liked, needs our **unconditional compassion** and the question to ask is, "WHAT do you NEED FROM ME to make this better?"

When Nicola and I discussed this training, we also discussed our attitude to the people who would be here.

And it is true that in the past I had a kind of war metaphor for conducting trainings. You go to battle with the punters. They want to tear you to pieces and you have to make sure this doesn't happen. That's a metaphor a lot of trainers have, even if they don't admit to it.

So we talked about this and what we came up with was to be simply - **be kind**.

Just to be kind.

What we have to learn is to be kind to our own conscious minds – and to other people's conscious minds. When you have someone there for energy therapy sessions and they say, "Oh I don't believe in energy," it's so easy to go, "Grrrr...."

We don't need this. None of us need this

We've all been **beaten up enough**.

We are NOT going to get any better people by beating ourselves or anyone else **any more**.

Things have gotten as bad as they have exactly because we've been beaten as much as we have been, by the system, the teachers, the priests, the state of affairs.

Well none of us need any more beatings and the conscious mind is a part of that. So our job, really, in order to make this whole thing happen, this whole thing work on a personal level, AND on a practitioner level and on a teacher's levels, is to somehow find a way to get the conscious mind back on board, to **answer its questions**, to **listen to its objections** and to **find a way to fill its needs**.

That's an interesting thing to be saying on an energy therapies training but it is actually core to the whole thing.

The conscious mind needs to be active as we've already discussed.

You can be active in paying attention, and seeking answers, and questing, and questions and running experiments AS WELL AS in thinking repetitive old thoughts. The term of "active listening" is an activity, make no mistake, and so is our paying attention.

The ET Level 1 basic technique, where do you feel this in your body, tell me if that hasn't greatly increased your own personal awareness of what's happening in your body. Where you are feeling things, how you are responding to things, how you feel energy shifts, how you are responding in situations.

THAT is a brilliant, brilliant gift and a wonderful thing and something that we should all practice even more, and get our clients and trainees to really go for – feeling these energy movements and **following those energy movements with your intention and attention**.

That is what ET Level 1 does – it **re-trains** the conscious attention to **follow** the energy flow in the body. Not to guide it or direct it or shove it this way or that or make it into red walls or pitted swords, but to **follow** where and how the energy is moving.

As soon as you do this you learn all these new things, and the conscious mind is actually happy.

We want the conscious mind to be **happy**.

Now here's something else that is really, really important.

The Need For Evidence

The conscious mind works on **evidence**.

To ask someone who operates from their conscious mind to take things on "faith and trust" is **impossible**, for the conscious mind works ONLY on evidence. And that is the exact loop which has held people back for at least ten thousand years or more, and it goes something like this.

In order to win the Nobel prize, you need to be a genius, right? But in order to be a genius, how do you know you are a genius? By winning the Nobel prize. Right.

So in order to win the Nobel prize to know that you're a genius, you **have to know that you're a genius first** in order to win the prize. You have no evidence to support it when you start out, and that's what fries the conscious mind.

It can't compute "faith" because that's one of those heart emotions. Our little theme tune, "Faith of the Heart".

The conscious mind deals with evidence, and it deals with evidence in the NOW. Not how things were ten years ago but how they are right NOW, which is an interesting trap and an interesting loop.

This has everything to do with how you present this stuff to yourself and to others, and I'm hoping a lot of you will go forth from this weekend and present this whole thing to some other people. Not necessarily what I am telling you here because that's a background thing that you might not need to know, but the basic ideas of EmoTrance:

X Yes, you have emotions.

It's ok to have emotions.

We're designed to have them.

They're a feedback mechanism.

You can learn to flow them so don't have to burst out into tears or have temper tantrums like a little kid and look like a fool in front of your colleagues or your troops.

X And the last thing I'd put on here for what the conscious mind needs is that we really need to learn to **fill the conscious mind's needs**.

The Conscious Need For Direction

One of the most important things the conscious mind needs is for **someone to tell it what to do**.

Because it doesn't know.

This is reason as to **why** human beings have been stumbling blindly behind these leaders. Why it is so **easy** for someone like Hitler to come along and say, "Let me do your thinking for you."

Because the conscious mind is structurally designed for someone else to do its thinking for it. It was never designed to make decisions by its lonesome self, and especially not decisions about life and death, what you're here to do, it isn't designed for that.

It isn't designed to make these decisions, nor even to remember all these things that it tries to remember – it is NOT designed to work out the Universe.

So this whole business in Life Of Brian, "I want you to think for yourselves!" where the crowd shouts back, "Yes, we think for ourselves, Brian!" – "I don't want you to follow me!" and they shout back, "We follow you, Brian!" is simply structural to the conscious mind. It is LOOKING FOR GUIDANCE from somebody.

70

- **And because it doesn't know about the HEROS system, it looks <u>outside of itself.</u>**

It looks for **OTHER PEOPLE** – that's the same deal with the "soul mates", some ONE to make it all alright, someone who will tell you what to do.

Of course, the one to tell the conscious mind what to do is in my system, the Heart.

In Chinese medicine as Ananga tells me the heart is the guy who gives the orders, which tallies with my system, my observations but most of all, with my personal experiences.

What we have to do is to **build bridges** – re-build the bridges between the conscious mind and the rest of the system, and the first step to that is to build a bridge to the Energy Mind.

The Energy Matrix

Now you've heard things said about the "unconscious mind", right?

It remembers absolutely everything you've ever done. Under hypnosis, people can remember the smallest little detail that was in their widest field of vision in any room they were in – sixty five years ago.

HOW is that possible?

There is this whole realm of phenomena, the hypnotic phenomena, that doesn't have any connection, or seemingly so, to all the rest of human endeavour. Like people having diabetes in one multiple personality, but not in the other. How cool is that?! People who get stigmata in their hands, people having instantaneous remission from cancer – there is this whole realm of these "weird" things that don't fit into the current constructs.

What I am proposing is that the energy mind is what is supposed to be storing all of this.

We are not actually supposed to store memories in the brain **at all** – it is not a storage device, but instead, a processing device. Memories and such are stored in the **energy matrix**.

This explains a phenomena you find in energy treatments, such as TFT.

Someone has had a memory and every time they have a traumatic flashback, they re-experience it all – they are right there, smelling the burning, hearing the screams and you do the treatment, and the memory ends up **crystal clear** – but there is no longer any emotion on it.

This really did perplex me for some years until I worked it out.

Once a memory is stored in the energy matrix, this "crystal clear" information is always at the conscious mind's command, so it can be reproduced, instantly, quickly, immediately – but it no longer has this state control of being a replica of "in the here and now" that is the hallmark of brain-stored materials.

The "here and now" quality, when you are physically re-living something, that is a memory stored **in the brain** which should be in the energy matrix instead. As soon as it is in the energy matrix, the memory has an overview quality – you can move around in it with the quality of a lucid dream, you can see all the components, you can see how it affected past, present and future, how it fits together with the rest of your timeline.

That is what happens in the tapping therapies when you deal with traumatic memories, and there was no explanation for it – but you bring in the energy matrix as a storage device for all our memories, it works.

One thing to remember the whole time about this is the question, this energy stuff - what **is** that? What is energy? Never mind, conscious mind, just go with the flow here for a moment! - **energy is inordinately more information dense** than words, or pictures, or Timothy Leary-type multi-media events, where he is trying to go for this rich information transmission. Energy is **incredibly** information dense. There is no computer in the World who can work that out, and including our brain, who can't – even though it has more neurons than there are stars in the visible sky, and the connections between them are to all intents and purposes, infinite. The brain was not meant to work it all out, the energy matrix does that.

So when you are dealing with traumatic memories, or memories which are troubling you in one way or the other still, where do they need to go?

For long term storage into the energy matrix.

In order to aid this, we came up with the idea of the Snow Globes.

Snow Globes

In Thought Flow, you take a single idea or a thought and put it behind yourself.

In the Snow Globe technique, you take a Gestalt, a memory, any amount of related information and literally put it behind yourself.

Let's do a Snow Globe exercise.

It is really quite simple.

All it does is to give permission for the content of a memory of some kind to be taken out from where it comes, and let's face it, these energy things are **real**. They are thoughtfields, and when you make a Snow Globe, you are making a thoughtfield and physically – with your hands! – taking this thoughtfield and passing it over for processing to the Higher Processing Systems.[5]

The metaphor of a Snow Globe is simply so that people can consciously participate in this process.

This is one of these Totality endeavours, just like Heart Healing.

You do it with your hands and your body.

You do it with your head.

It's a poem in Heart Healing so the unconscious mind comes on board.

These simple techniques like Snow Globes and Heart Healing are **totality techniques.**

They are trying to engage as much of the totality as we possibly can.

So what we'll do is to work in groups of two.

One person produces a memory of some kind they would like to pass over to the Higher Operating Systems for the cleaning thereof; once they are gone, they are not in your face anymore, they are not clouding your vision anymore, you can see the future and you can see the now, rather than having Aunt Mary, the child abuse, the war, September 11th, all swirling around so you are mostly groping in the dark because the past is always in front of your face.

---

[5] For diagrams & explanations, see "Snow Globes" in Addendum 2, Articles.

So take one of those, make sure all the tails have gone in and pass it over.

Just have a go.

Personal Development Rather Than Therapy

Now the deal with techniques like Heart Healing and the Snow Globes is not necessarily that you should do them with clients. Of course you can, and they are fun and often helpful, especially when you are dealing with large, sweeping gestalts that are really haunting a person.

People call themselves abuse survivors or abuse victims, and concentration camp survivors. Guys, that was 60 years ago. That shouldn't be there like that anymore. Unless that's cleared out of the way, this stuff, there is no future. As long as you are an abuse survivor, you are not over it.

Matrix Globes

By all means, the Thought Flow and the Snow Globe, and I might mention there is a version of this called the Matrix Globe, which is probably most nicely used by the hypnotherapists and the NLP practitioners, whereby you are putting a **datastream** into the globe so you don't have to look at the pictures. With a light bit of hypnosis it is actually quite easy to get people to stream the content into a globe in pure data format, this avoids abreactions. You can put a whole lot of things into one of those very, very quickly and the relief to people is enormous.

But let us very quickly remember the main point, namely that EmoTrance Level 1, the main techniques, Heart Healing, Thought Flow, the Snow Globes, the Matrix Globes are NOT what this is about. This our trail of techniques, if you will. These techniques are NOT what this is all about, and when you are training people in these techniques, don't let them get away with thinking what this is because that's not it.

These are all techniques to teach the conscious mind to get with the programme. The techniques are all **trainers** for the conscious mind to start using some of the things that it can do - **if only it knew that it can**!

Not only is the conscious mind this poor thing which has had this bad rap all these years, it is nowhere near running at the effectiveness that it could, which is one of the reasons why people get themselves into these repetitive thoughtloops or worry themselves to death about nothing all. Just so they have something to think about.

People are **designed** to consciously think at levels exceeding a thousand times than what we're doing.

The conscious mind is hyperactive simply because it is under-used. It is working nowhere near as fast and as hard as it should.

I had a lovely example of this deposited on my doorstep just a couple of days ago.

A young lady of 19 in an art class, who has anger management problems. She goes into the art class, which lasts an hour and a half. All the students arrive, sit down, the teacher declares, "Ok, you've got an hour and a half to come up with a design for an apple carton."

The girl raises an eyebrow, gets her pencil out, goes, sketch, sketch, whacks the thing on his desk, grabs her bag, thumbs her nose at the teacher and storms out.

Of course, duly the parents of said girl get the phone call from the tutor about her terrible attitude.

But here's the thing. I advised the mother to say to the girl, well this may be so for everyone else in the class that they need an hour and a half to come up with a design that takes you 10 seconds, but she should then set **her own standards and targets**.

So instead of one design, she should challenge **herself** to do a hundred.

See if she can manage a hundred different ones. For apples, pears, oranges, bananas – everything and anything that comes to mind.

The others may do just the one – but **you**, I want **you** to do a hundred.

Because you can.

But the thing is, all the students can.

They just don't know they can.

They've never been asked to produce that kind of thing. No-one has ever expected them to be able to do that. Lowest common denominator. It's horrendous how that works. I was not aware that mailshots that draw in more than a 1.5% response rate are celebrated as very successful in the industry. I didn't know this. So I used to do mailshots and get 65% response, and I was devastated. What happened to the other 35%? What did I do wrong? Seriously, this is true. I was working towards the 100%

all the time and completely unaware of the fact that you expect a 1.5% return!

The conscious mind is in the state it is in because it has never been challenged to do some things.

Interesting things. Things that it can do well. Things it is **designed** to do and which it **needs** to do in order to get back on track with the HEROS.

The energy mind, the environment is information dense and it is **fast**. It is really **fast**.

Hacking a piece off a frog so you can stare at a slide for 6 years is an anathema to every part of our being, every part of our being, including the conscious mind.

So I have a range of techniques that masquerade as therapy tools. But what they really are is to get the conscious mind to start working a bit. Do some useful things. Get some experience. Because it is the conscious mind which needs to really **speed up** in order to get with the programme.

Now you will have to forget **everything** you were ever told about being slow learners or stupid and all of that stuff. That's just bullshit. The conscious mind needs to re-set its standards and expectations of what it can really do, and we have a whole range of techniques, and the basic EmoTrance technique is a real baby tool for the conscious mind to understand that, "Oh my God! I **can** track my own sensations! I **can** make a change in this! I **can** encourage this! **I can make an effect!** Whoa!"

Yes, indeed!

Well done, conscious mind!

And it gets better with practice, and faster, come on!

The Thought Flow idea of taking an entire gestalt and throwing it into a globe, and throwing it over the top is another one of these applications.

Another range of systems I have for this are the zoom movements.

Zoom Movements

Where the conscious mind is in the most trouble and the most out of sync with the rest of the Universe is because the Universe **moves**.

All the time, everything is in flow.

But people behave as though that was a bad thing and they try and stop the flow.

So you get a car delivered, and now it's your job to make it look after ten years of heavy use as though it never left the showroom. Polish it, clean it, repair bits – just keep it frozen in time.

Keep your body frozen in time is the same story. Keep yourself at the same look and the same weight and the same levels as though you were 16, holding back, trying to reverse the flow all the time.

Healing is so terribly remedial, it is horrendous. Return the body to the same state it was in before the accident ever happened. That is fighting **the creative order** tooth and nail, it is so much useless and pointless energy expenditure in the wrong direction, it is horrendous.

Things need to flow. And one of the things the conscious mind of a human being – and remember, the consciousness is the bright white sword the Archangel Michael carries. Its a big bloody deal. It is a fantastic device, I can't begin to imagine what we could actually be doing with this once we've learned how to wield this. But in order to use this tool, the conscious mind needs to learn a few tricks.

The zoom movements are an example of that, and one of those is movement through time. Letting the conscious mind detach for a moment out of its cage of this frozen weird place where when you go to work it has to be exactly the same as it was yesterday so we can forget about the passage of time, I call that Constructville, and to zoom around a bit, to bring movement back into that game.

Timeline zoom movements are a particular part of this.

Energetic TimeLines

Have you ever wondered what an energetic timeline might look like?

Does anyone not know what timeline therapy is?

Ok, I give a brief overview.

Hypnotherapy people from long ago noticed that if you go back in the memory to an event that occurred a long time ago, and you find just the right point, you could change that memory and then, 30 years later you have an actual effect, for example that a person wouldn't be afraid of dogs anymore. That was called Pin Point Hypnotherapy.

The deal was that you would travel along this person's timeline, and found the point of disturbance, and you would take that point of disturbance. This is no different from doing EFT with opening statements like, "Even though the dog attacked me when I was 4 years old," it's a version of Pin Point Hypnotherapy.

So, what's a timeline?

That's a conscious attempt to compute something extraordinarily complicated.

Here, look at a person.

Imagine you could see his energy system.

All of it. Everything. One place, one time, all together.

Now imagine I took him into my hands, and I made him smaller, and flatter, and he became a pack of cards. Then we pull this apart longer and longer and longer – now, we have his timeline.

But in reality, put all the cards back together into the pack and look at it straight on, his timeline all exists right here in this one man.

A timeline is a **device** to allow the conscious mind to get with the programme with something that if you were to read the energy matrix directly, you would be able to see it **all at once**.

We have been told, and taught, and had it modelled for us, that the conscious mind can only handle 7 plus minus 2 bits of information. I don't think that's true. I think that's cultural hysteria along the same lines of, "If women think too much, their heads hurt."

Let's just consider for a moment what they thought when they thought of thinking.

Women think too much and their heads hurt. But my God, what are the men thinking? As though THAT was worth having?

Ouch, ouwh!

But the energetic timeline exists in a person **all at the same time**.

Just imagine what would happen if you had big breakages in that?

State changes?

Let's say we have a nice young man. He goes to war, let's say to Vietnam. He has this horrendous thing going on and now this **other person** comes home who isn't that one who went to war.

It is **not just** that he has a phobia now, or post traumatic stress disorder.

It's not Peter just with a new problem.

This is so bad, there's a school of thought to explain this that they say aliens come to land and they take over your body, and call this new person a "walk in". This is true, I saw it on the Internet. People really hold this to be a possibility, that aliens come and the original soul has left altogether, in order to explain such a personality change.

I'm just mentioning this both as an exercise in conscious stretching and zooming, as well as a form of methodology you might consider to use with a client, who has had such a cataclysmic event, which is stored in the entirety of their energy matrix, that has resulted in this effect of being two different people altogether – the person before, and the person after. And clearly what one might want to do is to re-establish a flow on that level.

Obviously, it is a technique you can use with clients, but it is about conscious **flexibility**. That is how the conscious mind gets to get out of its "cages of entrainment", to quote Krishnamurti, and to get back with the programme as the Creator designed it.

And we're going to do quite a bit of that in the next session.

Going Past The Demon Guards

Now that we've established the basics of the things we're going to be working with, we are going to do some interesting things. We are going to do demons and stuff! Yes, demons. I promised it to a lot of people. See one of the things with this energy stuff, this reconnection of the totality and that it isn't happening naturally or far more frequently, is because people are so afraid. Of a lot of things.

Some things they are afraid of because they are actually worth being afraid of. But other things they are being afraid of because – well, for no good reason really. Because mummy was afraid of them, for example, which I don't consider to be a good reason. There are a lot of people who are phobic of thunderstorms simply because their mother was, and not because they are inherently fearsome.

EmoTrance gives us the ability to go to places where everyone else fears to tread, because if we get afraid, what do we do?

Well, soften and flow. Of course.

EmoTrance gives us the ability to go looking in the energy mind for disturbances, vortices, problems – such as demons. A lot of people wouldn't go there, for love or good money, with or without a priest at hand because they are simply too afraid.

EmoTrance gives us a shield, a guide, a **resolving mechanism** and it is **all** up for grabs now because of that.

All of it is within our reach now.

There isn't a place where we cannot go.

Isn't that interesting?

What people tend to with things like demons, whatever shape or form they want to be, like, "my heroin addiction demon" would be an example of a demon, or a part of the personality which was shut down because it was deemed to be "too evil", these things are not stored inside the physical body, because if they were, they would create havoc, obviously.

You can't have your demons inside your physicality. That would cause systems failure.

So they get stored in various other places.

81

No-Go Zones

These no-go zones in your energy body are – what shall I say? – the most powerful keys to human development possible, on a very personal basis. On a very personal basis! You **know** what your own things are you've been wrestling with all your life. At one training, someone was talking about a "shadow" over their lives the entire time. Another thought they were not complete, there was something missing, and they'd always thought this, even when they were a little kid.

These are things – also family burdens sometimes come into this – which are stored in the wider energy system. This is a wonderful thing for us to experience and to do, but whilst we do, I want you to bear in mind that it is an exercise in flexibility for the conscious mind yet again.

Of course we're going to get benefits from it. Of course it is going to help ourselves get to know ourselves a lot better, and get to be a whole lot less afraid of who or what we actually are as a direct result. That is the absolutely essential first step, this fear of finding out who we really are.

When we've got **that** out of the way, then the road is clear.

So let's go and take a look ...

The Energy Buffet

<Audience member> Some of us didn't get any lunch, and we're feeling hungry now and find hard to concentrate. Do you have any ideas for us?

<S> Sure. That's easy.

Imagine if your energy body had a shape and it could walk around like a real body, so imagine, if you would, that this energy body would walk into a room which had this huge buffet.

And it's a buffet like you've never seen before,

never smelled before,

never sensed before.

There are more than

one hundred thousand items

from all across the Universe

right here

and you may choose,

and anything

and everything you are choosing,

will be **exactly**

what your energy body needs,

right here, right now

to help you,

to energise you if you need this,

to nourish you if you need this,

to warm you if you need this,

to boost your energy system

and your auto-immune system if you need this.

Eat and drink.

And this may continue while I speak, and whilst you open your eyes and come back to me.

The Energy Of Learning

One little thing before we get started with the demons. Someone asked me a very good question. He was referring to "The energy of learning", which in brief is the idea that learning is actually an energetic process, that things come from the person who speaks and the environment and the entire situation, and that all the information can go straight into our energy matrix, without us having to think much or try to remember anything much, and that we learn things so much more profoundly in that way and, "I was wondering," he said, "If you had any tips to make this process work better for me ?"

And this is what I said to him, and I thought it might be nice for one or two amongst you to hear this.

You could check yourself, if you wish, for any shields to the incoming energy which may be remaining, or any blockages. Now, when I say "incoming energy", I mean the content of what we are doing here, the content and the experiences of what we are doing here, not me personally, because I'm but a flawed human being, and I have weirdnesses going on, and I don't expect yourselves to open yourselves to those, just the energy of learning itself.

So if any of you have any shields against learning, just learning new things, the environment, because learning doesn't mean that you ever use it, or do anything with it. It's simply just accumulating a range of things like a collector would.

I thought I mention that because it is of course a very nice application of the basic EmoTrance shields principles to help you get the most out of this day. This is not only about learning what I am saying, but also from also from all the people around you, what they are doing, what is happening to them. That is in many ways much more interesting than any words I could speak.

Now, to the demons.

Demons

Demons is a generic phrase for an extreme disturbance in someone's energy system.

One of the problems with emotive language such as "demons" is that as soon as you say it, everybody freaks out. And a freak out is a technical term for even more disturbances in the energy system.

However, a demon is only an energy.

A big black vortex in somebody's energy system is only an energy.

If you remember from the EmoTrance practitioner training, even the oldest burdens or the longest, most gruesomely horrible things are at that level, only an energy.

So really, there is no need to be afraid of that.

Let us briefly remember the two main parts of basic EmoTrance, namely that:

1. Energy needs to flow and,
2. Things need to be where they are supposed to be.

When things are somewhere where they are not supposed to be, they create havoc. You can take a lovely, lovely demon and put it into an angelic dimension and you have havoc – and of course, vice versa. That is the whole deal with "a rose in an onion garden, is a weed".

Things just have to be in their rightful times and in their rightful places for most things to work perfectly. That is for memories the same as it is for components of the energy system.

In people's energy systems, we have **displaced systems**.

Evil CDs

One of them we had a lot of fun with were the so-called "evil CDs", which were energetic shards and entities which have entered your energy system **from the outside**.

They were never yours. To give an example, you say to someone, "You are an idiot." It enters the energy system – and this is why we have shields, to stop that from happening. We build the shields as a response to people throwing these energetic shards at us, and not because we're weirdoes. What happens though once a shard has entered into our energy system, we think it is **ours** – it becomes of ourselves, and the energy system deals with it as though it were a part of you when it isn't.

And these things create absolute havoc. And they are extremely resistant to treatment from the outside, such as a therapist trying to persuade this guy that he is not an idiot, because they are **of him** and now have the same protection as everything else that belongs to the totality.

But of course, they never were his, they don't belong there, they are best removed whenever they are spotted.

Evil CDs. What a term! Just like demons – but you can call them what you will, at the end of the day it is an energetic occurrence that has to go somewhere, it has to soften, it has to flow and go **where it belongs** wherever that may be.

That is as much the case for some huge big nasty disturbance in someone's energy system, something that if you were of that mind or nature, you could call it a demon, but we don't do that, because what good is that? People get scared and it makes everything even worse.

But that big black disturbance **will** soften and flow just the same as the "Oldest Burden" or the "Deepest Darkest Secret" or the terrible injuries that were done – it is quantum stuff and moves and flows most beautifully.

I don't expect you to believe me until you've seen it and done it yourself; so we are going to this wider energy system, demons exercise.

Would you like to see an exercise?

Yes?

Nicola, would you be so kind.

Demons Demonstration

<Nicola joins S on the stage>

<S>: Have you ever had the sense that there was something that was clouding your life, as it were?

<N> Yes.

<S> Have you had that for a long time? Yes. How long?

<N> Twenty five years.

<S> For 25 years you have had the feeling that there wasn't something quite right. Where is that, show me with your hands? Ok, so you can feel it in your solar plexus, but how is that connected to something in your wider energy body? Where is that coming from? Ok, it is high up to the right and connected to the Solar plexus. How do you feel when you look at it?

<N> Terror.

<S> Ok.

So what we have here is something that has been put out into high orbit, quite a way away and has been put there in that way so that it wouldn't be so close up.

Now the first rule in working with such energetic structures is to not stand in them. You stand right there and you become Nicola's demon! It will be overlaid on you.

That's the deal with people who go with dating agencies. They don't actually see the person in front of them at all, they see this energetic composite or all the weird people they have ever dated.

So when you are dealing with these sort of occurrences is to know that **just because they are invisible doesn't mean they aren't there**, and deal with them respectfully.

There is Nicola's demon and a direct line going into her Solar Plexus. I'm not going to cross that line. Imagine the reality of that thing. They are real, and they are certainly real to Nicola.

Ok, the basic theory of this thing is that it needs to go somewhere to be in its rightful place.

So where does that need to go?

<N> It needs to pass through me to get to where it needs to be.

<S> Any reason for not doing it?

<N> I'm afraid what it would do.

S: Interesting you should say that. There is a pattern called the Diamond Transformation. Most of you will know this from ET1. This is someone to fell in love, and rather than to let the experience pass through them, when it felt so good in the heart area here, they held it there. They fixed it. So it could not finish its path through. If it could have done that, it would have **changed** them. Experiencing that love and having it go all the way through and out would have changed them in the process. This is one of the reasons why people do this reflexive movement of holding things back. So now then, this fear that it would change you, where do you feel that in your body?

<N Indicates top of the chest>

<S> Soften and flow, and I will assist.

Now, let us look at your demon again. Is the idea that it should come in, pass through you and then end up in its correct position on the other side?

<N> Yes.

<S> Any conscious objections? See it is important, we are taking the conscious mind with us on this trip here. If the conscious mind has any objections, we will listen and talk about it if necessary.

<N> No I'm ready.

<S> Okay in your own time, this is your energy field. Just let it go where it needs to go, to its rightful place. To its rightful time and space.

<N starts smiling brightly> Whoa!

<S> You look happy. How did that feel?

<N> Wonderful! <laughs> Thank YOU!

<S> Excellent. Thank you very much.

Now here's a question which I want you to ask your practice partner when you're done, "What did you **think** it was before you started?"

<N> Something horrible, something hideous, something terrifying.

<S> And the actual energy required to keep it that far away? Because its natural movement was to always press in towards you.

<N> Oh enormous energy! I feel incredibly relieved, so much more balanced. Like a big weight has been released that threw me out of balance.

<S> The interesting thing about that is that it was the **misplacement** of this energy, whatever it was, that was causing the problem Not much fun having a dying star in your energy field. Not useful. But in its own rightful place, it is perfect.

Demon Exercise Instructions

So, this is what we do.

1. Ask your partner about a major disturbance. Don't use the word demon necessarily but ask them about something that they are aware of, something that has been haunting them for a long time, and if that was put in its rightful place, it would drastically help them in all ways.

2. Simply use the basic EmoTrance technique to move the energy occurrence.

3. If they are terrified, you might have to do the pre-step of dealing with that terror first.

4. If **you** get scared about what that is, you as the practitioner might have to do some EmoTrance on yourself first. Long history with fear of monsters and such.

And listen guys, this fear of monsters is nothing to be ashamed of. It is a **child's totality fear**. It is not reasonable, it is not rational and it is a full-body event – it is literally the fear little kids experience and that retains its resonance in your neurology. So should you be afraid, please deal with it. And really help each other out here. There is the two of you to help with the transformation of that thing.

Q: How do we know if it is inside or outside of the body?

A: The setup asks for something that is stored outside of the physical body. But also, this is not something you just do with everybody just off the street.

But some people will tell you about this. They talk about burdens and shadows, having an evil twin. Sometimes they come in and they have a literal distortion in their physicality. They walk as though they have something on their backs or they're leaning heavily to the left or to the right. A gentleman I saw not too long ago had his entire chest displaced five inches back from the line of his hips and legs, like he had grown around something that was sitting on his chest.

Q: Does this have to do with psychological reversal?

A: That can be an effect but we are dealing here with a massive distortion in someone's energy system, which will affect – well, all of it. It sets up distortions, massive gravity wells, disturbances and the energy invested in keeping this thing at bay is of course taken away from your life energy.

Q: I've been working with something in my body with EmoTrance but it doesn't go away. Could that be connected to something like that?

A: Yes, that's a possibility. In the demonstration with Nicola, the place where she was most aware of this was where it hurt in her body, where the pressure was – the blocked pathway the energy **should** have taken but could not. Just investigate, try it out, see if it helps, would be my suggestion.

Alright, let's discuss this further when we've had an experience of actually doing it. So off you go, work in groups of three, and remember to have a nice positive attitude. Works a treat in exorcisms.

<Audience laughs>

It's true. I've always found that to be case.

Re-Gaining The Balance

Now, I only saw some things but I did see some very wonderful things during these exercises.

I have to ask all the conscious minds here to find **some** way to handle the fact that such things can be dealt with this easily and this quickly. That it really is a case of when you find the right leverage point you can move an entire pyramid with a very small crowbar and a tap of your finger.

Just because it has been such a lot of suffering, and such length of time, complication and intensity that it cannot be resolved elegantly and easily.

A couple of things I'd like to mention.

There was a lady curled up on the floor with her team and her team stood there and went, "Help! Panic!" Simple. Person on the floor, go immediately and **join them there**. Standing watching them doesn't do any good. Rule No. 2, person on the floor denotes a person in need of **direct physical contact** and stabilisation. If you are working under psychotherapy rules, I can't help you. Sorry about that. But it's a fact that a person on the floor, curled up in a ball, just needs to be hugged or held, they are in a storm and they need something to hold on to. Now, the hug doesn't need to develop into a long romantic snog – this one did, but that could have been just me ...

Actually, it isn't a drama anyway. Just a brief moment where stabilisation is simply required. This particular person, they had experienced a shift of something that had been there for a long long time, and all they needed was a moment to help them find the new order of things, their new bearings. Another team I saw, they were all swaying with the person who was doing the release, which is a minor version of the on the floor, "My goodness my balance is all new!" experience.

When you move something like that in the energy system, of course it has an effect, and if it is a big deal like it was with the person on the floor, then of course they need a moment or two to stabilise. All you have to do is to be there for them, on the floor with them, hold their hand, give them a glass of water and wait until they are ready to get up.

Innocent Energy Evocation

Evoking innocent energy also helps with this as well, and I think I will do this for all of you before we go into the break.

You can do this with your eyes open or closed, or you can even open your night eyes now, as I am going to evoke the innocent energy.

Innocent because it doesn't care what it falls upon.

It is simply clear and so refreshing,

it can touch any part of your energy system.

It falls through

your energy system

providing moisture,

life,

replenishment

and washing away

any debris that is no longer needed,

and of course,

allowing your

energy system

to find its new

and rightful balance

after the interventions

we have done today,

breathing deeply

as this innocent energy falls

through your energy system,

all parts of them,

demons and angels alike

and everything in between,

assists the process.

All and everything you are,

is of this world,

is of this Universe,

all and everything you are

is beloved by the creative,

it could not

be any other way.

Now, if this would be useful to you, you might like to go for a walk outside in the fresh air, blow some of the cobwebs out of your head – if you find this useful.

Otherwise, do what you need to do instead during this break so you can come back refreshed and ready for action.

Congruency When Helping Others

One of the things I find particularly amusing about EmoTrance, this I also found amusing about Hypnotherapy and EFT by the way, so it is not just something about EmoTrance, I remember one of my very first ever EFT clients I ever had, she just vaguely gestured on the points most half-heartedly and stopped and said in this weak, whiny voice, "Naaah, it's no better ..."

I could feel myself losing it there somewhere, so I said to her, "Just sit there and think about spiders, I need to go the toilet." I went into the toilet and sat there, with the lid down, and thought, "What would Gary Craig do?"

So I burst out of the toilet, like a natural disaster, stormed back in there and went, "RIGHT. NOW!! Altogether, with feeling, Even though I'm afraid of spiders!"

And guess what, it was all gone in a single round. But I think she got a new phobia from that, one of Meridian Therapists.

But you know how it is with young Jedi, they get their first light sabre and they go berserk with all that power, create havoc when they first have it.

Anyway, back then it took me THAT much energy to get myself back from the brink of, "Naaah ... its not working ..." whinging into some form of proactive movement - **congruent movement** where you are actually calm and centred.

EmoTrance, EFT and Hypnotherapy are in that way exactly like an exorcism. You stand there quaking and you have no hope in hell. You have got to keep your centre and you have to keep **yourself** focussed to provide the client with the stability and guidance and space of safety they require to take that leap of faith and do something to change their problems.

The deal with EmoTrance is that nothing will move anywhere at all **unless the client gives permission** for it to do that. Now you can go and re-arrange people's energy systems against their will, and a lot of people make their living doing this, but the clients will just put it all back – shuffle, click, click – as soon as they walk out of the door. "Oh hang on, I've forgotten one important reversal!" Snick! Back into place with it.

"Well that didn't work," they say. "It lasted for all of ten seconds then it was all exactly as it had been before."

Right, so the client is the guy who is doing this, you are only assisting the client. That it the deal. And the EmoTrance chant, "It is only an energy!" is one of most useful things we have.

When people are crying and freaking, **they are not in a place where they can change themselves**.

They have got to be in that place where it is "only an energy" – ONLY when they are in that place does it work and the shifts really happen.

Something I noticed a number of times is the question of – well, it isn't even testing.

Please, do ASK if there are any objections left.

Conscious objections. Physical symptoms. Feelings of dread or emotions of uncertainty. Any little bit remaining is – something **remaining** and we don't need to put up with that.

One gentleman I saw had a "significant improvement" in something he had for a long, long time.

But a "significant improvement" doesn't mean its finished.

And we **can finish** this.

If it took three minutes for a significant improvement, then we can take ten minutes to make a complete and tidy intervention.

Ask them for their objections freely and openly, because that is of course **your client's ecology**. If they say that there's something there, but they need to keep the something for if they didn't, something else over there would go freaky ... we need to know about this to make a tidy intervention.

Sometimes you don't need to ask about such things. The client's jumping around all over the place, going, "Whoohoo! This is the greatest day of my life!" in which case there's no need to ask.

But if they're just standing there and looking around or looking scared, then clearly there's more work you need to do.

Remember the energised end state!

Working With The Wider Energy System

Now, the demon exercise was a multi-level experience for you in a number of things.

- The first and most important learning is that the basic rules of EmoTrance energy work do not stop when you get to work with the wider energy field;

- that no matter how scary or old, it is still an energy and no matter what someone may call it, and it softens and flows just as well as anything else;

- that the feedback mechanisms **are not as direct** any longer as when you have something stuck in your forehead;

- and most importantly, all the time, to **pay attention** to people showing you their own internal realities with their eyes, with their hands, with their bodies, with their clearly perceivable emotional responses and state shifts.

Physiological Feedback & Evidence

What that is when you see someone looking up at the ceiling and going pale with fear and starting to tremble, and when you've dealt with it, they don't anymore but they are beaming instead, this is the **evidence** we talked about the conscious mind needs to understand and compute energetic reality correctly.

This evidence is all around us.

"My boyfriend does my head in," they say and show you with both hands a pushing inward movement on their temples. It isn't a figure of speech, it is an actual and deadly real reality that's going on there.

That is **evidence** and that is what the conscious mind needs to start looking for. And the more you look you will find that we are living in a

...

Imagine for a moment if you could see this room at the energetic levels, you could see everyone sitting in this room, all that information about them, past, present and future. And not just these people here, right now, but everyone who has ever danced here, imprinted in the floorboards, inscribed in the very structure of the walls themselves of this 100 year old building. It is all there.

And best of all, there are parts of us which can read **all of it**. And that is normal, and easy – even though it is such an overwhelming seeming flow of energy. There are parts of us which can read it, compute it, understand it and navigate it, and when it does and **you remember that it does** then the world is no longer a frightening place.

It becomes predictable; it becomes logical and completely **reasonable** – and we don't have to be afraid anymore. Now, is that not nice? I certainly think it is.

A Better Connection With Your HEROS

Something that I would like to talk about a little further is the energy mind, and perhaps my energy mind can come up with a suitable exercise on the topic before we go into the break.

Something that I didn't know was just how very **practical** a good relationship with the energy mind actually is. Now it is true that I have had a good relationship with my energy mind over the years for such things as paintings and poetry, metaphors and hypnosis, writing books, giving lectures, sure.

But practical things?

I allowed my HEROS to decide which fridge-freezer to purchase for my kitchen.

I walked into this big warehouse full of the things, and they all look the same, big and boxy and mostly white, and I just followed my own pointing finger and said, "That one."

It fits.

Now you may laugh, but that is exactly the kind **of action** to bring these systems correctly on line. Some religions call it a leap of faith. Putting your money where your mouth is. Acting in accord.

And that's the title of this weekend, namely "Living Energy".

This doesn't mean so much that energy is alive – of course it is! – it means, actually **LIVING IT**.

Living energy consciousness.

Not just giving lip service to it, not just doing it on Saturdays in meditation classes, or after work for five minutes in the bath, but **ALL THE TIME** – ALL the time.

Now, our HEROS are waiting to support us, have been waiting to support us, because they are there to serve our totality. That **is** what they are there for. It is not a favour on their part.

We have them by courtesy of the Creative, build into our standard model of a human, and they have only one single purpose – **namely to serve our totalities.**

But we don't use them, because we think we have to do everything the hard way.

I've got to get a tape measure and measure the space in my kitchen, up and down. Write it down on a piece of paper. Take the piece of paper to the shop and then take the tape measure to ALL the fridge-freezers there, one after the other, up and down, and compare it to what I've written on the piece of paper, and worry that I didn't measure it right, that I didn't write it down right. And what will happen if I get it wrong, oh my God!

I've got a very small kitchen where I'm living at the moment and needed a dining room table. Hundreds of them in the shop, all different shapes and sizes. I just walk in and say, "Pack me – hm, THAT one."

"But it won't fit in your car."

"Yes, it will."

And it did, by a fraction of an inch either side.

Car auction. Two and a half thousand cars. What do I know about cars? I walk in, straight in, immediately see one, say dreamily, "We'll have that one if we can get it for under £6000, that'll be a good buy." We got it for £5,850 and then afterwards looked the make and model up in one of those used car guides and yes, it was a very good price.

Now, the HEROS can calculate complexities which are a million, million times beyond what the conscious mind can do.

This is not a guess. It is not a gamble. It is a **certainty**.

Calculating the dimensions of a fridge, I'm sorry, Ladies and Gentlemen, is a piece of piss for that system!

It is designed to be aware of the movements of the stars, and the sun, and the seasons, and the deer, the birds, myself, my entire family – that is what it's for, survival. Past and future, all of that.

It is the easiest thing for it to work out which book you should be reading – that kind of thing is NOTHING for that system. Really!

But we don't use it for that, we use the old fashioned hard work methods of to-ing and fro-ing, and one of the tasks I have for you tonight is for you to devise some things you are going to hand over to your HEROS to do.

It is up to you what level of importance you are willing to gamble.

Now I have gambled my entire financial construct-incarnation on certain things, and that was long before the fridge and the dining room furniture. But you really need to do that, because if you don't, how will you ever get **the evidence** the conscious mind needs to start the process of leaving more for the HEROS to do?

And particularly the energy mind is so unbelievably useful in that context.

You save so much time! You don't have to try on 500 suits to get the one that is just right. You just point. "That one. Thank you." All done.

So this is really the deal.

Use it or lose it.

I think that's the deal with the soul.

It is the deal with the heart.

And most especially is this so with the energy mind.

But it doesn't even stop there.

We have to also start using our conscious mind to a whole new level of using it.

Not one painting or design for an apple carton in an hour and a half, but a hundred instead.

We need to really re-set our expectations of what we can do, really stretch ourselves a bit at last and in that context, to devise a way in which you can start gambling some things on **your own energy mind**.

The hypnosis teachers always say, "Trusting, trusting the unconscious mind ..."

But you cannot ask that of the conscious mind.

It needs **hard evidence**.

I personally have some interesting evidence starting to pile up – **but that is ONLY because I've run the right experiments.**

Try it out.

Simple things like NOT trying to consciously remember something, and seeing if you still know it when you get there and the time has come, I think, to step out of the HEROS closet, as it were.

Nicola and I have both – yes, it is funny! – we have not had a scratch of preparation for this. Not a single piece of paper between us. I've just turned up here, and I have absolutely refused to worry about what I was going to say here or what order and sequence I was going to present this in. And I haven't run out of words today, have I.

Did this flow?

Yes.

Have I ummed and ahed?

No.

Not one single line of preparation for a three day training weekend. In fact, this is the other way around. What I am saying here will be recorded and transcribed to produce the book and manual.

I guess that's what Richard Bandler means by "trusting your unconscious mind".

For Nicola that was particularly impressive as she hasn't done this before. And funny, too. She'd get a sheet of paper out and say, "Oh I must, must write something down ... at least an outline .... else I'll forget ..." but then, there was the sheet of paper and she'd laugh and say, "Ah, it'll be alright!"

Things like being able to stand up and just talk for days on end coherently and congruently – that's worth having. In fact, having the HEROS in your life is like having your own personal Super-HEROS! I can't begin to tell you what they can do for you. What they can give you. Not just the support you've always wanted, but so much more beyond that.

I want to give you one more example – credit card bills.

I used to see them there on a pile and worry about them. Worry about them every day but not do anything about them, until perhaps one second before that "pay by" date was critical, but then you miss it anyway and have to pay an extra fine, you know that sort of thing.

About three months ago, I passed the whole thing over to my HEROS.

The result is that I don't think about them at all anymore. Not at all, and thus I don't worry. Yet this really strange things happens that I get up one day, and the thought just drifts through my mind, "Oh I think I'll do the credit cards and bills ..." and just there and then, I do them all in about ten minutes, walk them lovingly to the postbox – and then forget all about them again until a month later. No more late fees. No more stress.

Can you imagine how much stress this could take out of your life? Do you think it would take even further stress out to wonder if now would be a good time to do something or not? Oh but does it! I didn't actually realise how much stress I actually was under, all the time, worrying about when to do the bills, or if the fridge fits, or whether to wash up before or after watching TV – the most ridiculously stupid things like that.

You take that out, and what you have left, is ... space.

To create your own reality in your own special way.

Exercise: A Better Connection With Your HEROS

This is a partner exercise where we will help each other to get into a better relationship with these higher energy systems.

However you do that.

- Whether you need to remove barriers;
- whether you need to rescind fears as to what would happen if you did;
- whether there are permission issues;
- whether it is ideas of pain.

Whatever it is for each and every one of you, help your partner on their way to have a better connection within themselves and to help them become a better functioning totality.

Q: What about soul loss?

See I don't really think you can lose your soul. You can't sell it to the devil either. It's one of those things. I think it is a term that is used but it might be better to say, "There are big parts of me missing," or, "I haven't got access to parts of my energy system," or totality loss might be a better word, because I really don't think you can lose your soul. It's kind of stuck.

I had a four hour rolling on the floor argument with a Catholic not too long ago until I finally came to the understanding that he didn't mean soul at all in the same way as I did. At which point we tried to redefine our terms and things improved from there. I apologise to everyone who has a problem with the term "soul" but you have to call it something, and when it came up I probably didn't feel I was well qualified to re-name souls.

When I say the word soul, let's just remember I mean nothing spooky by it, just a functional, integral and absolutely **really existing** part of the energy system of every person, which exists at the quantum levels where time is all time, which makes it structurally immortal and does factually survive the death of the physicality. Nothing more and certainly, nothing less.

Q: How often do you expect to have to use Thought Flow before the thought stays gone?

A: Me personally, as often as necessary and with some things, it seems like a million times before it gets resolved. Some of my repetitive thoughts, they come really quickly all the time, and I throw them over real quickly in response. But the next day, it is usually already markedly less frequent. What I am noticing now is that sometimes, I can literally feel a thought going there automatically – it just slithers off that way as soon as it has occurred! Now I really like that. That is the same as with the basic EmoTrance process. Sometimes you notice something but it is already slithering off before you have a chance to even think, "Soften and flow."

And that's how it should be, anyway. Rather than going into a shop and thinking all laboriously, "I shall allow my HEROS to find me a fridge ..." it should be automatic. Fast. So you got your hands free to do something else, something you like, instead of all that worrying.

Q: Are there limitations to the HEROS systems, or the human totality?

A: I think that there are limitations, but I think they are way beyond what we can imagine. I think that we are in the position of a refugee child who has found a Mars bar wrapper and licked it. And that's the first time they tasted anything else but gone off porridge. And we are going, "Whoa! There could be something else out there!" I would say that it is my idea that life is so horrible is that we are not starting at 0 at all, we are starting at minus 600 on the Richter scale. Our happiness isn't actually happiness at all yet, we just think it is in comparison to the misery.

Summation: The Evolutionary Spiral Of Life

Let me sum up today's adventures in energy land.

A human being is a totality which consists of many components; there are some which are more essential for survival than others.

For long term survival and immortality, the HEROS system is of the essence.

The pathway which includes the conscious mind, namely that the questions from the conscious mind are given to the energy mind, and the experiences and observations; the energy mind codes and stores this; the information then goes via the soul to the heart which decides the next course of action, and this gives new thoughts, new directions, new orders if you will to the conscious mind as what to do next; I may speculate **in response to what the soul needs us to do whilst we are here.**

It makes sense in this flow system; if the information flow passed through the soul, and that was just some sort of funnel, that would be quite pointless. You could go from the energy mind straight to the heart and there would be no need for the soul-system at all but I would propose the idea that the soul requires certain experiences to have had, to be fully actualised.

So the current experiences get passed down to the soul, the soul asks for something else, this gets **translated** by the heart into something the conscious mind can understand and so it thinks, "Oh yes! I know what to do next! I have to explore a new continent!" Then it thinks, "Oh, but HOW?!" and that gets passed then again to the energy mind for the next circuit through that system, only it isn't a loop or a circle.

This is an evolutionary spiral.

It is a wonderful spiral that is evolving as this stream of energy changes all the time, and what changes it is the incoming energy streams as we interact with the environment through our physicality. It changes all the time in direct response to the environments you find yourself in.

Every single thing you experience, every thing you do moves this whole system **forward** on its path – as the creative intended it to be doing.

Tell me this is not a nice model!

It is friendly, it is workable, it allows us step stones to get into it, to collect evidence – our own evidence! – what the conscious mind needs to come on board.

This means you don't have to believe anyone else, only your own evidence, which is always correct and once again, as the creative designed this to be. We don't take some guru's evidence, or some dead prophet's evidence, but ONLY **your own life experiences**.

Those dead prophets, they've lived, they've done their thing, and there's nothing to be gained by doing **their lives** all over again, is there.

That's a bit of a waste of time for all concerned – instead, we have to do **our lives** correctly in the flow.

Now, some of these techniques and exercises we've done (and they're all flow related, EmoTrance related, and in the end, it is only energy!) are all designed to bring the flow of this totality system back in motion.

Whether I ever talk about souls, or whether I ever mention this at all, all the techniques are directly designed to re-establish flow in the totality.

EmoTrance Level 1 is designed to re-establish the connection between the conscious mind and the physicality. The HEROS system is the re-establishment between the conscious mind and the higher energy systems, especially the energy mind, and tomorrow, we are going to do be doing something especially nice, and that is to turn towards a particularly neglected aspect of ourselves, namely the poor old physicality.

The RSPCA makes a lot of money by going round showing people pictures of mistreated dogs and cats.

Now I can show people pictures of mistreated people.

Popstars and models. Any fashion magazine. Look at these poor bastards. Look at them! Just look at that SHIT they put on their faces – poor misguided fools, do you really think you can improve on what the **Creator** made you by adding some paint?

It is sad what they put their physicalities through.

Poor, poor people.

But not to fear. We are here to the rescue!

We shall give them a different model, a different approach.

One of kindness and of caring, which is long overdue.

And one of compassion, which is what is required if we want to come to a point of forward momentum and dancing.

I will mention this before we conclude here.

I was going to do a Project Sanctuary CD which was called "Energy Dancing". The idea was for people who were so obese that they can't walk anymore, people who don't have legs, who are in a wheelchair, so that they could go into Sanctuary, and in Sanctuary, they have a body and they can dance, right?

Ha! Fool that I am.

I arrived at Sanctuary, and I looked at people's bodies – and they couldn't dance, hell, they could hardly crawl. And these were people WITH legs and not in wheelchairs.

We're not ready to dance.

But we will be.

That is my intention.

PART 2 - THE AUTOGENIC UNIVERSE

Welcome to this second part of our journey here, which is about the body, the autogenic body, the conscious mind and how it all hangs together.

I developed Project Sanctuary to reconnect the conscious mind with the energy mind. Then there is EmoTrance Level 1 which reconnects the conscious mind to the physicality and the energy systems; and EmoTrance Level 2 which reconnects all of that to the higher energy operating systems.

So now, we have only one major system left to be dealing with, and that would be the physicality directly.

The Physicality In The Totality System

The physicality is actually what people have the most problems with, in general.

Even if they say they are having emotional problems, or business problems, in the end it is all about the body being stressed and unhappy, for it is really difficult to say that you are having a problem when you are lying somewhere, pleasant and warm, being stroked lovingly with oils and told how wonderful you are.

It is difficult to be stressed out about your life under those kind of circumstances, and so the body always reflects and causes, one way or the other, one's life's experiences.

I love the comment Oscar Wilde made, "By the time a man is 50, he has the face he deserves."

Role Models

If you remember, I have spoken at some length in Part 1 about learning to have compassion for the conscious mind. It has been berated and accused and blamed for all the bizarre problems we experience in our societies, from the unbelievable one way system in Brighton that drives hundreds of thousands crazy each and every day, to the characters of our construct world leaders and all the other nonsense that is going on.

I just saw a perfume advertisement on the television last night, with your requisite half dead heroin addict anorexic in their last stages of decrepitude being held up as a role model to ourselves and the young of today. They had even put pink and purple eye shadow underneath her eyes to make her look as though she was even more at death's door than the poor anorexic bitch was already – she literally looked like a three day old corpse. Super-expensive Christmas market advertisement, that was. I looked at that and couldn't help but shake my head and sigh.

I thought, if she goes on like that, she'll never get to fifty to have earned that face she deserves! By the time she's fifty, she'll be maggot fodder. And will of course thus have, the face she deserves ... oh dear ...

But of course, that particular young woman actually DOESN'T deserve that. **No-one does.** It isn't her fault. She was just born into this madness and unlucky enough to have "a good bone structure" and be over 6 foot tall.

Now one of the problems for all of us in what we are doing here is that we have no **ROLE MODELS.**

There are no role models for us people to look up to and say, "Yes, that's a good example of a fully actualised human being who's really got it together, who's really glowing and shiny and intelligent and showing this in their physicality, in touch with their creative forces, the soul is shining, and you can see a lovely bright white light over their heads, everyone can see it, be they enlightened themselves or not, to the degree that these people get invited down mineshafts when the lamps run out."

Where are these people?

We hear of them in song and tale but where are they in reality?

There simply ARE no role models.

So what the conscious mind does which doesn't actually manufacture new ideas of its own, not ever because it can't, because it needs to draw on the creativity and imagination of other parts of the totality to get anything done at all?

What does it do?

It has to take existing things, things it has seen before, and copies them, makes them more intense without changing their structure or essence, so that's how we get our generations of perfume models getting ever more intensely anorexic and generations of young girls role **modelling THE SAME INSANITY** as a result.

And it doesn't stop there.

The conscious mind, devoid of original solutions to existing problems, can actually map across one thing to another, so now we also have anorexic boy models. Now, the same hollow heroin addict starvation look is on the male models, just as well. I could hardly believe it when I looked up the Top Ten "male models" not long ago. My God, they look sick! If you saw any one of them lying in the corner somewhere, you would call an ambulance!

So the absence of role models is a huge, huge problem for the conscious mind and left to its own devices, it can only go "harder and faster" and create situations of absolute travesties.

But let's get personal here for a moment.

Who ARE YOUR personal role models?

WHO do YOU want to grow up to be like?

Someone said, "I want to be me."

Right, but the problem is, what exactly does that entail?

Do you have any idea who "me" could actually be?

Can you understand the problem, and how enormous that is?

And I do believe that one of the core reason for things being as desperate and remedial as they are, is exactly because **GOAL POSTS AND ROLE MODELS ARE MISSING** which **draw development towards it.**

If you show someone something, and you say to them, "There it is, there's your goal. Now go get it!", that is easy. They know what they want, and they can then figure out just how to get there, to get it.

But if there's nothing there at all, where do you go?

This way? That way? That way over there?

And the problem with that is that every step you take, IF IT IS IN THE WRONG DIRECTION, will actually take you further and further away from the true goal – which you don't know where it is. So structurally, you can truly never take any steps in ANY direction at all because the fear is always there that it might actually increase the distance.

This of course causes endless stress and anxiety on oh! so many levels.

113

What people do is that they use devices to alleviate this endless anxiety and day-to-day stress, because you have to CHOOSE actions and paths and such EVERY SINGLE DAY. It is never ending. So what they do is to use devices like Guiding Stars to help them have some form of guidance towards what they might actually want. The way traumas and guiding stars direct someone's incarnation is a direct result of the absence of a role model, or a goal, to draw them towards itself.

The Other

I very well remember the night when I was having a glass of wine with some very good friends in my house. I had received a standard advertisement for "low rate interest loans" that day and the letter was still on the kitchen table. On it said, "Dear Homeowner. What would you do if you had £12,000? What would you spend it on? A lovely holiday in the sun? A new car? Or perhaps ... that home improvement you've been waiting for so long?"

So? Is that it?

Is that the menu? What's the next item for me to choose from?

But there wasn't anything else. That was it.

Now that may have been sad enough all by itself, but when I put this to the party, even my best enlightened intelligent, creative friends would come up with things such as, "I'd buy a piano." But surely, that comes under home improvement! "I'd go to a Tibetan Monastery and meditate for a whole year."

That's the lovely holiday in the sun!

So it went on and the horrible discovery was that we couldn't actually come up with ANYTHING AT ALL that wasn't either a version of travel, car or status symbol, or a nice holiday EITHER!

Now, don't get me wrong. We did really try. One person said they would do an NLP practitioner training with the money. But I had already seen how it works and said, "Yeah but what will you do when you come out of the training?" – "Well I'd be able to get a better job, earn more money – and finally, be able to afford that holiday in the sun ..."

Gotcha!

But this is it. Those three things, that is ALL Constructville has to offer its inhabitants.

That is IT. What else is there? What can I do?

Become a guru and sit on a cushion all day whilst the lepers file by?

As a job description and the end accomplishment of your career path?

Dear Jesus! And whilst we're there, perhaps I should get myself hammered to a cross, or burned alive as the outcome of the career path?

Well I can't of course know about anyone else but that just isn't **MY** idea of joy.

I'd even rather do home improvements if I had to.

So that night, I got very angry and I stood up and said, "I don't want ANY OF THAT SHIT. I don't want to be a guru or a healer or a priest or a teacher or a millionaire who has endless holidays in the sun – I want to be ... ANOTHER!!"

AN **OTHER.**

And what, pray tell, is an **OTHER?**

It is someone who I have never seen.

Not in my town, not in the big city, not on television, not in my trainings.

I have heard vague whispering about them across the centuries, but they must exist because the potential is there **in the template of the human totality.**

People who can come up with something better than having £12,000 and either spending it on a holiday, a car or home improvements. Or avoid the whole horrible issue by just giving it to charity. What a cop out that is.

It MUST be possible that there are people who would be able to do better than anything I've seen so far.

It is built into the very structure of the human being BY DESIGN.

It is like you have this computer and its programmes. Now of course, YOU PERSONALLY have never managed to get that programme to run, and you don't know anyone who got it to run either – but just by being there, the structural possibility exists that it can work.

There's hope.

So I want to go straight to the jugular with this one.

If we were to find a role model for ourselves – and we are all different, bear in mind, even though we are a similar base model with eyes, ears, noses and such – but in the context of that, if you look at your neighbours, and even bearing in mind that we are quite cohesive in our genetics, where we come from, the time we were born in and such, people are quite different.

How are EACH ONE OF THESE VERY DIFFERENT PEOPLE to have a role model that fits them perfectly EACH ONE?

Now in the past, prophets and such have been held up as role models.

Which is understandable, because the conscious mind operates on the Highest Taste Principle.

The Highest Taste Principle

Here's a simple example of how this works.

You might meet a man (or a woman, if you are not that way inclined) and he is just the best thing you've ever seen. You fall madly in love with him, get married, live happily and then this other guy walks in, and he is actually even BETTER than the first one. What happens is that then you leave the first one, because he is no longer the "Highest Taste" and run off with the second.

Until a third comes along.

Then, you have a baby, and that is even BETTER than all the three men put together. And in fact, all three men were rather abusive so you take the baby and live by yourself.

This goes on for a while until one day, our person has an enlightenment experience – and leaves the child in an orphanage to go and become a nun!

This is how it happens that some guy can simply don an orange robe, and leave their 4 wives, 18 children, the cows and the goats, their aged

116

mother and father, after a total full-on lifetime's entrainment of having to be a good family man behind to just walk out and go sit on a mountain top, regardless of the wailing.

What motivates all these behaviours is the **Highest Taste Principle.**

But don't think that this is only in action with such things as love affairs that **shape entire incarnations.**

It is in fact **a basic and entirely content free organisational device that RUNS EVERYTHING.**

It works for everything. It sorts out for you what you like BEST and how to behave. You used to always buy Nescafe, and then you try Nescafe Gold. That tastes better and now you ALWAYS buy Nescafe Gold instead. The principle of the Highest Taste applies to all and any decisions we make – consciously.

This is a operating principle of the conscious mind, and indeed, of the totality – we are DESIGNED to always seek and always strive for the Highest Possible Taste.

The best experience, the brightest star, the most wonderful feelings.

Now, isn't that the most wonderful thing to know about our own neurology? That it works automatically like that? All of us, every person, everyone – even dogs do it! That's how they train their owners what to feed them. From cheap dog food to expensive, then into cat food, then into proper gravy, into lightly stewed lamb's liver with j-j-j-ust the right amount of garlic ...

That is not actually the pain pleasure principle but instead, it's the **"pleasure – more pleasure – even MORE pleasure" principle.** And it is always directed towards the very best on offer at the time.

But here's the thing.

If you had said to the first lady, the one with the three husbands I mentioned earlier, that there would be at LEAST four more higher tastes coming along in the next ten years, she would not, could not have consciously believed me.

That's like trying to tell a teenage girl with a major crush that there is anything else beyond that, better than that, more than that.

You cannot convince **a conscious mind** of the validity of this – **IF THERE IS NO EVIDENCE.**

And there cannot be any evidence of the coming Higher Tastes yet – **because they have not yet arrived.**

Now, in fact the truth is that logic and intuition actually belong together. They are not at conflict at all. They must be one system, and they work together perfectly well if we let them.

There IS no conflict when you put logic and intuition back together, it just seems that way when you look at things in isolation.

How can we re-set our higher taste?

Well, the truth is that we don't actually have to.

All we need to be able to do is to make the conscious mind understand that there is a pattern there, and then it can **EXTRAPOLATE as it is designed to do that there LOGICALLY MUST BE a next step, a new sunrise, a next higher taste – in and for ABSOLUTELY EVERYTHING!**

AND that this goes on for as long as you live and never, never, ever stops – AT ALL.

If you can go honestly through the evidence of your OWN life and track how you have followed this higher taste principle – in shoes, in records, in flavours of breakfast muesli, it really matters not, your conscious mind MUST come to the logical conclusion, and it really **MUST** come to that, that no matter how much you like something right now, or no matter how right you think you are **right** now, there is **ANOTHER STEP.**

No matter how great the house you're in ...

No matter how great the health you're in ...

Even though I really believe right now that this is it ...

... there is always a next step.

Can you understand just how important that is?

It isn't bad being wrong. But staying wrong, is.

Now, people work and learn by trial and error, by experiments, and sometimes they work, and sometimes they don't.

However, being wrong has been tainted with the idea that it means you are bad when you are wrong, possibly even evil – good and bad, right and wrong, good and evil.

So if you're right you're good and if you're wrong, you're evil. This causes people to sometimes stay on in situations that they full well know are wrong for them, simply because **they can't admit that these situations are wrong.**

There are people staying in marriages for years that they knew on the second day had been a mistake. And 22 years later, they're still there, nursing their various cancers and wondering why their lives aren't working.

This is the principle of why being wrong isn't bad, that's only human, but staying wrong is bad, because it is so very destructive.

We couldn't be talking about any of this at all or even consider such concepts as this if we didn't have something to help us deal with the fear. Not the conscious fear of being wrong, but that gut churning fear when you start thinking about your marriage and your relationships and that really only stops when you eat something or you really, really concentrate on your developing database.

This is why EmoTrance Level 1 is the key to so many other things – they just tumble like domino-stones when you confront this gut churning fear and resolve it.

You can't address thoughts and feelings like, "My God I've been solidly wrong every day for 25 years ..." without having something to help you deal with that sense of doom, of gut wrenching horror, and you can't even look at it, you can't even go there because it makes you feel so sick and uneasy – and so it seems a better option to deny it all and stay with the old crap. But we now have a method of dealing with this problem, and more importantly, once you get your head around the higher taste principle, the Universe is more or less at your fingertips.

It means that things are NOT as good as they get the way they are.

Which is at the basic root of the desperation in Constructville to keep things at the Status Quo.

You know, the car you just bought in the showroom, that's the best car you've ever had. It is the greatest car in the world. There cannot be a greater car after it. So we mustn't lose this car. We must keep it in "showroom condition". We must dedicate our lives to make a shrine of this thing and polish and best not even take it out for too many drives in case it gets a chip in the paintwork – this is the best car in the Universe!

This is the best marriage, the best job, the best I can do – this is my best thought.

This is how people get stuck on having a single good idea and then spending the rest of their lives telling others about it, cause they'll never be having another, right? My wife just left me, and I'll never have another wife as great as her because she's the best there is. It's all highest taste principle. Ok. And there's no better coffee either. And the showroom has no other car. There are 9 billion people – **think logically.**

This of course conflicts massively with many Constructville rules and regulations. Monogamy is one of those. And I'm afraid I don't believe in it, I think it's completely ridiculous. It doesn't work, it causes complete misery, unnecessary contortions and endless heartache – the entire contents of every single stupid daytime television soap opera you could ever possibly begin to want to watch. And until we get rid of this preposterous notion and get all of that out of the way, how can we begin to think about something else for a change? Take the whole adultery, illegitimate children, bored with husband, jealousy intrigues CRAP out of Constructville, you'd leave a hole so enormous, you'd actually have to **start thinking** to fill it. Just imagine it. Societies starting to think. Girls not worrying anymore about boyfriends, their bodies and their make-up and how to attract them and endless chatter about who's going out with whom and instead discussing the creative, or their own designs as to how to make the world a better place, where would we be?

Anarchy!

A population of thinking human beings!

But for now, let us simply note about the highest taste principle and that staying locked in the last-highest taste because you think it doesn't get any better than that is not a good idea.

If one understands this principle, not only does the world immediately become a far more exciting place. We – and especially our conscious minds! – **can also turn forward and begin to actively SEEK OUT the next highest taste in anything.**

Now this really and truly doesn't mean that one should be dissatisfied all the time with everything.

In the contrary.

The current highest taste **is** always most rewarding and wonderful, it is a great state of being. But for evolution and **TRUE evolution,** to not and never get stuck there, to try and then close one's eyes, ears, intuition and such, batten down the hatches and make decisions like, right here I am and I'm gonna stay here forever, THAT is the wonderful escape from the previous cages of our own makings, that is the way forward and **into states of being, of accomplishments and works that have NEVER existed before at all.**

The Template

Our consciousness needs a guiding star to orientate itself by, and the question is then of course, in the absence (and impossibility!) of any role model, where do we get a template from to become our own guiding star for each one of us, individual to each one of us individuals, to become our personal guiding star and pull us forwards and towards a new future?

When faced with this very question, here is what I did. I was so frustrated with the lack of available guidance that once again, I was having a discussion with friends as to what my mysterious "others" might do during the day, what they eat for breakfast, what they do for amusement, where they go on holiday. If they are not like us at all, how can we know what they do?

In the end, and as I absolutely couldn't it figure out consciously, I asked the HEROS.

I asked for a role model.

And do you know what they showed me?

They showed me a template of my – MY! – design as intended by the Creator.

And it was very different from what we are looking at here today.

Because what you see here today, is what we have after that template has been through the ringer for 45 years. I wasn't designed to be this fat. I was NOT designed to be this short sighted. I wasn't designed to be this stupid, this conflicted, this unhappy, depressed, mad – I wasn't designed to be this mad, I was driven mad after the fact.

And the HEROS showed me the template of this other.

I thought, whoa.

And I wanted to **be her** so badly I thought my heart would break. I wanted an affirmation, something, some word to say to be able to shout out aloud, yes, yes, that's who I want to be, that IS who I NEED to become or move towards, please give me a word, give me an affirmation.

And the answer shouted back so loud it nearly deafened me – **"SILVIA!"**

The ultimate affirmation – not for you, of course, but for me.

The ultimate template is YOUR OWN inherent design, your Creator template.

That is the ONLY possible role model for each and every person possible. You can't take someone else's template and try and grow into that, that is totally wrong.

At one time, I tried on the Jesus Christ jacket. But it just didn't fit. Might have been the breasts. The Mother Mary virgin thing wasn't much good either, having two children.

I needed my template. And I got to see it and it has become my guiding star.

What you might like to do in a moment is to

> close your eyes if you wish,
>
> and just consider for a moment
>
> if you had some idea,
>
> let some idea build up
>
> of your own

original
design
as the Creator
intended it
to be,
your original
totality design
with everything
working together,
what might
you
look
like.

At this current age,
or even
a little bit older
than you are right now,
what might you be
moving like?

That template
is actually stored
in every strand
of our DNA,
in every part
of our energy system –

who YOU

were supposed

to have been

in this incarnation,

your template

in the perfection

of the Creator's design,

not made by some guy,

but by the creative order itself.

Get a really strong sense of that,

as strong as you can allow

yourself to sense that,

see that,

note the location

and also note

what you are thinking

when you

are getting in touch

with it,

whether you want

to be like that,

whether you want

to become

THAT person.

Now we can go

on a little bit further

and if you were

that person,

and allow yourself

to consider that

for a moment,

to get a sense

of how different life would be

for you,

and those around you.

Allow yourself

to experience this

as fully as you want to,

and retaining

the sense of connection,

let us return to the here and now.

I wonder what that was like for you.

Many people find it totally amazing.

This template, if you are working as a practitioner, or as a trainer of a group, if you can get your people to get some sense of their own template and orient them towards THAT template, rather than towards pictures in a fashion magazine, or pictures in their own family photo album when they were 16 on holiday in Spain, with that lovely 16 year old face, and **take them away from the orientation to the past, or to someone else**, and orient them BACK to their own template as the creative designed them to be, and then say to them, "All that hard work you've been doing, trying to be a good person, now put it into becoming THAT, becoming ONE with that," then you're actually giving people something worthwhile.

This is probably one of the most profound personal experiences I've ever had with that kind of thing. I can't believe that I have actually seen a version of me that I would want to be. I have spent an entire lifetime NOT wanting to be me! In every sense, in every way and shape you can possibly imagine, and to see this version of ME that I really want to be – wow! It has done a lot for me.

But it is a practical thing.

In moments of doubt, we often ask ourselves, what would the template do?

And the answer usually is, she just wouldn't!

She wouldn't BE in the situations I am finding myself in!

And that is fun to see.

Something else that I find extraordinary about my template is that she is so light. Joyous and light. She is so alive. And I want to be her. That's who I want to be.

So now, when someone asks me what I want to be when I finally grow up, I have the answer.

I want to be Silvia.

The Template Exercise

This is a very important thing. I don't think that this makes people selfish or that it takes them away from the Creator. Quite in the contrary. The state we are in, we haven't got much chance to do anything worth doing rather than just lie there and perhaps squawk once in a while.

This other, on the other hand, has a chance at a real close connection with the creative. This other can serve the creative, if you will, like we now never could. We are too full of doubt and misery and pain, hamstringing ourselves, and whatever your life's work is, **that other would do it better**. It is really as simple as that. You often hear it said that we mustn't try and sort ourselves out and have to wash leper's feet for the rest of our lives because it is only in the service of others that we can make our way to the promised land.

Ok, fair enough, but **let us get to a place first where we even can begin to give service to others.**

We're not ready for service. This isn't selfishness but survival. Survival first, helping others after.

So this is what I want you to do.

Give this your best effort. Have your partner connect to their own template. Help them all you can. If they have fears or doubts, help them out with EmoTrance or any other energy therapy. Have them make it clear and strong and connect with it.

Also, help your partner to find an affirmation or an evocation to call up their template. If you have changed names since birth or have other name issues, you need to figure out just what you are going to consciously say or think to call up your template when you need to remind yourself or you are seeking guidance.

The Template & The Physicality

The template is the essential pre-requisite to start working with the body.

Because of the way we are not consciously factoring energy things into the maps of our Universes which everyone tries to build as they are growing up, trying to make sense of things, finding out things, conducting our experiments, because we don't have this energy realm to consciously compute, what happens is that our physicality, or what we think we look like, or what other people tell us we look like, or smell like, sound like, whatever, feel like, bears our main brunt of our dissatisfaction as human beings.

It is the first place the torturers will go to break you.

The physicality is the first thing that gets attacked, the first thing that gets warped, the first thing that people will go to with their interventions if they want to do something to and with you. In the army they tell you to stand up straight and put your body into a uniform.

As a result of this, we've all ended up with a completely idiotic idea of what our bodies are and what they are for; I don't want to even use the term of "body image" because it is much worse than that, goes much further than that.

When we have the guiding template and look at it we begin to recognise that the body is not this fixed thing, it isn't a model.

It is a developing group of cells that are working together and they are organising themselves towards an end.

Just like a strange fish-like embryo organises itself to become a human being, our bodies organise themselves to become anew as they are going through time, **all the time** – that's the core of Deepak Chopra's Quantum Medicine, and this makes people very excited and very happy, because it gives them hope that even long standing and old injuries may be reversible.

But it's not a question of reversible.

It's a question of all these cells and they are all individual swarms of cells – it seems to be this one body standing here but it is a hugely flowing, interactive system, constantly developing, constantly in movement, constantly in motion – that's what physicality is, and what it didn't have was to have a proper organising principle, **something to organise it TOWARDS**.

The problem is for us that our conscious minds interfered in the organising principles MASSIVELY.

When I say massively, I mean MASSIVELY, **causing massive disturbances to this template** towards which the physicality tries to arrange itself and grow towards.

Reversal Disturbances

One of the first ones I saw was this reversal disturbance when people try to hold back time and they try to remain 15 or 16 forever. The Peter Pan psychosis. It is amusing until they're 65 or so, then it becomes painful. And it causes all sorts of problems, it is painful. Even more painful when you take the whole plastic surgery business into consideration.

But trying to hold back time and direct towards a past time guiding star is the least of the problems.

What interferes so horrendously with the physicality and causes this in the first place is what I call the Autogenic Body – the conscious mind's idea of what the physicality is like, right now.

And that, ladies and gentlemen, is nothing less than Frankenstein's Monster.

Created out of dead parts.

You have your father's eyes and your mother's nose. Viewed from a certain angle, you look like Miss Piggy. You're too short, too tall, too fat, too thin, your legs are bendy. Your ears are sticking out. Your hair's too stringy. Too curly, too thick, too straight. It's falling out. It's growing in places where it shouldn't.

Well you know.

As people gain consciousness as children and they take these things and they try and piece them together into a body.

And they end up with Frankenstein's monster.

That's the **Autogenic Body Template** and we will discover more about it and ways of coming to its rescue in the next part.

The Autogenic Body

Let me begin by quickly paraphrasing what we have already discussed, namely that the physicality, or the body, THE body – well that is a piece of Korzybskian insanity. It is not a solid block, but it is a flowing thing, a malleable thing, that is **shaped all the time by our consciousness**.

If you remember the diagram of the three HEROS, with the little box that denotes the conscious mind, I said then that this is what is causing the problem – the ONLY thing which is causing the problems. And it isn't causing the problems because it's evil or has anything to do with Lucifer or anything like that but because it isn't being used correctly in the context of the totality.

The conscious mind isn't understood at all and no-one seems to know how it really works, probably because evolutionary speaking, it is quite new. It is quite a bizarre thing to be finding yourself with all of a sudden, a consciousness. You have to figure out how to use this thing and humanity hasn't done too well with that for the last 10,000 years from what I can see.

But we can use this thing.

So I came at this whole autogenic thing from a personal standpoint, namely weight loss.

Well I said we have to find evidence, evidence that makes sense to our own conscious mind to bring it back on track, allow it to co-operate properly; I have my own convincers and you will have your personal things. One of mine is to make fire in the palm of my hand. Not hypnotically, I can make you all see that if I wanted to, but a real fire so you can then take a candle and light it from my fire here. Not just one, either. I'll be doing this all day when I first figure out how to do this.

Another one of those is weight loss. Well, not really weight loss. The truth is that I have always disliked that term so intensely. This is not just about weight loss. It is about me being more of my template. And I know this isn't it. There are people who are sturdy or stout, and that is their template, but this size isn't mine. Never was and I always knew this. Interestingly enough, when EFT first came out, a lot of people tried to apply it to weight loss programmes, but they weren't particularly successful. And in fact they were exactly the same in outcomes as the K-

Diets and all of that, they showed an improvement in the first few weeks and then it all went away, nothing structural had changed.

This was most disappointing to the people who worked with that and that's why they don't want to talk about it anymore and it isn't really a topic anymore. So yes, you can tap your cravings away but it doesn't seem to make much difference over the long run because you just find yourself unconsciously eating something else. Damn unconscious mind! What a saboteur! I could be healthy, I could be happy, I could be beautiful, I could be loved if it wasn't for my unconscious mind! Shut the fucker off!

No, no! That's the wrong way!

Then we have weight loss and the energy system. That really never made any sense to me in energetic terms even though I tried to figure something out with that over the years; not in some kind of driven investigation because I'm actually not that well connected to my physicality in any shape or form as I usually spend my life floating about ten meters above myself but it's been something that I can use as evidence procedure as I'm monitoring myself doing trips to the fridge or refusing exercise, or whatever they tell you to do to get in shape, get fit – there's even a word now they're using to replace beautiful, "Oh look he's fit!"

So, I'm just playing with it. I'm never applying willpower to it because I'm interested in my own processes, how it all works. I don't actually eat that much. Now a lot of fat people say that, but I actually really don't, and still generate all this energy for all these things I do, it's a marvellous testimony to the fact that there isn't actually a linear cause and effect relationship between what people eat and how fat they are.

So I'm standing in front of a fridge and I'm not thinking anything in particular for once, which was a very good thing so that the HEROS had the space to send me a little insight into the thing, namely that it wasn't my energy body that is fat, **but my autogenic body.**

The Body Thoughtfield

What's an autogenic body?

The autogenic body is the construct that the conscious mind has created from the external incoming evidence over time.

Incoming external evidence.

Like when you're a little kid and you're just wandering about and you have no concept of anything really and someone comes along and says, "You're a nice little girl." that gets put in as a puzzle piece. So I'm a nice little girl. Then Aunty Mary comes along and says, "My god, you look just like your uncle Joe." Who is 6 foot 5 and has a red beard ...

Well the conscious mind takes these puzzle pieces and tries to make a map out of them. That is what the conscious mind does. It just tries to organise things into some form of logic. And over time these things build up into a denser and denser thoughtfield.

The more attention you give a thoughtfield, the more dense it becomes.

If we all went on a lovely retreat together and sat in circles and hypnotised each other, we'd all be seeing angels by the end of the first day. By the end of the third, you'd been having stigmata, full blown psychosomatics, reverse your cancers, see spaceships – and you'd swear that it was all absolutely real. Mass illusions and group delusions are very powerful. The more attention you give to a thoughtfield, the more real it becomes. It is one of those facts of life, it is one of those things that you can do with consciousness. To create thoughtfields from nothing.

Especially a person's **body thoughtfield** can become incredibly dense, right up to the point that when they look into the mirror, they don't see the physicality anymore, they see the thoughtfield instead, or sometimes they see the physicality overlaid with a shadow of the thoughtfield, but in the case of anorexics for example, or people who suffer from body dismorphia, who take razor blades to their faces in order to cut of those protrusions that they can see in the mirror, the thoughtfield has become so dense that it is absolutely real to the person in question.

This also explains this sense of unfamiliarity when you look into the mirror and don't recognise yourself. Cause you are expecting to see the thoughtfield.

The thoughtfield is not one thing. It is a writhing, churning mass of conflicting weirdness. Right from, "You ugly bitch, get out of my sight," to "Oh my god, you're the most beautiful woman I've ever seen."

These things are with us in practice and practicality in every way. It is with us in the concept of inner beauty where the attraction or attractiveness of a person cannot be explained by their physicality alone. It is with us everywhere. This is of course the picture of Dorian Grey. A beautiful young man who really is behind the scenes a writhing atrocity. This is one of the core reasons for people creating shields and cocoons because if you know you are a writhing atrocity, then of course you have to hide this from your fellow men and women. That's that whole business with keeping your true self inside and no-one must ever, ever see it. When there's finally someone you really, really trust you open it up just for one second and you can see the horror in their eyes ... they've seen your "true self" and it's not a pretty sight ...

Imagine a little baby with their senses and eyes to see these things still intact. Night eyes still wide open, and here comes monster-mommy ... oh dear ... and that's what I'll grow up to be ... role model ...

But this is where it finally begins to make some sense.

I was married to this guy who for 22 years told me every day at least 20 times how fat I was. I'm actually quite pleased, I've done well that I haven't ended up being the size of the Universe. I must have had some thing in there to keep it to these manageable proportions in spite of that.

So I thought, cool. I've got this autogenic body, I know where it comes from, how it works. I just saw the whole thing in a flash, I know why I've always felt so ugly. See this is it. Another one of those – I love it when that happens. **See I was RIGHT to think that**. I wasn't deluded, I wasn't wrong, I wasn't having low self esteem – I was completely correct. My autogenic body is a nightmare! Uncle Peter's belly, pig ears – oink, oink! All these things! God almighty, all these things! I even know why I often play with the idea of having a tail. Because I had an aunt when I was a very small kid who thought it was funny to tell me I had one. And I kept trying to turn round and round in circles trying to see it. Everyone thought it was highly amusing. So now I have an autogenic tail. Thank you, Auntie! People may have horns if they have been told repeatedly that they are the son of Lucifer.

But there we have it. So I'm standing in front of the fridge with my brand new discovered autogenic body and the intention is to eat a piece of quiche. I often do this. But here is the beautiful thing. As I am picking up the piece of quiche, I become aware that what I am eating isn't actually quiche at all.

I am eating AUTOGENIC QUICHE!

Magic quiche.

Quiche where one little triangle piece like that contains more calories than can be found in a hundred buckets of lard.

Magic cake. One slice of chocolate cake the size of a matchbox, and someone puts on 30 pounds!

Now the cause and effect relationship of this has never actually been properly established because that middle step of the autogenic body is missing. You know somehow that this is so but logically it doesn't make any sense because you need that in-between of the autogenic body to make sense of it, to make the whole thing work.

It is the autogenic body which shapes the physical body.

The physical body is a mass in motion, looking for some guidance to tell it where to go.

And the autogenic template is in between it and the normal procedure whereby a dog just grows up to be a dog and then dies. The consciously created autogenic templates are in between this.

But it is actually much, much more interesting than that.

Do you think the autogenic quiche is the end of it?

Of course not! I went, "Oh my god, I'm in the matrix!"

I am standing on autogenic feet on an autogenic floor in an autogenic house that I have given all kinds of meanings and all kinds of attributes – magic all around. What does that fridge mean? What does that floor mean? What are those things on the wall? What are they? What meanings have I attributed to them? How have I made them magical, like I made that piece of quiche magical? That piece of quiche has the power to put on ten pounds in the absence of actual nutritional value.

Ladies and Gentleman, THAT is magic!

I have turned a harmless piece of egg and pastry into an energy bomb! And my body responds to this. Now of course we could have freakouts at this point as we are beginning to question if anything is real. The answer to that is, "Hey that is a very good question, and never stop asking it!" Cause if you believe things are real and they are not, you will go astray and do all sorts of strange things, and further, many things in the Universe will never make any sense. But there's a vice versa, because when you believe things aren't there when they actually are, you're in trouble also. If there really is a monster under your bed, then you will lose your legs.

Well it is all a bit much to take in all at once but don't worry, the real horror of all of this will hit you sooner or later.

I was standing there staring at my piece of quiche and the whole thing had just unfolded for me how this works, how this actually physically works – see **autogenic quiche makes the autogenic body fat.** Now, the autogenic body's fat and the **physical body tries to fill that fat template**.

This takes a little while which breaks up the immediate cause and effect and that's what used to be the trouble. We've bee told that **if you think** something makes you fat, it does make you fat but where is the evidence for that? The conscious mind can't hang on to the cause-and-effect because it is broken by the intervening step of the autogenic body. Which you only get to see when you factor in the energy dimensions. You don't get to see this if you don't factor in the energy dimensions like thoughtfields and the ability of consciousness to create actually real reality.

Here is an interesting thing. Animals and especially companion animals such as dogs and cats and horses, they of course don't really have autogenic Universes – but when you put them into ours, they respond to the rules of our Universes. As do plants. And there's your evidence procedure.

If it was JUST people, you could talk it all away as just being a hallucination and one of those weird things people do. But it isn't just people. Animals and plants and even mould and yeast ALSO respond to people's autogenic interventions such as praying over mould and loving your houseplants or being completely convinced that this concoction you are feeding your pet is good for it and so it lives for 24 years when the average life span is actually 12.

So now, ladies and gentlemen, what we have on our hands here is MAGIC!

It is magic.

You don't know anymore what is good. You TELL it what's good. This hemlock chalice is indeed, everlasting beauty and glorious enlightenment. Cheers!

This also goes again to our anomalies. Things like Seneca. Couple of thousand years ago, this guy fell out of favour with his current prince and they send a couple of soldiers round to force him to commit suicide by drinking hemlock. He drinks the hemlock but he doesn't die. So they put him in the bath and open his veins. It's got to be suicide so there won't be riot, it wouldn't have looked good if people thought he'd been executed. So he goes in the bath, they open his veins, but they just heal over again. This is well documented. In the end, they just chopped his head off. These anomalies where poisons don't kill people as they should. But we can also go to the other anomalies if you like, which are rampant, namely whereby totally harmless substances cause people to do this weird stuff. They die or their heads blow up like a balloon, or they get rashes all over themselves – also known as allergies. What's wrong with a grain of wheat or a peanut? What is causing that?

What is causing that is an instruction that this is poison. And it poisons the autogenic body and the real body has to follow suit.

In preparation of the horror of all of this, and please do your EmoTrance if you have to, I want to give you a useful tool.

When you have found out that you have done something very wrong in your life, that you have made a real bloody mess over the long term, the thing to do at that point is to think or say the following:

And now, knowing that this is so, HOW can I use this to my advantage?

If you have found out there is an energy dimension, and your autogenic interventions have caused your loved ones to die of cancer, and you have come to realise, "Oh my God, **I** did that!" and yes, you're right. It really WAS you. Welcome to the autogenic Universe and the power you actually have because of it. Now at this point, of course there is a moment of horror and "Oh dear, oh dear ..." but then we must stop and think or say instead,

And now, and knowing that this is so, how can we use this to our advantage?

If I'm standing there holding quiche which can make the inmates of a starvation camp eventually become fat, what could I say instead this does for me and have it be so?

What could this BECOME for me? What could this DO for me?

I was pretty overcome by the occasion and of course, it was all pretty new to me. But what I ended up saying was in the end was, "This is the most life giving and nutritious piece of food that has ever passed my lips."

And then I ate it.

And I felt a huge rush of energy.

Now you can call this a post hypnotic suggestion or a self hypnotic suggestion if you want but even so, then let's ask how do they work?

How do suggestions, affirmations, hypnosis and all of that work?

They work by influencing the autogenic Universe, that is how they work.

Hypnosis and all its manifestations, placebo effects, spontaneous remissions, faith healing – all these anomalies make perfect sense when you bring in the autogenic Universe and the autogenic body. That is and was always how this worked, and now, and knowing that this is so, how can we use this to our advantage?

Well, we can take control of this thing.

Which is of course was what the conscious mind was always supposed to do.

When in the olden days we were told to do affirmations, "I like myself, I like myself," and "Every day in every way I'm getting better and better," what stops that from working is **a conscious filter of disbelief which disturbs the cohesion of the thoughtfield you are creating.**

When you are making a thoughtfield, it has to be pure, for the want of a better word.

For example, let us imagine I wanted to create the thoughtfield of a small chalice just there. If, during the making of this little thoughtfield I'm thinking that I'm not doing anything at all or questioning whether I should even be doing it, the best that's going to be made at the end of the day is some form of wiggly, weaving weirdness that never takes on its real form.

This takes us back to evidence.

You have to find your own way to bring your conscious mind on board. Everyone has to find their own evidence procedure and some of the things that I use in preference are behavioural evidence.

Is my own behaviour, visible and measurable, different before and after an autogenic intervention?

For example, I was making a cup of coffee.

There are three things of which I partake generously. One is red wine because someone once told me it was life giving and the only thing that makes life worth living. And I always found this to be so; I drink a small amount of it and I just brighten up and feel more alive. It just takes a little tiny bit of it to do the magic.

Another is black coffee with one spoon of sugar.

And every spoon of sugar that goes into every cup of coffee comes with, "Oh my God, I'm going to get even fatter than I already am."

Every one of them. 10, 20 cups a day. Every day. So and as I was done with the quiche and making a cup of coffee, this time I caught the thought because I was in that frame of mind. I caught the thought by the tail and went, "Oh for fuck's sake." Talk about affirmations! 30 years, every single spoon of sugar! Oh please! Even if you leave the whole autogenic body and all of that out of it – what HAVE you been doing to yourself, Silvia?!

So I just looked at the sugar and asked for a different meaning, a different magic, a good magic to replace the old voodoo and because it looked like snow, I thought, "Hmmm .... Glacier energy. Pure. Cold and bright." But then it went further. I thought, "Well what if I didn't actually put that in the coffee at all and was to say instead that coffee without sugar is the taste of the NEW?"

I tried the coffee. It tasted unusual and I couldn't really for a moment think as to if I liked it or not, but then the thought came, "Oh the taste of the new." and it was amazing. I really, really liked it and for a time I was quite fascinated by the experience, right inside it until I woke up and thought, "My, THAT was easy?"

That's not struggling with willpower. That's not putting Post-It notes on my fridge, that's not practising it a hundred times. It was so easy.

This happened about two weeks ago and now I'm not putting sugar in my coffee.

I don't mind if someone else does, after all, it is bright glacier energy. The only thing is the effect is a little too much for me, I get a bit too hyper. But that's ok, and still the black coffee is the taste of the new. Re-affirming itself with every sip.

It really is that simple.

It is really only a thoughtfield. I made it and I have the power to change it.

And finally, after all these years, the things the affirmation people were saying clicked together in my head and I understood it. Yes, they had an evidence procedure to satisfy them to the point where the conscious mind came on board, and when that happens you are congruent, and when you congruently saying to a piece of quiche, "YOU ARE LIFE GIVING and re-shaping my autogenic body to perfection," and you are doing this deliberately, and with power, and without doubt, well then it works. **Then you are making a stable, powerful thoughtfield that will last – probably forever.**

How far does this go?

How far can you take this?

I don't know because it is pretty new to me.

But yesterday, a lot of people came in and said they didn't get their lunch. And I did this little thing with an autogenic buffet where your autogenic bodies could go and choose what they wanted to eat and that did the trick, didn't it.

I have noticed in myself that often hunger pangs are not what they seem, they are autogenic, not physical. So I eat quiche but really I wanted strawberries and melons, exotic red oozing fruit, but you wouldn't find that in my fridge. Even so, and even if you had alien fruit in the fridge, that's not what's required anyway – **AUTOGENIC or energy food is what is required.**

It is some sort of magic potion energy food needed somewhere and doing this has alleviated at least three out of four trips to the fridge. It is frightening to think that what I thought were hunger pangs were really no such thing and that these could originate from anywhere else but from the physicality had never occurred to me.

This is even though we have the concept of Energy Nutrition in ET Level 1. That a whole heap of things we are hungry for and needful of **are not actually hard in origin but instead, they are energy forms and non-material in nature.**

And the autogenic body, being the appalling mess that it is, of course needs all the nutrition and all the healing it can get its hands on.

Now, I'd like to do an exercise.

Think autogenic body for a moment.

Re-Connecting Our Broken Bodies

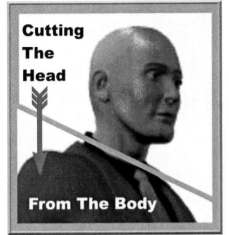

Cutting The Head

From The Body

For the first thing, we have a distinction between your head and the rest of the body. Breaking up our own body into parts is already a major problem and it causes major disturbances and distortions in the energy system which is much faster and more direct in responding to the autogenic disturbances than the physicality which takes its time to have cells migrate and morph from here to there, from this to that.

But apart from the head, there are other major demarcation lines. You can see them when you look at someone who is dressed like "normal people" are. The head sticks out. The hands stick out. The feet have demarcations where the shoes end, where the socks end. All traditional clothing is worked around those demarcation lines of course in the first place.

But of course, the worst breakages are around the so-called bikini line or where underwear or swimsuits are being worn. Outside those areas, we have "publicly acceptable", inside we have "shameful and must be hidden at all costs".

So for this exercise, with a partner or by yourself, the affirmation or intent is, "One body."

At the same time, **stroke across these demarcation lines to literally re-unify your own body** (or that of a partner) for the first time since you were a child and **your body parts got disconnected autogenically** when you learned to name your hands, your fingers, your knees and they all became separate bits then.

If you are doing this by yourself, the affirmation is, "One body, my body," and you should really **touch and stroke in long sweeping strokes across these barriers and boundaries to erase them now.**

When you are doing this with a partner, one should do the stroking, only for sake of propriety and for now, we float the hands and don't touch and we focus on, "One body." The person who is being re-united joins the process and they think, "My body," as the other makes the long sweeping passes.

One Body Demonstration

<With demonstration person> Pick up your partners hand and start there. See, there's a wristwatch. Another demarcation line, a distinction between the hand and the wrist, but it really is one body instead. The same with the so called fingers. It is just one body. <Strokes fingers up to hand, across wrist and arm.>

That is a simple little exercise for the person who is experiencing this from the inside to simply think, "This is my body," and to reject the distinctions for a moment.

This is important, because these breakages, these distinctions **directly cause disturbances in the energy flow** and major problems in the energy body, because **the autogenic template doesn't just pull the physical body out of shape, it pulls the energy body out of shape.**

See, the physical body is slower to react to this. The cells are hard, they have to migrate to form all the things they need to form, but energy is quantum. This causes disturbances instantly.

<Points to the demonstration person's chest> Here is another distinction line, where the bra is. Up above this line, it's alright to show this "bit" of the body in public; below that, a different story, a different world altogether. This is so more so for women than for men, but men also have this because a man without a shirt on is not welcome in a good restaurant, right? What is he going to do? Express breast milk over the food? I don't know. Sweat and shake?

But this is why we have to put it back together. Not this is my chest or these are my breasts, but **this IS my body**. Not this is my organ heart, this is my spine, this is my spleen and all that baloney, but to allow your consciousness to really flow clearly through all of you for once, as **we undo these boundaries**, as your partner makes these passes and assists you with this.

Ah, and then of course, if we go further down, then we really get into the most terrifying territory!

Genitals!

Seriously, use EmoTrance if you have to, your willpower – just don't be afraid!

Genitals!

And it's round the back as well!

Now, if I was a male practitioner, I'd probably be sued within an inch of my life, and frankly, ideally, this really should be done with touch so that she really feels this, it makes all the difference. But I shan't be asking you to start massaging each other's breasts and genitals, and it's a shame that I can't because that is actually what is really required. By cutting these things off as we do, putting them into certain situations but not having them at all in other situations – like, every day, all the time! – cause **massive disturbances** in the autogenic body and in the energy system, and especially this whole genital area here, and the back end of it, that is so **massively** disturbed in most living western human beings, that the energy system doesn't have a snowflake's chance in hell to do enlightenment flow.

Now if we were even leaning to the Chinese idea of "Dragon Rising" or Kundalini rising, as the other term goes, there is some energy that is supposed to flow from the base of the spine all the way up – how the hell is it going to do that with these breakages, these boundaries, these vortex disturbances?

It is literally impossible.

Which is why we can understand why these religions try and get the body out of the way, or the mind out of the way, so that there is some hope of energy flow. This is also why they say one shouldn't do this before you're ready, because imagine, just imagine what would happen if that sort of lightning strike energy was to hit these totally distorted, freaked out, mal-connected systems. Oh my God what's going to happen? Anything. You can turn into a serial killer or a rapist, or a schizophrenic, or one of those who starts wanking in the streets and gets carted off to a lunatic asylum. And that is **exactly** what happens, and that's exactly why it's been said that the whole enlightenment thing is too dodgy and too dangerous, don't try it. Exactly because of that.

So this basic reconnection of the body is absolutely essential and really, really important. I really can't stress that enough.

And also, for the practitioners who are making the passes over the other person's body, this is of course an excellent opportunity for you, say if you were sexually abused at some time by a person of that gender, as you are doing this to flow **your own energy** as you are hitting these areas.

If you get afraid, ashamed, freaked out, uncomfortable, use EmoTrance immediately and let's help each other out here from both ends, inside and out.

<To Demonstration Person> How does that feel to you when we do this?

<Person> It feels strange ... warm, pleasant ...

Pleasant. Yes, it is. And the reason it feels pleasant is because it is **right**. It is **right** to have one single functioning body, and it is wrong to have it all cut up into bits like this, with some being worse than others. Everything needs to flow all the way through.

Now, to the exercise. Find a partner. Be a little experimentative. Pick someone you wouldn't normally choose and do this simply exercise, for seeing this body for what it is, a simple malleable physicality without boundaries, in flow, given to you by your Creator.

Affecting A Change In The Autogenic Body

For adults, the power over the autogenic body resides entirely in the owner of the autogenic body.

To hold the autogenic body cohesive, shields are erected. Exceptions are when people are children, or under extreme circumstances, such as being in love with them and dropping shields, other than that, the autogenic body is shielded from intervention from others.

This is superseded in moments of stress when the shields are not available. For example, when a doctor tells someone they have 6 months to live.

A hypnotherapist gets people to drop shields so that their words can become a part of the autogenic Universe again, like they did when the person was a child.

Different body states have different shielding parameters.

I'm particularly happy about this, because this brings hypnosis back in from the cold. It was sitting there with its phenomena, way out to the left hand side, and it never made much sense in spite of all the evidence accrued; now it does.

A hypnotist affects the autogenic Universe of the person.

If the hypnotist says to someone, "This quiche is healing quiche," then this will affect the person's autogenic Universe as the new instructions **become a part of the LAWS** of that person's autogenic Universe.

I've been extremely interested in the fact that things like beliefs and values – and people do know this on some level, again, but once again, the cause-and-effect of how someone's beliefs and values shape their lives doesn't take the step of the autogenic Universe into consideration and becomes too tenuous for scientific evaluation and doesn't make sense.

You have no idea yet just **how much** you can do with this just yet.

How much **you** can do with this, you personally. Don't think about your clients, think about yourselves.

I posted a nice little pattern to the StarFields list about turning one of my drinking glasses into a Healing Chalice.[6]

Re-Setting The Laws Of Our Autogenic Worlds

Now if we're living in the matrix, then we get to write the rules.

I get to decide now how I feel here, what attitude I have to you people, who you are.

It is NOT left to accident or chance any longer because I can say who you are.

I can say that you are wonderful people, and that you will support me, and that you will listen to me on these two days, and that becomes a law of my autogenic Universe, and no matter what you are doing, that is **what my perception will be**.

The conscious mind then seeks the evidence **to support the decision that has been made**.

I can't tell you how pleased I am about this.

I used to be in personal development for donkey's years and there were all these things – these tempting things like affirmations and goal setting, hypnosis and self hypnosis, and autogenics, especially autogenics, because there is so much research about autogenics. Like basketball players visualising scoring goals and growing muscle tissue without having moved an inch. There's a movie about some piano player who didn't get near a piano for years because he was in a concentration camp. He came out, put his fingers to the keys and played beautifully. He was asked, "How on Earth is this possible without practice?" and he said, "I practice every night in Sanctuary." Now he didn't say Sanctuary, he said, I practiced in my mind, but he practiced his autogenic body.

This goes much, much further.

What do you take into Sanctuary?

Your autogenic body, of course, and that is **completely** under conscious control.

---

[6] See Witch Proud, Addendum 1, Articles & Essays

God has literally NOTHING to do with your autogenic body.

Free will, ladies and gentlemen.

Conscious mind decisions.

I'm beautiful, I'm ugly – it is entirely up to you.

Now, remember what I said.

You cannot use this successfully **until and unless you have convinced yourself** using **your own** experiments, your own trial-and-error procedures and you have learned **how this works for you**.

I have my own evidence procedures, and I've been a hypnotist for many years, but it was never really evidence for me.

Hypnosis & Autogenics

I had a friend who came in and said, "Oh I can't join you in a glass of wine because I'll have a terrible hangover tomorrow morning."

That is a **law from <u>her</u> autogenic Universe**, and that is the law under which **her autogenic body operates**, and which in turn **will produce the physical sensations** of a hangover.

She will feel as though a bear is sitting on her head, even though **there is no bear**.

There really is no bear.

It is just energy.

So I said to her, "Ah, but what you didn't know is that this doesn't apply for bottles of wine that are cheaper than £1.50 per bottle. And this one so happens to be ..."

It was only a bit of fun a couple of years ago, but her shields were down, it went straight in and this is still a reality to her. Up to £1.49, no hangover. £1.50 and over ... the whole morning, not being able to see clients, feeling like death warmed up.

I used to do these things and marvel at them, but then put them aside because I really couldn't understand how this would work. I knew it worked, I did it, every hypnotist knows it works, but we didn't know **how**.

We didn't know what we were doing, and this is what makes this so much fun and so interesting.

So when a different friend came round, many years later, and I produced a bottle of life giving, nourishing red wine, and she said, "Oh I couldn't possibly drink THAT, that will give me a migraine!", **I** had that **congruency** that the old hypnotists used to be talking about which you need for power hypnosis.

I looked her straight in the eye and said, "But this is **different** wine. This is **life giving** wine. You'll feel so good, you won't believe it."

And of course, she did.

How difficult is that?

Like, it's not!

It's amazing. But again, back to that evidence procedure of the conscious mind.

You have to find your own evidence procedure.

Let me say something about this body exercise.

It isn't actually possible until the person in question you are doing this with knows how to do EmoTrance, or you know how to do EmoTrance, or preferably both, because if you are kneeling in front of their genitals and they are going inside and saying, "Oh my God I can't believe it, there's a man kneeling in front of me, that's just exactly what happened when I was three years old and Uncle Bill used to sexually assault me in the cellar .... aaargh ..." of course, absolutely NOTHING is gained.

Don't do that with people like that. All that would do is to trigger all the old things. And if you're kneeling in front of some guy and going, "Aaargh this is so embarrassing and horrible ..." as a therapist, it's not going to help either.

This can't actually be done properly until both of those can feel this weirdness coming up and the old stuff coming up and **release it, there and then**, or stop the other briefly and say, "Stop, I'm having a moment, I need some help!"

See **if you just re-play your old games with new actors over and over again, nothing is learned.** Only the old is re-affirmed. "Somebody kneels in front of me, and that feels terrible." Nothing is gained. This exercise is one of these realms of things **you can't even do** until you have EmoTrance. You can't even get near it.

But once you have a hang of feeling these things coming up, and you can feel them and get rid of them, THEN you have this tool of having the consciousness flow through the entire body and accept it for once, and break those old thresholds, break those old barriers, and that's what restores your autogenic body and brings it back towards the idea of the template.

Questions?

Q: If you are doing an energy based intervention, led by the therapist's unconscious mind, and someone has a real big experience that seems to have changed their entire world view, what happened there?

A: What happened there is that you made a direct intervention in that person's system. Because if you can **get in** like a hypnotist does, or an authority figure, or a priest, or like mommy and daddy used to be able to when you were small, **if you can get in there, you can <u>re-write the rules</u> of their autogenic Universe according to your <u>own gospel</u>**.

Cult leaders, religious leaders and teachers have been doing this since the dawn of the ages.

You **create their Universe for them**.

- **As they don't know that they can re-create it or un-create it, they will run with those rules in their Universe until they die.**

And those rules, that autogenic Universe, that is the "cages of entrainment" that Krishnamurti talked about.

The autogenic Universe IS the cage of entrainment.

That is what keeps the conscious mind stuck inside itself and keeps that other bigger Universe, where we have the creative order, the star fields, the souls, all this magic we've been looking for, outside.

Questions on the Autogenic Body

Q: What is the difference between the energy body and the autogenic body?

A: The autogenic body is made by the conscious mind. It is made out of thoughtfields. The energy body comes courtesy of the Creator, as does the physicality.

Q: Is that like "the map is not the territory"?

A: Exactly. The autogenic Universe is the map, and it is NOT reality.

Q: Is the autogenic body shielded from the view of others?

A: Yes, it is. People put layers on the outside to hide the autogenic monstrosity inside. Sometimes like onion layers, at that. They don't want other people to see it. Much like we hide our breasts behind a piece of fabric. It's one of those things.

Q: How come we get it so wrong?

A: When you're small, you don't know you are doing this. It happens chaotically. The rules derive from bizarre computations. I used to have good and evil completely reversed for a long time. I had good defined as quiet, lying, lying more, lying lots more, only doing evil things when others weren't looking, and generally being a completely two faced, evil bastard, that was being good. Evil was being noisy, intelligent, creative, and asking questions. I didn't figure that one out until I was nearly 35.

Now it's time for lunch and I might ask you to become that observer who watches their thoughts go by, because these thoughts reveal your rules in your autogenic Universe relating to food.[7]

That should be interesting.

I'm not asking you to change anything, just become **aware** of it and start plotting and planning.

---

[7] Reference Essay "Good VS Evil" 2000

Fun & Games with the Autogenic Universe

Now I've written down this headline, "Fun and Games with the Autogenic Universe."

If we were to consider for a moment if it were true that **we can write our own laws** and if you've come from an energy healing, body orientated background, and you haven't done much with values and beliefs and attitudes, and words and neuro-linguistics, don't fret.

The thing is this. How fast someone heals depends on a rule they have on how fast someone can heal. Or if you can heal at all. Or if that particular thing can be healed. Of if it can be healed by you, through you, whether a healing can be experienced depends on the rules of their autogenic Universe. It used to be called beliefs and attitudes, values and such.

I call all of these "rules".

And some things which are entirely resistant to all forms of energy healing, massage or allopathic interventions at that, are resistant to healing because there is a rule in their autogenic Universe which doesn't allow the healing.

It's not all in the mind.

It is the reality for a person.

Re-setting the rules in the autogenic Universe in which I live has been, for me, the most profoundly useful and user-friendly and fast change methods that I have ever experienced.

- Because when you re-set rules, you can re-set **basic rules** that influence other rules.

Many sub-rules can all hang on one underlying thing. For example if you have an underlying belief on how long it takes for a simple flesh wound to heal, that sets an underlying **general healing** rule against which everything else is measured. That rule then runs your entire operating system.

So if you could change rules, you could change **all kinds of rules**.

Just off the top of my head, how about, "I can change people."

If you had that rule in your autogenic Universe, how would you use it? On your children, on your parents? Your lovers? Your clients? Or people in your trainings?

What would that do for your experience, or for your evidence feedback of the reality you are experiencing?

Here's where playing with the autogenic Universe becomes interesting.

When you change a rule, the conscious mind goes to work and **collects evidence in accordance to that rule**.

That's like before, when you had a rule that you must be ugly, and all these people tell you you're beautiful until the cows come home, and all that was simply discarded because it was **contrary to the existing rule.**

Is anyone going to ask me what this has to do with **real** reality?

Have you all seen that movie, The Matrix?

Well you should because it's an interesting metaphor. There are these people all asleep in pods and in order for them not to go nuts, they have this virtual reality programme. If you KNOW that it is virtual, you get to change the rules – you can fly, jump enormous distances, stop bullets with your hands and you're great at martial arts. That's the best they could come up with as examples of the benefits when you change the rules, but we shall forgive them. Anyway, in there they have the usual idea that it is better to be in the matrix, because **real** reality is actually terrible.

This is an ongoing hallmark metaphor throughout story, fable and tale that the illusion is better than **real** reality.

I don't know how many movies I have seen where people found out there were in some kind of virtual reality, and when they got into the real reality, it was so much worse – eating rats, and everything had fallen down and everything was distorted, disfigured and horrendous.

It is a real idea that the illusion is better than reality.

Well, I think that is a lie.

And I think I can prove that.

Have you ever seen an illusionary cardboard moon hanging over a cardboard sea?

Does that even come close to a real moon over a real ocean?

Right.

That is my evidence procedure.

I have **never** seen a painting of a sunrise that comes close to a real sunrise. I have never seen a painting or a photograph of a man that comes close to a man.

- And I put forth the proposition that **real** reality is better than any illusion could possibly be.

However, we are in an interesting in-between state, because I don't think we can get into real reality without first getting out of Constructville. Illusion city. Out of the cages of entrainment. Out of insanity, as Korzybski termed it. Lots of people have noticed this apart from me and I think it's actually true, because you can't experience real reality before you have woken up to the fact that **there is** an **autogenic reality** – and you're in it! And you are in charge of what you are seeing, that you have created illusions around you and you understand that they are thoughtfields and that you created them.

Then you can become the master of these thoughtfields and you can ask them to step aside and clean the doors of your perception; and all things will appear, as they should be, namely infinite.

I am hopefully now laying to rest all doubts about playing with Constructville, with the autogenic reality.

What the conscious mind really needs to arm the trigger on this nuclear device of reality creation this actually represents is **evidence**. It won't arm the trigger until it is convinced that it works, that it is correct, and in your best interest.

One of the ways to help the conscious mind is the Magic Jelly Bean device.

The Magic Jelly Beans

Magic Jelly Bean Demonstration

Let's have a demonstration of this technique.

Listen to my wording as I'm setting this up. Is it hypnosis? I don't know ... it's just straight talk. It's true, the two can overlap entirely.

You know that there is a structure in people that causes the formation of beliefs. And one of the main structures that people use is a **"What if ... then ..."** scenario.

"If I step onto a pavement crack, then my family will die," for example, or, "If I get first prize in this swimming competition, then that means that I will make it to the Olympic games when I grow up."

That's magic words, that is **magic phrasing**.

It is magic because our neurology knows exactly what to do with that. If you're not an English natural, please re-phrase this into your own language, you must recognise the pattern, "If I don't flick this light switch 20 times, my family must die."

It's an "if – then" combination of components that have fuck all to do with each other, but that the neurology treats as if there was a real cause and effect.

And now, that we know this, how can we use this to our advantage? I love that sentence!

<To demonstration person> Here, have a magic jelly bean.

<D> Thank you.

<S exclaims> My God! It's an orange one! It's a sign!

<D, shocked> I meant to take a green one!

<S laughs> Ah, I'm just kidding. Ok, so now this is a magical jelly bean. Don't eat this yet, but **when you do**, I must point out to you **that this cannot be undone** because the jelly bean becomes a part of your very fabric. **You cannot un-eat** this jelly bean. It's a big deal. Do EmoTrance in all ways if you need to.

<D> Yes ...

<S> Now the question is, **what will it mean** and for example, I could say, that "If I eat this jelly bean it will mean that I will find a new lover within a fortnight".

<D giggles> Oh! I don't know what my husband would make of that ...

<S> Little pointer here. When I said those words, I had an emotranceable response. I wasn't congruent. I was afraid and went immediately into a "what if ..." spiral ... oh my God, oh dear <demonstrates shaking in fear>. Now this Magic Jelly Bean exercise is again one of those things that you couldn't be doing at all, it wouldn't work at all if you didn't have EmoTrance **first** – you have to be **congruent**.

- **The rule has to be accepted by your entire neurology, by your physicality, by your energy body, it has to be congruent.**

So I noticed when I thought about doing the Magic Jelly Bean for finding a new lover that I had a pressure in my chest, in my head, something else went on at the back of my neck.

<S takes a moment to do EmoTrance on the ereas and takes a deep breath> Ok, so once again, if I was to eat this jelly bean – and I know what that means, I've done this before! – this will mean I will have a new lover within two weeks. Eeouwh! <shudders then laughs> Secondary problems!

<S to D> Have you started thinking about yours yet?

<D, laughing> You have me worried now, seeing the effect on you!

<S> Ah but you see this is what stops affirmations. This is what stops congruency. This is what stops ... you can override it with will power and **make** myself eat the bloody thing – but all that would happen is that **nothing would happen** and it simply wouldn't work! Like all those New Years resolutions and all these times I cried and smashed my fist on the table ... Ok, one more time.

<Audience member cries out> But – you could say **anything**!

<S, laughs> Yes, you could! Welcome to the autogenic Universe, ladies and gentlemen! Free will! The free will kind that lets you choose anything.

<Audience member> But you could choose evil things!

<S> The repercussions of your actions are between you and your Creator.

<Audience member> Getting a new lover would be adultery!

<S> I don't have a husband.

<Audience member> But this is terribly dangerous! Evil people could do anything!

<S> That is between **them and their Creator**.

<Audience member> But if you had a husband ...

<S> Ah monogamy. I don't believe in it. Structurally. Also, they get their own jelly bean. This lady could eat her jelly bean and make it into a reality that her husband has eyes for no-one but her. Whether that is any more moral than me asking for a new lover is - **between you and your Creator**. It's one of those things.

<Audience member2> So I could choose to become a criminal, and if I felt bad ...

<S> ... you could emotrance that away ...

<Audience member2> ... and commit a crime and get put into prison ...

<S> That's nothing. They are just constructs. They have nothing to do with your immortal soul and your redemption. It is nothing. What really happens and what is really important is **between you and your Creator**. It's up to you to think about it, what you're actually doing. Makes it into a nice little ceremony.

<Audience member3> But it changes things ...

<S> Yes, of course it changes things. **It is the very act of emotrancing yourself beforehand which changes everything.** This is reality creation at its finest. Whatever beliefs stand in the way – that I'm too ugly or too old, that it is unlikely, that I don't hang out in the right places such as singles bars or whatever else may be in there that is causing conflicts is simply being put away, clearing up the room for a miracle if necessary – which makes this into a very, very interesting process to try out.

And I don't know why I came up with that thought, it came, I had said that I would speak whatever would come, so here we are.

Let's see. And remember, it cannot be un-eaten. It becomes a part of my very structure.

<Audience member4> Will we get feedback on what happened?

<S> Depending on what I do with my body image until then, you might get to see the movie!

<Audience laughs>

<S> And by the way, I didn't actually stipulate a physical lover.

<Audience laughs, someone shouts> But that's a cop out!

<S> Yes it is. Ok, ready? <Eats jelly bean and bursts out into a huge big smile> It is just such an extraordinary sensation on every level when you do this. And a really fun way to do it.

Talking about totality interventions again for a moment, the physicality eats it. The energy system gets its emotrance workout and gets to register its protests. The conscious mind is formulating the words and directing the hand to the mouth. It's a ceremony. I can just see this being completely perverted from the happy fun event that it is to be done at parties and with friends, to some sort of mega weirdness with bells and whistles. But we leave it as the fun that it is. <To D> So, have you got one?

<D> Yes.

<S> And are you willing to share it publicly?

<D> When I eat this ...

<S> If! If I eat this.

<D> Oh, ok. If I eat this, I will be totally in touch with the energy world.

<S> Ok, and how does that feel? Any resistance anywhere?

<D> No, none at all.

<S> Because we don't want you to take this step unless you're really sure.

<D> No I made the decision.

<S> And you're aware that once you've eaten it, it cannot be uneaten.

<D> It is good.

157

\<S\> Ok, go for it.

\<D eats jelly bean and starts to laugh\> It means your lover becomes my lover!

\<S laughs out aloud\> Does that mean that, indeed!

\<Both laugh for some time\>

\<S\> Ok, that's great. Give our friend a hand!

\<D laughs and leaves stage\>

Magic Jelly Bean Exercise

Now, that is one of those things you could watch and you could think that we were acting. But we have some Jelly Beans and I've also purchased some M&Ms.

I'm going to ask you to do an exercise.

How seriously you are willing to take this, **is entirely up to you**.

It is between you and you.

You can just pretend and just eat the thing. Waffle something totally meaningless.

Because that is **absolutely** your prerogative.

I can only show these things; what you **do** with them is entirely up to you.

You can really have a go at this, find some rule in your world that would make a mega difference.

Set up an evidence procedure for yourself using this "what – if" principle. If I eat this jelly bean, it really will mean this or that. And immediately, the conscious mind goes with all the objections as usual, "Squawk, squawk! it would take a miracle! You've never done it before! Save yourself the disappointment!" General freak out in the energy system, all sorts of fears and madness. Do the EmoTrance. Try the statement again and **when you are totally congruent and happy, eat the thing.**

Allow yourselves to experience that. Your training partner, make sure to remind them that "once this thing has been eaten, it cannot be un-eaten – it becomes a part of your very structure." That's the "as I will so mote it be" part which cements the whole thing in.

We are just using a structure which happened randomly **to our advantage.**

So, ladies and gentlemen, let's use the Jelly Beans, or the M&Ms, and if we run out, you might have a mint in your pocket or some other thing that you can eat.

Find something you wish to stipulate and let's take charge of that autogenic Universe!

Personal Development For People

I haven't worked as a therapist with a client for five years. It doesn't mean I don't do stuff with people, I just don't consider myself as a healer or a therapist, that never worked for me.

I play with friends.

Which means that I am an individual who doesn't know, and they're another individual who doesn't know either, and we have a bunch of jelly beans on the table, and it is like, "Ooooh that was weird! You try one, see what you feel! How cool is that!"

This jelly bean thing isn't something you do with clients, might even be weird to do it with clients.

Seriously, not unless you develop some kind of meaningful ceremony around it, with chalices and knives and stuff, because that always gives that air of authority, and people accept it, because they have been entrained to, believing the most appalling things. The first time I went to see a witchcraft coven, they were dancing about with antlers strapped to their heads and stabbing knives into chalices. I just couldn't believe my eyes and thought, "My God! Is there any hope for any of us!" and turned my back on that whole Golden Dawn thing in that instance because I wanted nothing to do with people who thought that that kind of thing was necessary to create change, or imprint your will on the Universe – it's bloody ludicrous!

Anyway, if you are dealing with a group of those, by all means, strap on the antlers if you feel that it helps, morph it if you have to.

But at the end of the day, this is for YOU – not as practitioners, not as healers, it is for you AS PEOPLE. To work with, to play with, to try out for yourself and with your friends, as a party trick.

I brought it out at a party the other day with some friends of mine, and it was bloody brilliant. It was excellent. We also developed this idea that you give a trusted friend the opportunity to give YOU a statement to say and eat the magic jelly bean with because mostly, your worst problems you're unaware of.

One of my friends gave me one and said, "If you eat this, you'll finally stop putting yourself down all the time."

I would not have thought of that, but I did it, and it was way cool.

We did some really nice ones. One was, "If you eat this, you will never be old." They were just so nice. One was, "If you eat this, you will never again doubt my love for you." It took some doing but he ate it, and what a lot of stress that will take out of our relationship, at last.

It was such a nice thing, and really, none of it is therapy. These are PEOPLE things. Heart healing, thought flow, the jelly beans, the autogenic Universe, making your World what you want it to be. Reconnecting your body from the inside.

They are PEOPLE things, one person at a time.

There is no bus that goes to the Holy Land.

The truth is a pathless land, which is why I've been going on and on about **your own evidence procedure**. I could suggest evidence procedures but I won't because you need to **convince yourself**.

What we have here now is a superb set of starting techniques – kindergarten tools to really get to play with, to really have some fun with.

This is not a dour thing, this is – every time Nicola and I figure something out, there's this joy about it, this lightness, this friendliness. WHY did we expect it to be hard? WHAT is wrong with us that we still don't get it? Well I guess we all still have our own various cages of entrainment.

We have our various outer constructs, designed to hide the autogenic monstrosity from view – look at me, I'm this great teacher, healer, I'm ever so tidy, I'm ever so rich, you know, that outer shell behind which the monstrosity quivers for fear of detection. But at last, we can do something about it and sort these things out, from the inside out as is right.

The key to it is to lighten up and to have fun.

The autogenic Universe is truly nothing, it is meaningless.

What our neighbours think of our car is truly not worth thinking about. It is nothing – it used to be something when we were inside of it and we looked around and that was all there was and there was nothing else. So you take what there is and make it as important as you can to fill your time and stop yourself from going insane.

But now, we've got this other Universe there – with a creative force, with a soul, with immortality and we don't even know it yet.

Whoa! And the more I find out about that, the less I care about the other. I truly don't care anymore if anyone thinks I should wear a push up bra, for the love of God. I just really, really don't. I am trying to figure out how to connect up souls and I really can't be doing with this nonsense anymore. When someone comes along and says, "The police will come and put you into prison," I can't take that seriously anymore. Who cares? Who cares if I die in prison? What is important is what happens next, and whether I've learned enough to have attained my personal immortality, whether I've contributed something important, not campaigned to have a new traffic sign put up outside a school.

I understand how that comes into being, we want to contribute something real as people. If we don't know what we are supposed to do, we just take some thing that everybody says is real.

It breaks my heart. All these good people, working so hard every day, wanting so hard to help and make a difference and really be a decent human being. You'd be surprised how wide spread that is amongst people. It is extraordinary. And it is nice to think that we now have a way out of it.

So if you were to drink a cup of tea, or coffee, or a glass of water now, that would mean that you would really remember everything we've said here today.

Congruency Competitions

One thing I'm looking forward to finding out is what happens when many people at the same time try to create divergent autogenic realities and real realities.

As this has never happened really so far, it would be interesting. Normally the deal is like in playing poker – the guy with the best construct-mask wins, and in reality creation, the guy with the most congruency wins.

It is as simple as that.

The person with the most congruency wins.

I love David Bowie. I've been following his career with interest since about 1967 or thereabouts. That guy used to be not very popular. Everyone who had any sense used to say that his music was atrocious and his lyrics were even worse. However, he is so astonishingly congruent that fifty years later, he is hailed as the greatest creative rock genius England has ever produced. How did that happen? It happened because he was simply more congruent than those people who said that he was crap. I love that as a role model – the power of reality creation.

So what would happen if you got a whole lot of people who were all congruent together? You could have this field and the task is to design a tower and the one whose design actually gets built, is the winner.

But mostly what I want to do at this point is to round up what we've been talking about here so that everything gets put in the rightful places so that when you take this away, you know what we've been doing and not just have a clear memory of all of it, but also get to **use it** for real with great elegance.

Was that a post hypnotic suggestion? I think it was!

Reality Re-Evaluation

We started with EmoTrance Level 1 which is simply feeling the energy body moving around. And noticing that energy follows intention, responds to intention.

That is New World Reality Creation Sidereus Style 101.

If you teach this to other people, that's a good place to start, namely that you have a conscious mind, you have conscious attention and that this conscious intention influences energy; but more than that, **that you can feel it** when it does – because that becomes the **evidence procedure** for the conscious mind and opens up a helix of learning.

"My thoughts really do have an influence on my own reality."

This starts a process of **reality re-evaluation** from that moment on.

Because you could **feel** the difference, you know it was real. This is the real breakthrough with EmoTrance. Someone had a big energy shift, they had a big blockage, it went away, someone shouts the insult - **and it doesn't hurt anymore**.

- **THAT is PROOF.**

It proves all these things in one fell swoop.

It proves that we have an energy system. It's proof that old burdens can be released. It's proof that we can do **something** about it.

AND that **we can do this ourselves**.

You don't have to go to a guru or someone with magical powers that "I wasn't born with".

Yes, we can learn to do this ourselves. It opens up the whole thing. It certainly did for me and my investigations.

From there, I went to this idea that the heart, the energy mind and the immortal soul. That alone you could spend years on, designing strategies and techniques but I will leave it entirely up to you how you apply this to your own challenges.

You could always, before you go to bed at night, tap EFT if you wanted to – "I want a closer connection to my soul." – "I want to learn about my soul." – "I want to find out more about my soul."

That's one way of doing it.

These simple techniques of Thought Flow and Heart Healing are from those realms, and they are designed to start this process from these realms by **noticing the changes** when you call on your heart of energy – consciously.

Now, as you are doing this, "I place **my own** healing hands on **my own** dear heart," there's a lot of pre-suppositions in there.

MY OWN healing hands. Not Dr Martian's. Not Ramah Swaktibugera's. MY healing hands on MY heart.

Once again, the **evidence procedure** comes in the feelings afterwards as you are **doing this**.

The feelings afterwards, and as you are getting better at this, as an individual human being, not as a therapist, not as an energy magician, but as a human being, there is evidence that **increases your congruency on the reality creation that MY HANDS ARE HEALING HANDS**.

Thought Flow is particularly designed to begin a process of getting to be a little bit less fed up with our conscious mind – including Snow Globes and so forth – because they really can drive us crazy. And anything that drives us crazy, husbands, boyfriends, pets, children, whoever, we get angry about, and negative towards, and we **shut down communications between us and them.**

And the very last thing any of us need is a bad attitude to our conscious minds which create our reality and directs our consciousness. Thought Flow is one of those where we calm the crying baby to give mummy a break. This will give her a chance to love her child as she calms down and isn't so disturbed anymore.

Our thoughts have been driving us crazy for a long time and we need to get to a point where we can be loving towards them.

Now, then we moved on one step further and talked about an interface device between the energy systems – all of them, including the meridian system and the physicality as well, which is the autogenic body, which is created by our thoughts, so real that other people can "see it", so real that if you look in the mirror, you can see it too.

You can shape this autogenic body with Guiding Stars – that's a nasty, nasty thing when that happens. Michael Jackson had a guiding star with

Elizabeth Tailor when she was about 35 years old. He looks in the mirror, and what he sees doesn't match that Guiding Star picture and he's trying to bring his physicality around to match that template. Not the original Creator template for a beautiful, elegant black gentleman, powerful and strong, but instead, he's trying to match Elizabeth Tailor at age 35. It is particularly intense because he has the money for all the surgery this requires, and of course because the base-mismatch could not be more conflicted – he is a black man and the template a white woman. But I feel we should give him a sainthood that he has put himself through this, so we could see it in action and it is so clear, and such a piece of evidence, not just for the Guiding Star/Highest Taste principles, but also for the role models and the templates principles and that if we don't have a template to move ourselves towards, then we just don't know what to do.

We don't know what to do.

Our bodies and our thoughts run in circuits and we simply create havoc.

Meaningless havoc. Addictions, repetitive behaviours, the whole system just breaks down.

Next, we went on to the physicality.

The physicality which got the blame for EVERYTHING, for everything that went wrong and in some cases, that would be everything.

To begin a process of re-evaluating the physicality, of what that is. Some thing that is in flow, something that is malleable, but at the basis it is a fantastic Creator-given system which will try and follow the guidance YOU are giving it by your templating and Guiding Stars procedures as best as the poor thing can. I could burst out into tears, it is so sad. Like people trying to turn a poodle into a little boy, its a horrible thing to do. It is so pathological. What people – we – have done with our bodies is so pathological.

It wasn't our fault, it is not because we are bad people but still, it is just such a mess.

When instead we need to love our physicality properly, **support it** properly, just like our conscious mind. Like all parts of ourselves. That is a hugely powerful thing. And like all things, physicalities respond to a little bit of care and attention in the right places, rather than endless beatings – "You stupid plant! You're not growing! Well I'm not going to give you any water today either, that'll teach you a lesson!"

That's not how you get to grow a good plant.

You grow a good plant by looking after it and finding out what it needs, and giving it THAT, and it responds by being a beautiful plant which wins you prizes, and that is very simple.

What this gives us, all together, is an interesting model of the Universe, which may be slightly different from what you have heard before but I am particularly excited about the **many avenues of exploration** for each one of you this opens out.

I don't know which is your own favourite thing, where you would like to start; with your mind, with your soul, or with your body, or all of it at once – it doesn't matter where you start.

This totality system gives us ideas and tools, and what is even better, and I really like this, is that it is **your own exploration**.

It is your own personal exploration with **your own challenges**, with your own existing physicalities, with your own histories, rather than to look to some guru or to me, for that matter.

I wasn't even going to do this unless I had something I did not have to trip around for the rest of my life to the starving in Africa because "they really needed to hear it".

Sorry, I'm busy. I'm building my own soul. I'm trying to sort **myself** out, I can't be doing this every weekend.

And this is the truly exciting thing. I hope you have some ideas already as to how to apply this in your own life. I don't want you to go away from this completely convinced. What I want you to do is to use this totality model as an alternative to the ones you've had existing, and see if your puzzle pieces fit, like a shape sorter. Do it for yourself, every person for themselves – not for your clients, not for your children, not for posterity but for YOU – for yourself.

The better YOU are, the more use you are to anyone, including the Creator.

Q: What is the relationship between the autogenic body and the energy body? When we are doing meridian therapies or other interventions, what are we affecting?

A: Now you have to bear in mind that these three things are all a part of the same system. They are three horses in front of the same carriage. So one of them is on its knees, being dragged along by the other two. You target an intervention at one of the other two, give it more food and hay, your carriage will increase in performance briefly, that will eventually peter out again, and you're right back where you were when you started. Or worse than you were off before. Which is exactly what you find for example with diets.

And this then forms the idea that things don't work long term.

That is the autogenic body on its knees. That is what is setting the rules and regulations, dragging the whole system back. This is always been one of my hobbyhorses, that something **stays done** so I can build on it and get **more done**. It is no good if you have to re-build the same thing over and over again, it's just atrocious.

Q: How do you know just where the problem lies?

A: A change in one always reflects through the levels. But don't under-estimate people's relationships with their autogenic bodies. It is the **autogenic body**, not the energy bodies, which are producing stigmata, eczema, heart attacks. The physical body and the energy body is just reflecting the **distortion** that the autogenic body is bringing to the entirety of the system.

Q: Is the autogenic body like the self concept?

A: That's right. It is a body map you create and manufacture. I'm sure that children don't have any bones until you're told that you have them. It is just that thing which gets constructed of what people tell you from the outside, a very weird map. But now we have this other map to compare it with, which is the Creator's template, which is something to move towards.

Rather than saying that your template's shite, that's no good, how are you going to fix it? You need something positive to compare it to and move it towards.

Q: Can your autogenic body create illness, like cancer, in those around you? Family, friends?

A: Your autogenic body doesn't create cancer in your friends, your consciousness does. Thoughtfields. We are broadcasting thoughtfields the whole time. If you are a big producer of thoughtfields, you are going to have a powerful influence over your environment, such as plants and pets. Whatever **you** are creating, **they** get shaped into. Like, you must know those people whose pets are always ill. Skin diseases, what have you, they are always down the vets. All that is to autogenically **put your own problems onto someone else.** Like saying, "It isn't me that can't go out at night, it is my husband who won't let me go out." You know all this stuff from family therapy. There's this family and they pick one kid, and everyone puts their shite on that one kid. So as long as he is still alive and crawling around, he's the stupidest in the family and so it doesn't have to be me. That is that kind of thing which causes in children or people who are not well defended against that autogenic problems in **their** autogenic bodies – which then leads to **their** cancer.

Q: I've got a dog which has Addison's disease, and of course he'll never get over it completely, but is there something I could do with that autogenic influence?

A: Okay, stop. What you need to do first of all is to re-write the rule that it can't be cured completely. That's the first thing I would do. Then, let some ideas come to you as to what to do next. Animal experimentation with energy. See, once an owner has created an autogenic body for a pet, it is stuck with it and has to carry it around wherever it goes. The only animals who have a self concept are human pets, of course. Rescue pets, at that. You could go mad with what people do with animals through autogenics. Just by naming a dog, "Satan" they cannot ever have a decent relationship with it – especially if they were Roman Catholics! And the name is just the tip of the iceberg – the name is just the label on the jar in which the thought-forms live. Wow. There is so much you can do with this.

You can use this to **set your environment to be much more supportive, much more loving to you**.

Consciousness is not actually a bad thing. Bodies aren't a bad thing.

People aren't bad. They're not even misguided. I'd say they're fucking desperate and doing the best they can. Including myself. And whatever they do, it isn't their fault. It is completely systemic – a great big screw-up. But we can put it to rights. Now.

Talking To The Body

This is something that is really quite wonderful.

This is something you can do with people without having to get involved in the whole autogenic body theory. It is a superb intervention and if you are a massage therapist, it is the most extraordinary thing.

This is the deal.

<Invites Nicola to join her on stage>

<S> This is Nicola's physicality. And we can work on the energy body, and we can work on a whole load of places, but actually, in her physicality is the memorance of all the things that were ever done to it, all the injuries it ever sustained, all the things that were said to it, and about it. All the unkind treatment the physicality has ever had.

And what we can do is to take it out.

<N stands, eyes closed. S lightly touches N's face and says>

All the memories, every incident across time and space, back and back and back.

Any incident, any unkindness and with total support for the physicality, we take it out.

Now.

How does that feel?

<N nods, clearly very moved>

<S> Now that is not just for faces. Or heads, or hair.

This is for shoulders and for hands. For feet. For all the body, for the autogenic body. By touching the body in this sense, we're not naming the autogenic body but that is who you are talking to, that is who you are impacting with this.

By saying, "There is a part of you that keeps a memory of all the burdens you have ever had to bear ..."

And they need to go. They are old burdens which belong to the past. And this exact exercise or rather experience is how I got to the autogenic body in the first place.

<Turns to N and lightly touches her head> You know the ears. All the horrible things that people have ever said to her. All the horrible things she had to hear. All the lies. Screams. Take them out. Let them go to the past where they belong. All remembrances rescinded, all taken out, leaving the physicality as it should, just ears. As the Creator designed them.

<N near to tears but smiling>

<S> This is nice, isn't it?

<N nods wholeheartedly>

<S> And you don't just have to do this with people who have body dismorphia.

This is a very nice exercise. Before you do this with anyone else, I want you to do it with yourself, in the shower. And take that third party stance on yourself of, "All the insults - **I banish them**." Everything that ever happened. You can go further than that, even. "All the loving things that never happened."

I did something like that when I was in the shower after the German EmoTrance training and I ended up **thanking** every part of my body.

Thank you, hair. Thank you, eyes. Thank you, face.

That is extremely moving, especially after what I have put them through.

It is bad enough when other people kick the shit out of you, but when you then turn around and kick the shit out of yourself as well, that's when it turns into a tragedy.

I get angry, and I won't berate myself for that, I still have use for those kinds of energies. And sad. Very sad. Because when you get a sense of the shit that has been piled upon people, just even from a distance ...

We didn't really go into it just then, and even what we did was already enough to near enough overwhelm your energy system, and hence this is again something you just can't do if you don't know how to do EmoTrance. It's just too much. Just too much. Just one single person's foot, all the horrible shoes they have worn, and standing when they should be sitting, being forced to walk when they should not have ...

That's where I got the whole deal with the autogenic body from. When you bind a Chinese woman's feet, it doesn't matter when you take the bindings off after five minutes, but after thirty years, just look at what the feet become! That just goes to show just how **malleable** the physicality really is. Seeing these babies whose heads get strapped up and they end up with these long cone-heads. And these women whose necks get stretched – the physiology is **incredibly malleable**, and in that lies our saving grace.

I wouldn't bring any of this up, the horror of what has happened to us, if I didn't have a solution for it. I couldn't even talk about it. And I think that's why **they** haven't talked about it. Not because they are bad people or they want to hurt people, but because they didn't have the techniques to deal with those kinds of emotions, those kinds of occurrences.

But we have them now, and we can make the changes, make the difference – one person at a time, and we are first. Not letting other people do the healing for us, **we** will heal.

Go first, be brave, have the courage.

> I place my own healing hands on my own dear heart.
>
> I pay attention to my heart's messages.
>
> I am willing to learn.
>
> what my totality has to teach me
>
> about this world
>
> about my life
>
> about this creation.
>
> Thank you.

172

I had to pause a moment there to receive my own heart's messages as to what to say to you. And often, a conscious statement of intent is all that is required.

You don't have to know how to do it, you just have to state that you are willing.

And on this wonderful note, I am going to conclude, and I'm going to ask you that you have **a lot of fun** with this.

ADDENDUM 1

Patterns In Brief

Resolving Conflict - The Rainbow Connection

The Rainbow Connection is a simple Erea pattern to begin to flow information between certain thoughtfields or Ereas in order to structurally change them both and "widen a person's horizon". This pattern is perfect for the more advanced ET applications.

Like many Sidereus patterns, this is unbelievably simple and straightforward - but that doesn't mean it isn't highly impactful.

Quite in the contrary.

Don't just read it, do it for yourself and try it with others.

Based on the Sidereus parts model, we do not try and integrate energetic realities or neurological realities that are in very different places and don't wish to be mashed together in any shape or form.

For this exercise, and especially if you have holistic leanings and tendencies, choose the two concepts of Love and Money.

We're going to use these so don't cheat and try to go with "Light" and "Abundance" or suchlike; Love and Money are a nice conflict that few, if any living human beings have successfully resolved or even aligned, for that matter.

Firstly, point to where in space you would find love, and where you would find money.

This may be near or far, inside your body or way outside, left or right, back or front, up or down, it matters not. Just locate the two concepts in space as is right and proper for you.

If you wish, you may describe them to yourself, or, if you do this pattern with others, have them describe how the reality of these concepts appears to function for them.

Note what hand gestures and body postures accompany these descriptions - warding off motions, waving away motions, blocking manoeuvres or physical backing away can be observed, amongst many other responses to the ereas (existing energetic realities) as labelled by those two concepts, money and love.

Once we have them established in space, all we need do now is to make the "Rainbow Connection" - a strand of interactivity through which information and energy may travel from one to the other and back again, setting up a communications system, if you will, whilst keeping both respectfully and ecologically where they are.

You can help this along by physically "painting the rainbow bridge" into the air with your hands or gesturing to that effect (as though you could draw this with your hands/fingers functioning like a laser pointer).

Observe yourself/your clients for physiological feedback as you do this and also note how the Rainbow Connection touches and lights up the regions that lie between those two concepts.

Notes:

I prefer this method of creating ecological belief changes and "horizons widening" to the standard NLP techniques related to swish patterns, parts integrations and EFT treatments that seek to physically move and/or destroy existing ereas for it is my understanding that ereas themselves are never the problem, but their placement in the system and greater scheme of things.

It is a highly generative pattern that is also subtle - although there are usually direct behavioural feedbacks during and after the implementation of this pattern, the change it causes is gentle and very ecological as it unfolds over time and both ereas become changed through their information/energy exchanges.

This pattern is safe for use with children and can be used for any conflict that involves separate ereas, and not just two at a time as in the simple example above.

Connecting ereas for information exchange is generally an ecological intervention; "nice" ereas or "rose coloured spectacle" ereas truly benefit from an injection of counter examples as do in turn the "depressing" ereas to which they may be connected for the truth is that neither type represents reality as it stands.

Rainbow Connection II

Following the re-connection of the original conflicted ereas, and this could be more than two opposing ones, and may also include family systems, for example, re-establish communications/energy flow to yourself, i.e. let the now combined energy pass through you as well.

This creates the energised end state and completes the intervention.

1. Find something you wish to improve your relationship with or communication to - a person, a pet, a topic ("Pure Maths", "Computers", "Geography"), a skill or ability, an object, an addictive/allergic substance etc.

2. Where is this topic located? Point or describe ("Show me with your hands")

3. What is causing disturbances in the flow of information or energy between you and the topic? (Shields, injuries?)

4. Resolve the disturbances and re-establish information/energy flow with the topic fully, all the way up to the "energised end state".

5. What insights have you gained, what have you learned and how do you feel now about the topic?

Some information fields cause problems in the energy system, simply because they are not **IN THEIR RIGHTFUL TIME AND PLACE.**

No matter how big, problematic or fearful these are being experienced as, they are still ONLY AN ENERGY and simply need to be returned to their own original flow states to cease causing further disturbances or problems.

Question: If you knew, is there something somewhere in your energy system that is causing problems, you may have had it for a long time, that is casting a shadow over your life or that represents a burden to you?

Show me where that is.

1. If the question causes a fear or pain response, deal with this first.

2. Now, find out where this needs to go - it is an energy and needs to flow. Trust your intuition.

3. Deal with any shields or injured ereas which are blocking the flow or which are preventing the energy from going where it needs to go.

4. Establish the flow to the energised end state.

5. Reflect on how this feels now and what you have learned from this.

Energy Weather, Energy Storms ...

This is a version of invoking innocent energy from ET1.

To remind us, innocent energy is particularly fine and light, gently refreshing like a fine summer rain, and this is of course extremely useful for all and any purposes of instant "energy body refreshment".

Innocent energy may be evoked at any time, in any place, "in the field", such as being in an unpleasant room, situation, in the car, or just in a listless or dull state, and it may be confined to one's own energy field or cover an entire situation which may contain many people.

For more advanced users, far more powerful and many different options are available, and these can be used to clear rooms and houses, create change, destroy existing thoughtfields in an environment, and of course for self help in any situation.

Such energy evocations can include:

- Powerful rain storms and hurricanes (particularly useful for room clearing and to wash away major disturbances, permanently);

- Heavy and prolonged "rain" to really re-fertilise barren or toxic ereas within and without;

- Snow storms and in general, different *temperatures* for different purposes.

- Colour storms as well as gentle colour rains, sheets, mists.

- Upswellings and downpourings of any form of essence, such as luck, joy, beauty etc.

There are no limits to the use of raising such events and with a little practice, extremely useful environmental events can be produce which can brighten and sparkle the most depleted environments and energy systems.

182

Autogenic Body Exercises

Re-Unification

Simply make sweeping passes across the major breakage lines and re-affirm, "One body" as you do so. If you can touch, this helps.

Note: Another affirmation which may be used is, "One body, one mind, one heart, one soul."

Note 2: This is an excellent exercise to do in the bath or in the shower. In the shower especially, the flow of the water from the top across all the divides creates a powerful affirmation.

Note 3: Pay special attention to the "head-body" divide across the neck; this is particularly important if you are given to disassociation , "live in your head" a lot, or don't feel things as strongly as you would like.

Mirror Exercise

Find yourself in front of a mirror.

Take a moment to simply acknowledge your physicality as a malleable group of cells in motion which is organising itself to the creative template.

Do ET on any sensations of pain, loss, disappointment, shame, anger etc. until you can be with your mirror-image and be at peace.

Now, stroke and love your physicality, making contact with it, in unconditional acceptance and affirm your heart's desire to love it, take care of it properly and as the creative order intended it should be.

Continue until you have reached the energised end state.

Removing Injuries From The Body

1. Pick any part of your body you know holds memories of injuries, pain, injustice in particular (i.e. eyes, ears, genitals or a body part that has been declared to be less than perfect, i.e. nose or thighs etc.)

2. Stroke the body part lovingly and say, "I remove from you now all memories of hardship, of pain, of suffering; any unkind comments, attacks, all mistreatments and I restore your loving perfection as the Creator intended."

3. If necessary, do any secondary ET treatments for fear, pain, sadness the treatment brings up.

4. Continue until you can begin to feel the part glow.

5. End with re-affirming the entire body as a physical totality, and let the loving charge of healing spread throughout your entire body from the freshly restored part.

6. Take a moment to reflect on what you have learned and how you feel now.

NB: This is an absolutely fantastic exercise and superbly healing, regardless of whether this is done by one person for themselves, or with a healing partner. PLEASE try it at least once to experience the power of this.

I have recently taken up painting once more, but this time from a different standpoint, approach and reason altogether (See Energy Art Solutions).

It came to my awareness as I was painting that I was tensing up for fear of making a mistake with the brush. The autogenic universe slipped into my mind and I thought, hm, one might reverse the thoughts of fear to make a mistake which caused the tension, into a nice positive hypnotic suggestion, such as, "I am painting accurately and confidently."

It worked surprisingly well, with the help of a little subtle EmoTrance-in-the-moment-of-movement and after half an hour or so, where I had to repeat the process of Micro-ET (sometimes as subtly localised as just ONE sinew on ONE finger!) plus repeating the statement perhaps half a dozen times as old habits kicked in again, I got to thinking spontaneously all of a sudden, "I paint accurately, confidently AND FAST."

I had never really noticed before that I paint slowly as that was the max speed I could do without the fear of mistakes or losing control (clenched fist country here!) would become TOO GREAT - a sort of very distinctive threshold I could never cross before, no matter what the time pressure. Of course and conversely, if I DID go through the threshold with willpower, I would immediately then MAKE LOTS OF MISTAKES as that is pre-supposed and re-affirmed by the entire OLD setup!

So, I am now "painting confidently, accurately AND FAST."

Do I have an increase in speed? Yes, I do.

Do I have a decrease in the amount of mistakes that need fixing and compensating for? Yes, I do.

Do I have a noticeable increase IN ENJOYMENT OF THE ACTIVITY because of the added confidence and stress reduction? YES I DO.

These improvements are measurable, noticeably, AND provable to anyone else who would care to either watch me do it, or check the mistakes from previous attempts and what is happening with the new painting. This is reality checkback and the perfect CONSCIOUS CONVINCER for the parts of me who need that sort of thing.

There is a noticeable improvement after *just one session*. I have been painting for 40 years. Imagine I had done THAT from the start, what I could do now with a paintbrush! Probably brain surgery ...

Micro-EmoTrance on tiny old engrained movements, locked fingers and toes, neck and face, shoulders and back, is a truly fascinating thing and something to look forward to as a result of getting more practiced with EmoTrance. And lest we forget, the most practiced people with EmoTrance did not die in the 14th century. We've been doing it *for under 18 months*!! and always only as and when, so that's actually soon enough realised for anyone who wants to.

But even without that, the repeated POSITIVE statements during the ACT ITSELF are a very useful thing and I'm quite surprised I've never thought of it before.

But perhaps I had to become AWARE of the micro-tensions first, then unlock them, to have access to ALL OF THAT.

Micro-EmoTrance works for and with piano players, guitarists, holding a pen (left and right hand), knives, sports equipment such as bats, clubs and balls, body postures, facial expressions and has many, many more possible applications besides, such as any range of ritualised actions found especially in addictions. It may also impact highly localised tension ereas which can cross into physical pain as in the case of migraines, headaches, arthritis, etc. and of course, can be used to prevent "repetitive stress disorder" entirely if one can become sensitive enough and pay enough attention to small, localised "blockages" and "injuries".

It has also been suggested that Micro-EmoTrance might help with eye problems and sight problems that are not strictly physical in nature.

Micro-EmoTrance addresses tiny locks and blockages in tiny parts of the system which can unlock the most inordinate BIG systems. The question we ask is more specific to the body part, so instead of saying, "Where do you feel that in your body?", the question might be, "Where do you exactly feel that in your hand, in your foot, in your forehead?"

If applicable, ask to point to the erea with a fingertip and to use a "laser finger of ghost" if necessary to help another resolve these blockages in finer or smaller systems.

The Creative Template

1. Simply become relaxed and easy and set the intention that you wish to tune into the very real reality of your original creative template, which is stored in every cell of your body in the DNA, and which is further stored in every aspect of your energy matrix - the original creative design for you.

2. Allow a sense or representation of what this template would be like at your age or possibly a little older, and take your time to have this become clearly known and experienced.

3. Do any necessary ET treatments for sadness, fear or pain, disappointment, shame etc. knowing your creative template produces in you so that you can relate with it clearly in all ways.

4. Affirm your desire to move towards the template in all ways from now on and do what needs to be done that this should be so (shield removals, making energetic connections with the template, flowing away distortions etc).

5. When the template is steady, resonant and radiant and you are fully aligned in your will to move towards it with every breath you take, hold this for as long as is needed until you experience the energised end state.

6. Reflect upon what you have learned and how you feel differently now.

NB: It is useful to find a word, sound or name to evoke the template, like an affirmation, in a moment of crisis "in the field".

The Creative Template & Relationships

A superb application that is really stunning in its overall effectiveness on thought, mind and the environment is to use a template for guidance that belongs to someone else.

For our own personal endeavours, our own template is the best guidance; but when you are talking to someone else, interacting with them, and you really wish to make an impact of the unconditional nature upon them, **look to their template** before deciding how to proceed.

Especially in close/intimate relationships, this is a truly outstanding means of helping us break out of pre-established patterns and closed loops, and **assist the other** to become all the creative order had intended them to become.

1. Become aware when you are feeling helpless, anxious, unsure as what to do or say, or how to respond; exasperated, angry or generally out of control when thinking about, talking to or interacting in any way with **another individual**.

2. As soon as you become aware of this, **focus and look for THEIR Creator given template**. Even if you only catch the slightest glimpse of that, it **will absolutely** change what you say, what you think, how you feel and what will happen next.

3. Usually, looking to the other's template is enough to know immediately what to say or do next; if you are still unsure, ask yourself, "What could I say or do right now to help this person get closer to their template?" Sometimes, this results in saying nothing at all and simply walking away, but on many other occasions you will be truly surprised as to what happens next.

It is my contention that the people who can perceive other people's templates and respond in that context are those known to inspire others in a very specific, well recognised way and really help them to grow towards their own true self. Conversely, for another human being to perceive our own creative potential is one of the most powerful and rewarding experiences one may have, and one that can truly change entire incarnations.

Autogenic Universe Exercises

Setting The Autogenic Properties Of Food

1. Choose any kind of food item.

2. Become aware of your relationships with it, and most importantly, what autogenic properties you have already imbued the food item with.

3. Use ET to remove shields, reversals, problems and/or disturbances that exist between you and the item.

4. When your relationship with the food item is steady, affirm its new autogenic properties, i.e. health, energising, improving immune system functioning, being entirely healing etc. or whatever you wish to set from now on for this class of food items.

5. Continue until:

a) The item has the new properties, strong and steady; and

b) your relationship with the item has reached the energised end state.

6. Eat the item.

7. Reflect on what you have learned and how this has changed the way you feel and experience.

8. At least for one week, keep attention to your relationship with this class of food item and especially note how your physical reality is affected by the change.

Creating An Autogenic Healing Object

1. Choose any object you can hold in your hand. For this exercise, have it be a man-made object, such as a glass, a cup, a plate or such.

2. Contact the object and make sure that your contact is steady and resonant. Use ET to remove any disturbances within yourself.

3. Affirm the intention you wish to imbue the object with, for example, "This glass will imbue any liquid it contains with maximum radiance, maximum health, maximum benefit."

4. Continue until the object is radiant with your intention.

5. Check your relationship with the object, making sure your relationship is perfect and the energy flow sparkling clear and to your liking, and there are no barriers or twinges remaining to the energy of the object.

6. Continue to the energised end state.

7. Reflect what you have learned and how this has changed the way you feel.

NB: Keep this object around you for at least a week and check how your relationship with it progresses as time goes by, and how the object and its use is affecting your reality.

The Autogenic Detective

1. When there is a time and space of quiet and tranquillity, take a notebook and a pen and move about your living accommodations, room by room, and make a note of *the autogenic qualities* of objects, places, items etc. you have already imbued what there is.

On this occasion, please just make a note and other than instant ET responses in the field, move along swiftly to get an overview.

You may also want to leave your home and take an overview from the outside, if you wish.

2. Take your notebook and arrange an order and sequence in which to deal with the most urgent problems you have discovered. You would know what these are by how intense your response was according to your notes.

When you have the top ten most urgent items specified, ...

3. Deal with the objects/places etc. by facing each one, doing the requisite ET in yourself, then setting the properties of the object to your own desire.

NB: Some objects are not worth re-setting, such as a print of "The Scream" painting, and should simply NOT be in anyone's environment who is seeking to live in joy and creative harmony of flow. They are best discarded.

If the object which has such properties cannot be removed, create an autogenic energy cage around it instead to contain its emissions.

4. Note how your interventions have materially changed reality and pay especially attention to how behaviours of people who have no idea what you did, pets and houseplants for example, are showing evidence of change.

TimeLine Exercise

To re-connect a timeline energetically, the following beginning exercise is useful.

Create a biographical timeline by placing your name as the heading of a document, then noting down the main events just as a biographer would after the fact, avoiding any emotive words until you have covered the main events of your life up until now.

Example:

Susan Smith

1943 - Born in Manchester, UK. Mother Anna Smith, Father unknown.

1944 - Spent 3 months in hospital with chest infection.

1946 - Mother marries Peter Thompson. Brother Andrew born.

etc.

Doing this on the computer is particularly useful because it affords the opportunity to add important events later on.

Once you have "your life on a page", you can run your fingertips over the numbers and affirm the cohesion of your life, using words such as, "My life, so far."

Use ET to deal with any major disturbances this may produce.

Self concepts tend to lag behind in time.

Affirmations of wonders to come are a problem if there is an abyss between the existing perceived realities and the "future state" that is being called into being.

Further, if there is too much of a clash between the now states and the then states, the conscious mind simply refuses to draw the lines from point to point (or does not know how to do connect the dots).

So, a good stabiliser BEFORE embarking on any more change work is to do Affirmations 101, which states simply the truth of where we are at, RIGHT NOW, because often the passage of time is not being accounted for (in the autogenic Universe).

The format is simple. Look at the calendar to get a sense of where you are right now, and speak some simple true statements with affirmation meaning:

"I have been a mother for 24 years and both my children are still alive."

It is interesting how *shocking* such a simple statement of fact becomes as an experience; this shock is due to a "lagging self image" (or autogenic self creation) which hasn't caught up with the latest news.

Keep the statements simple, true, and avoid any judgements which will lead to counter-events, keep to the bare bones. In the above statement example, it is NOT claimed that the person was a GOOD mother.

"I have run and owned my own business for 12 years," is a statement which produces the re-adjustments of the self concept, whereas, "I run a great business and I am a total success," does not. Although ET can help there and goal-state affirmations are useful, they cannot be reached as a rule from nowhere - and if the fact that the person has "run and owned their own business for 12 years" is basically unbeknown to the self concept, the *foundation* for that further assessment is missing entirely.

This Affirmation 101 "statement of fact" device is also the stabilisation device that helps to move the *direction* of attention and energy from sorting for mistakes towards sorting for successes, via this step of unconditional acceptance of facts.

Simple as it may seem, it is a bridge from the then to the now and a highly beneficial exercise on any problem area in the self concept systems and indeed, a good pathway out of illusion and into a reality which is actually much better than the illusion ever tried to be.

Magic Jelly Beans

1. Decide on a future event, no matter how unlikely at this point, that you wish to manifest/create, and find a wording that is suitable for you.

2. Take a jelly bean of the correct colour, hold it in your hand and as you look at it, affirm that, "Once this has been eaten, it cannot be uneaten."

3. ET on any disturbance-responses this may produce.

4. Now, state the desire in the following format:

"IF I eat this jelly bean, this will mean that ..."

ET any fear or disturbance responses the statement has produced.

5. Re-state and ET until you really WANT to eat the jelly bean.

6. Eat the jelly bean.

7. Note how you feel when you do!

8. Keep an eye on the manifestation of your desire, and especially on unexpected events/changes which logically needed to have come along in order to make the desire happen.

ADDENDUM 2 – ARTICLES & ESSAYS

The Energy Of Learning

Is it possible to learn easily and swiftly? So fast it makes the teachers gasp? Everything and anything that can be learned - and not just human learning but learning deeply from everything around us - every animal, every plant, every rock and every person we ever meet? And learn not in a top level, "it's just a bunch of letters" way but in a deep knowing and familiarity with the topic? We think it is. Read on!

In NLP trainings one of the main challenges to the teachers and trainers is to somehow get the students into a state where they will actually learn something new, rather than to "filter" everything that is being presented through their old beliefs and understandings they already have; to get the students to interact honestly with the material, so they can actually learn something from this interaction.

Unfortunately, most if not all people do not approach learning in that way. They are critical, cynical and sit there with their arms crossed before them, tapping their fingers and an eyebrow raised, whilst demanding from the teacher to "show me what you've got".

This is of course a defence mechanism designed to keep various energies at bay and far away from oneself in order to protect the already existing order of things in the energy system; people even pride themselves in being "just open minded enough" to let a little bit of the learnings in, not all the way but just into some kind of holding area where it will be cynically and consciously dissected and where what is left must pass through even more hoops, loops, tests and filters before it is finally admitted into the system and thus, "being learned".

Here we are getting into something that is essential to learning. Which is the ability to leave one's critical facility at the front door altogether and immerse in the material exactly as it is being presented, at face value, completely open and not just "open minded enough".

As I'm contemplating this, it strikes me how very EmoTrance that is - not fight it, not side step it, not slow it down, not shield it out but **take it in completely**, let it do it's thing, through and out, just like an experience.

And learning **is** an experience or should I say, in my opinion it should be because it's one of the, if not simply THE most fun I've ever had with my clothes on.

On another list (which indeed was what prompted me to search my inbox for NLP and which turned up this message!) we are talking about different learning styles and I've said there just a few moments ago that I learn by immersion.

And I learn **fast**. Very fast. It sometimes frightens teachers just how fast I can learn what they are presenting and I believe this is so NOT because I'm especially clever, which I'm actually not, but because **I open myself completely to the material, exercises and thoughts** and let this become a **personal experience with the material**.

When I first got my EFT tapes, that's exactly what I did.

I sat down and said, OK, show me. Teach me. Totally non-judgemental, all previous knowledge and my critical faculty left completely at the doorstep to be picked up and used **after** I've had a personal experience with the materials **as closely to exactly as their Creator intended** as possible.

It is **extremely possible** if not highly likely indeed that the reflection/abstraction process most people engage in when learning is being offered hinders deep learning and full integration of the materials presented.

If we think of information fields, experience fields from an energetic standpoint and especially from an ET standpoint, those critical reservations and computations are shields to not learning but to **knowing** and **integrating** the material.

Shields are usually formed as protective devices because one thinks one needs them in some shape or form to safeguard something existing that might be spoiled in some way - often a very distorted self concept or strange beliefs formed by significant emotional experiences as it turns out, rather than anything actually worth protecting.

There may also be a time in a person's life when they are young and the "channels" to guide such incoming information in the right processing directions and to the right processing systems are not yet correctly formed and indeed, at that time such things should not be presented or else the child will **be forced** into constructing these shields.

As far as learning goes, I've at some point learned to drop shields - even to those some say are very scary gurus you mustn't let inside your head (and never mind your energy systems in toto).

But I haven't become a Satanist, a scientist, a scientologist, or a Moonie, or a rampant Bandlerite, or anything like that at all in the process. It doesn't work like that when the information is just allowed to flow straight into you, through and out - all that happens is you end up **knowing** so much more, not just with your mind either but with all sorts of you. That is, I'm convinced of this, why people keep telling me that I'm a natural at this that and the other, simply because I don't fight the "incoming" but just take it in without reservations and think about it **afterwards** when I've had some personal experience with the thing to help me make comparisons and form conclusions, when I have something to actually **base** the subsequent thinking **upon**.

This follows exactly the pre-suppositions upon which the EmoTrance™ system is based.

I've never thought of learning as an energy exchange before but of course, that's what it is. That energy needs to go into, through and out the students to actually and physically (yes! physically! different brain structure before and after learning!!!) CHANGE them. When that happens and **only** when that happens, has something new been truly learned.

And it is **total perfection** in a beautiful and really rather mysterious synchronicity that I got to write this article **today** and not a moment sooner, because just now on the EmoTrance trainer's list, the mail came in from that lady who has gotten it and is doing exactly that immersion move with EmoTrance - she dropped shields to it at last and now knows what it is and is getting the benefits from it.

She wrote:

"Things are clearing so fast it's disconcerting. I may transform into a totally unrecognisable being any minute. ET Romance you say? I think that's as good a quick description of EmoTrance as any. I am in love with the entire Universe, cause everything brings new change and all of it feels good. Either Silvia has invented access to ecstasy, or I'm succumbing to mania for the first time at the ripe age of 40."

And then ended the mail with what I consider to be the very best thing I've heard all this year:

"Nothing on earth has prepared me for the feeling of dancing wildly with my demons. And falling in love with them again and again."

This is a wonderful extension of the EmoTrance Principles because I KNOW that by opening yourself up totally to the learnings of a thing, of **any thing**, let me repeat that so it doesn't get overlooked - **THE LEARNINGS OF ANY THING** at all, you can learn faster, deeper, wider, more that you ever thought possible.

My head is literally spinning with the repercussions of this, big time and my fingers fast as they are can't keep up anymore.

First I thought of all the other METs - BSFF, TFT and so on. When I got it what Roger Callahan was trying to do and how he was trying to do it, vooom! my Universe expanded instantly. When I was studied at Larry's Nims BSFF seminar, the same. I understood something that goes way, way beyond conscious understandings, words and meanings.

Dropping shields to learning - to all learning? My God. Learnings from **anything** - a crystal in your hand. Teach me about your world. The night sky. Teach me what I need to know about you to understand you. An animal. Another person even - how scary would that be! But what an extraordinary experience and what unbelievable scope for personal development exists in that simple basic idea of dropping shields to learning, to true knowing, true understanding. Wow.

Now, we can start to talk **in earnest** how to make it so that those who want it and are ready for it get to learn that way - incredibly fast, incredibly profound, and not just facts and figures for the conscious mind but this deep knowing and sense of familiarity that you get when you open yourself to the energy of learning.

Brilliant. Perfect. and correct.

As usual when I get very, very excited about something I immediately phoned some friends to discuss this more thoroughly (and I was and still am extremely excited indeed by the whole hugeness of the repercussions for learning - I **love** learning! :-)

Something that we did talk about was the fear in the gut or the "NONONO" response when something or someone strikes a barrier that exists inside oneself. A systemic, directly consciously controlled reversal which in truth is nothing but an energy blockage in the systems and with this removed, Even Flow comes into being and all sorts of magic begins to happen - naturally, incredibly quickly, perfectly as it was always designed to happen to happen in the first place.

A part of my intense excitement about "the energy of learning" is my deep faith, knowledge, belief, whatever you want to call it, that learning is NOT about sitting in rows with dusty books and that people with their truly fantastic neurologies can learn so much faster, so much more, understand so much more and as a result, have and be so much more than is currently perpetuated.

Reversing The Flow Of Learning

What seems to be most important is to simply drop all barriers to the "energy of learning", wherever it may come from, and not to either shield from it or to move towards it in a selective fashion, bringing your own opinions into the field and ending up just being surrounded by your own original opinions again rather than learning anything new.

There's a rock on the table in front of you and you're supposed to contact it and learn from it. Basic Shamanism 101, same exercise exists in **every** school of magic cross culturally all around the World.

Now, most people try and get "into" that rock.

Only that's totally pointless because there is literally **NOTHING you can teach the rock.**

In order to learn from it, you have to open yourself up and **reverse the energy flow** - not from you to the rock, but from the rock to you.

It is **then** you learn what a rock is and what the world's like through the existence of a rock.

The "energy of scepticism" is a self generated, outgoing energy which must by it's very nature disturb the one way flow from the rock to you.

And THAT is the deep trick, the deep surprise and wonderful understanding which is opening doorways to unbelievable dimensions for myself, very personally.

Just give it a shot. Use ET on it. Reverse the flow, leave the river of scepticism for another day and do anything you got in your house - a pot plant, a crystal, a pet, just anything. EXPERIENCE IT to get what I mean.

Grant Connolly says, "I agree with the above statement completely and wholeheartedly. If the critical factor is not bypassed then I believe we see what is to be learned solely through the limiting lens of our beliefs. And if our beliefs are opposed in any way to the new learning, we find resistance and difficulty fully absorbing and accepting the new learning. Any beliefs that do not resonate with the material presented acts as a selective filter and inhibit learning.

"I have discovered that I can lessen the impact of my critical facility and its resistance to learning by focusing on that resistance and tapping with EFT. Somehow EFT clears opposing beliefs or at least the emotions surrounding those beliefs and allows me to learn easier and quicker."

Energy therapies have indeed already showed us many aspects of what happens when blockages in the energy system are being removed and "shields to learning" are being dropped. I had a client when I first started with EFT whose story I wrote up in Adventures in EFT under Learning. This was a 54 year old woman who called me from her office, first time ever alone with a computer, had never used one in her life but it was made clear if she wanted to keep her job, she'd have to.

She had had 3 days staff training on how to use it and she was in tears when she rang me.

She said, and I quote, "I'm staring at the screen and all I see are hieroglyphics, it doesn't make any sense, I can't do this!"

I got her to do basic EFT whilst looking at the screen and it took one single round and she said, "Oh god! Something's just happened! What is that - that looks, you know that looks like a little tiny picture of a paper folder? And is that a dustbin in the corner there? Do you put old files in there you don't need any more?"

It was absolutely extraordinary as an experience for both of us. After she got over her surprise and I got her to click a few things here and there, did a couple more rounds when a spreadsheet popped up, she said to me the following:

"It is so strange, it's like I'm having this feeling of FAMILIARITY with all this all of a sudden. Even as though it's FRIENDLY and I want to try some more things, find out what they do?"

Three weeks later she send me a thank you in an **email** (!!) all proudly and told me that as impossible as it may seem, the other people in the office were coming to HER now for advice on what to do with the new computers.

Shields To Incoming Information

Let's now talk about shields against incoming (information, energy, whatever).

These are **energetic realities** which really do **change the actual perception** of a thing - making things "unclear", "difficult to grasp", "like I'm in a fog" and so on. People say these things and in fact, they're actually and exactly true. They can't see through their own shields!

These shields are blockages in the wider energy body that stop the energy from coming in, dissipate it, swirl it up and make it impossible to learn and contact these things and get that sense of "familiarity" the computer lady was referring to.

EFT removes these blockages and these shields and that's why people keep saying things like, "It's becoming clear to me ...", "I can now understand this ..." "I have a whole new grasp of the situation ..." and so forth.

ET is specifically designed for the purpose of letting energy in and moving it through and out, and so it's a lot faster than tapping but certainly, EFT can be used **most successfully** for these things.

There are actual shields to learning, and they would manifest in thoughts like:

- I can't learn this
- I won't learn this
- I don't want to learn this
- It would be bad for me to learn this
- If I understood this, it would change me
- Knowing this would threaten too much of who I am.
- This cannot be learned by such ones as me
- It would take forever to learn this

On another level, and that's the EmoTrance level, it simply displays as procrastination, pain and reluctance based upon that pain, state shifts into physical discomfort at the very thought of "interacting with the material".

There are a million and one immediate and obvious examples as to the validity of this - i.e. if you somehow manage to "drop shields" you can learn so quickly, it's literally scary and throws our whole idea of education, memory, storage and all of that totally out of the window in an instant.

One of my personal favourites was "Shakespearian language". I was, like most, deeply traumatised by it at school and it was totally incomprehensible to me in all ways.

Then, I heard Mel Gibson had done a version of Hamlet. So I went to the cinema, having been a huge fan (and probably quite in love with the guy at the time LOL) and to my horror, it wasn't at all an Australian re-make but the real deal in full out Shakespeare talk - and without subtitles!

As this became apparent to the horrified audience, over half got up and just left. I watched them go and thought about what to do. At which point Mel made his entrance and I thought, oh sod it. Doesn't matter if I don't understand a word. I can keep myself amused by just watching him bend over, wipe a strand of hair from his face - lovely anyway!

Ten minutes on and I laughed at something and it was **then** that I became aware that I was absolutely understanding **every word they were saying** - easily, perfectly, logically, just as though it was the plainest English possible.

I was totally blown away by that and never could understand how I could have just shifted into this foreign language in just ten minutes so easily. I've so often wondered about that and how I could make it so that my kids and friends would be able to do it too and I wouldn't be left alone with how much I enjoy Mr S's sense of style, humour and expression now.

Because I was no longer fighting it, all shields dropped, it just came in and there's something inside my person that **has the ability to make sense of it perfectly** - just like the computer lady had something inside her person that just understood and became familiar and friendly with those symbols just like that after a round of EFT.

Learning, it seems, is totally **other** than we were led to believe.

I'd call to everyone who is here to test this for themselves, right now, stop whatever you're doing, call up a webpage containing something that frightens you, be it an article by Dilts or a mathematics site, view source on a webpage or find a geography school support page if that's what hurts you still!

Just look at the screen and do a round or two of EFT and of course, ET if you know it on everything. Then report back.

If we can **learn** - my God then we can learn to do things very differently from what we're doing right now in every way possible.

Heart Learning

I was talking with Ananga Sivyer (Author of The Art & Science and The Meridian Journey and fellow AMT Trainer) this morning about the "energy of learning".

She told me some very interesting things about how meridians are involved in the transportation of this energy and I asked her if she would write it down to share with you - which she kindly did!

In Japanese, "the heart" translates as "the centre". It's all coming together.

Ananga Sivyer says, "As I typed that in the subject line I remembered the expression to 'learn something by heart'. We really do know the truth already, don't we!

As far as traditional energy medicine goes, energetically there are channels in the body which operate as a feedback mechanism between the heart and the mind. They are depicted as a curved channel which loops out of each side of the central (or conception) meridian - that is the one that runs up the front of the body - and into the centre of the head.

The function of these channels is to relay information between the mind and the heart and vice versa. In the specific context of learning (there are many other areas influenced by this energetic feedback loop) knowledge is received by the heart and verified in conscious awareness by the mind - here it is processed and considered externally before returning to the heart for storage and recall.

Many texts cite the heart as the seat of intelligence and, beyond that, wisdom - and not the head!

In traditional Chinese medical reference texts it is referred to as the Emperor - the ruler and overseer of all other organs and energy systems and specific reference is made to wisdom and knowledge coming under the jurisdiction of the heart energy.

Ancient oral traditions passed on vast amounts of complex information from master to disciple as part of a relationship of mutual trust the disciple would offer respect to his superior and the master would, in return, offer affection to the disciple by imparting knowledge. As speech is the manifestation of heart energy (more on this in The Meridian Journey) it would be considered that knowledge would be passed from one heart to another."

Students & Teachers

Knowledge being passed from heart to heart? What would that be like? In the martial arts traditions, the teacher/master is more like a father to their chosen students and this form of "energy exchange" might be a very profound experience that might be either mistaken for, or indeed be simply a variation on the label of "love" - for what could this be other than a true exchange of the energies of the heart?

I have had the extreme good fortune just recently to have had a student who delighted me and vice versa.

For sure, the relationship was beset with difficulties because I didn't know where to place it - it didn't make any sense in the usual relationship definitions of "boyfriend/girlfriend" or any variations thereof, with sex or without. From the teachers perspective, I **know** what this student brought out in me - incredible flow and clarity of thought, insight, understanding.

When we were really at it, our energy exchanges went into a not dissimilar state of what I noted previously about the "true co-joint healing" where you just don't know who is healing whom, who the healer is and who is the healee, and who is being healed of what. The energy exchanges with my student can only be described as co-joint learning because I have no idea who was teaching whom what, and indeed, looking at the whole interaction with the wisdom of hindsight and in the context of "learning as an energy exchange", simply what one could say that both end up changed, which was if you remember my original definition of true learning.

In the movie metaphors, a favourite is the story of a bitter, crusty old teacher who is saved just as profoundly if not profoundly more so by the appearance of the orphan student with whom they make that relationship.

They need each other to heal each other and become changed people, real people, awakened people, whatever you want to call that. From Zorro to the Karate Kid, from Heidi to Star Wars, from Finding Forrester to Educating Rita, that's the story, time and time again.

And it's a GREAT story. No wonder we like it so much, find it so inspiring. It's true, that's why.

The terrible contortion, be in teaching or in healing in whatever variety and even including psychotherapy (!) AND with the caveat that there may actually be **no distinction between healing and learning** at all! - is that we have no full on societal archetypes and role models to fall back on when these relationships happen.

What do we make of that boy from Karate Kid who is hanging out after school with that old weirdo in his wooden hut? What would the neighbours think? In The Man Without A Face, they're coming round to burn "the perverts house down".

The people involved in these "Good Will Hunting" exchanges have the sensations, the feelings and emotions but there's nowhere to put them into a societal context, with rules of engagement and progressions such as we find in courtship, engagement, marriage and divorce to tell us what we are "supposed to be doing" with each other.

I can't help but wonder how many people "turned gay", into paedophiles or simply married their teachers/ students/ clients/ healers because they just simply didn't know what else to DO with THAT.

THAT kind of profound energy exchange. Which is way, way too rare anywhere and everywhere and which, if it wasn't, wouldn't throw the neurologies of those involved in them into such unnecessary contortions.

Conclusion

The Energy Of Learning, and using EmoTrance principles to remove blockages and shields to learning at the energetic levels, throws open a world of new possibilities. In the last section, that on the student-teacher relationship, this bridges into the most profound of human relationship possibilities and the truly unbelievable lessons that might be learned there, and the healings that might arise - if we have the courage to take that step from learning as the ancient scriptures suggest first with the heart so we can know in our head.

Thought Flow

The basic ET process continues to throw up some very interesting side effects and patterns - this one must be about one of the most useful things an energy worker could come across.

Simply put, this pattern is designed to allow the player to break out of infinite thought loops. There is a huge array of theory behind this very straightforward pattern but we don't need to get into this; suffice to say that the thought-loop pattern works to reduce stress, bring about relaxation of over-active mind circuitry and can also lead to some very welcome and surprising new ideas and insights.

Breaking Free From Thought Loops - The Thought Flow Process

What is a "Thought Loop"?

A thought-loop is a set of thoughts that go around and around without an exit point or any form of resolution.

A simple example of this phenomenon would be: "I need more money" - "But I'm already working as hard as I can." - "But I need more money." - "But I can't work any harder." - "But I need more money." - and so on, round and round.

In all systems flow, these endless loops need some form of exit point because unless such an exit point exists, there can be no forward movement.

In thought-systems, which may be quite complicated and include many sub loops but still don't have an exit point and thus keep behaviour stuck and the folk who run them awake night after night, the added problem is that these loops run faster and faster with practice, "overheating" certain pathways, unbalancing the energy system and indeed, are damaging to health and happiness.

The favourite way of humans to break out of thought-loops is by adding new material - also known as "learning" - in the hope that this might provide the exit points.

With very complex and personal thought loops, off the shelf advice is usually not sufficient to break out of a loop and also, the longer they have been running, the more entrained they tend to become.

Lastly, people do a lot of these virtually all the time they are awake and so what was needed was a method that would:

a) Allow someone to break out of thought loops fast and as soon as they have come to the conscious attention;

b) To have an intervention that is likewise fast;

c) To actually resolve the problem of the loop - by providing new and different insights but without having to rely on externally acquired added information.

Putting It Behind You

Now, there is a lot of energy theory involved in this pattern; indeed, far more than is necessary to know about in order to successfully use this simple energetic move.

I would briefly say that the system of human thought is an integrative and very important part of an overall system that is designed to learn and change constantly and that the reason for thought loops developing in the first place is a detachment of that thought system from a greater system that is required to complete the process flow which leads to new behaviour (and I include new thoughts as new behaviour too, as thinking is, indeed, a behaviour form in its own right).

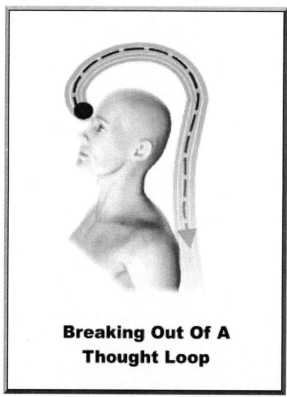

Breaking Out Of A Thought Loop

So, and to make what is a long story very concise indeed, what we are going to do is to take a thought and literally put it behind ourselves, from the emergence point of the thought into our energy field and taking this thought, sweeping it up and over our head and letting it flow down the back of our heads and down the back.

Try it, and in the beginning, by all means use your hands to make the gesture physically in order to set up this flow from thought to the requisite non-thought systems which are designed to process out of the thought loops.

Think of something that you have thought of umpteen times during your life - *I want to loose weight but I can't* is such a thought, as is *I should be doing something important but I don't know what it is*, for example.

Now, simply allow that thought to come, then physically take it, sweep it up and over your head, letting it trickle down your back and go where it would go.

Consider how that feels - and what a very nice way to get rid of troublesome thoughts this actually represents.

Questions On The Thought Flow System

Here are some questions and answers that usually arise:

Q: When I put a thought behind myself, it seems like its completely gone. Surely that is a bad thing? I must keep on worrying to finally solve the problem?

A: Well you can look at it in many different ways. One is to have some trust in the rest of the (little used) processing systems of your totality and which are actually designed to compute the answers for you that your thought has discovered. Another is that should you get tired of feeling relaxed and having space for once to think about something else, you can go right back to the old thought loops that got you absolutely nowhere for all the times you've run them.

Of course, whether or not you wish to make use of this system is entirely up to you in all ways.

Q: Is that the unconscious mind we are passing the problem over to?

A: No, not really. It is an energetic system of the totality we are using in this case. The unknown and highly misunderstood systems that comprise the so-called "unconscious or subconscious" "mind" are a part of the whole deal but that is not where the thoughts are going to in this technique.

Q: Will I get - finally! - some new answers to my old problems?

A: No guarantees. Try it out, find out what happens.

Q: How will I know that the system has started to work as it should? Where do the new answers come from?

A: I don't wish to prejudice your personal experiences with telling you what it feels like or what happens. I am very highly prejudiced in favour of people having their own experiences and their own learnings in their own way. Suffice to say you will know when it is beginning to work as it should. :-)

Q: Can you put other things as well "behind you"? Beliefs, memories, emotions?

A: Sure. As usual, just play with it. It is designed for thoughts, mostly, but it would be difficult to differentiate, as well as memories and emotions making up parts of these complex thought loops in which many of us are trapped.

Q: Is there room for all of that "stuff" back there? Are there thoughts you shouldn't put into that system (in case they turn out toxic or damaging)?

A: It isn't a store room but a flow system. It can take any kind of thought, any amount, and chances are it is glad to be able to flex its systemic muscles and be of use again. The more you use it, the more useful it becomes.

Q: Is there a meridian tie in with this process?

A: Yes, there is. The corresponding meridian is one of the strange flows known as the governor.

216

Beyond Questions

Now, passing over questions and conflicts is a nice thing. No, it's better than that. It is uniquely releasing and wonderfully relaxing, and sometimes even feels so good that I chuckle to myself.

As we have now noted, it also allows new and other questions to flow, including the old "silly" ones you were taught not to ask, and those you decided you could never figure out and gave up on (like the Zen riddles), and even encourages the idea as to what questions we're not asking yet but can now if we want to.

Flowing these questions and indeed, thus encouraging "question flow" rather than endless loops on the same old ones is really a most wonderfully welcome gift to me - and that is even quite regardless of any "answers" emerging.

But those "answers" are a topic for another time.

Here, I would like to consider what we do after we've set up the question flow with all that free time and space of mind :-)

So, and as I'm entirely unused to having all this free space and my own thought-mind is still operating at the speed of knots, or speed of light more like, I have found some other uses for the Thought Flow system, other things that can be handed over and when you do, make you feel real good too and cause some interesting effects.

First, some more thought-mind examples, a simple list really for you to look down and notice if any one of these catches your attention.

- Wishes. "I want a magic wand!"

- Needs. "I really need some more space in my life!"

- Forbidden Desires, wishes, wants and needs.

- Decisions and "Realisations" (which in NLP are interchangeable) - "I realised that my mother didn't love me."

- Knowings. "I know I'm just not good enough." Now those really rock if you allow yourself to consider what you know and have the courage to pass them on. (And if you don't, that's just as interesting in every shape or form imaginable!)

- Truths. Beyond knowings, there's the truth. THE truth. Can you hand it over? And the question as to what might happen if you did, likewise? :-)

Now, you may or may not have noticed, we are beginning to turn some kind of corner here.

"Giving" the higher processing systems a "truth" is actually structurally different from asking a question or making a demand - it's like you are passing on something **precious**, something **valuable** for a change.

Here are some more treasures and riches.

- Secrets. This is really, really powerful stuff. And the deeper and darker the secret, the more **precious** it becomes. Strange but true.

- Achievements. "I am an excellent teacher." - "I earned my PhD."

- Values. This can be tough stuff but what a gift, especially if they are YOUR OWN top values and really important to you. Examples are "the principles of love", "freedom", "health", "my love for my family", "actualising myself through my work", etc.

- Failures. No, I'm not kidding, real moments of deepest, darkest failures are extremely powerful in their own right, and the passing along of these is a powerful gift indeed.

- Talents. A word derived from an old measuring device, each one of us is said to have some talents in some areas (and by definition, not in others). I personally have always considered my personal talents to be both a blessing and a curse and of course, they are. Time to hand them over.

- Anti-Talents. That's all the talents you think you don't have and the more bitterly envious you are for the lack of those, handing them over once and for all will be the sweeter a gift for your totality. NB. If the term talents doesn't make any sense to you, they are also sometimes called resources or qualities or character traits.

- Life's Work and including Art. We all make decisions as to what we're doing here and those of us who think we've found our life's work might have a hard time passing this jewel over.

Now, we are moving into another class of "gifts for the soul" again.

- Dreams. Now by that I don't mean waking dreams but real "dream dreams" - things you've dreamed about and you have remembered, had them with you for a long time, whatever they may be.

- Memories. It's a really sad side effect from running entire incarnations via the thought-mind that we think we need to carve precious moments into some kind of stone. Taking photos of that family Christmas and this is just an external representation of what the thought-mind tries to do so "I will never forget this moment". Good and bad alike, this is an anti-flow device and a disturbance to how the systems of the totality should run of the highest order.

- Guiding Stars and Dark Night Of The Soul moments. You might need the Snow Globe technique for these as they have components that cannot be handled in thought alone but these are indeed, the defining moments and highlights of an incarnation - the greatest gifts for the higher processing systems I have come across so far.

This list is of course, by no means exclusive; but it is a start.

These are not instructions, they are only ideas.

Let your own self be your guide, and under all circumstances be kind to yourself in all your endeavours.

In Conclusion

Thoughts are but a part of an overall system designed to process information and return change states (which include behaviour and thought as well) as a result.

This system has become disconnected and is currently on many occasions in human usage, trapped in a feed-back loop where the same thoughts are presented over and over again when they cannot be resolved with the inherent capabilities of the thought system and get passed back to the starting point essentially unchanged.

The energetic movement of consciously ordering these thoughts into different channels as described breaks out of this loop and begins to engage other computation systems which has the benefits of reduced stress, less strain on the thought systems and better balance in the energy system, as well as allowing different and new results being delivered through different and other channels until they are presented back to the thought systems.

Thought Flow – Snow Globes

Part II in the Thought Flow system deals with the concepts of "your heart's desire" and introduces the Snow Globe technique to pass on complex thought-groups, memories and including guiding stars to the higher processing systems in order to kick start the flow in the processing systems of the totality. This is also a powerful technique for goal setting and in magical applications.

The Input System - Following Your Heart

I'm sure you've heard it said many times by many very highly esteemed experts that in order to have a meaningful life on this planet, you have to follow your heart.

That is something which I have found virtually impossible up to now.

When the heart asks for a direction or an action, a course of endeavour, this is what has happened to me.

There would be the idea but then, the thought system would begin to consider the idea and entirely fail to come up with any form of strategy to make this work. A simple example is being a creative artist versus earning a living, in my case. The very best my thought-looped mind has ever managed to come up with was a very unsatisfactory, very uneasy compromise with "earn money first, and if there's any time or spare energy left after, you get to be allowed to do a painting or two".

That is clearly not following my heart and the resulting heartache and living an entire life that is constantly unsatisfactory and which feels so very wrong is a pointer as to what happens when we get stuck in the thought-loop systems.

One of the main limitations and problems with the thought system is that it lacks the tools to understand, compute and navigate all the layers of reality, not just the hard.

You need strange qualities such as luck, faith, love and magic, not to mention creativity, in order to make **anything** work at all beyond basic potato planting for survival, or recounting the old solutions to the same problems that were picked up elsewhere and the thought systems cannot handle their complexities at all.

To compensate for this, people have been trying to make symbols and labels and use these instead, but without a real understanding of these things, it is just simply so that we're left with a strange mess that doesn't work. The thought systems, which learn linearly from past mistakes and experiences then go on to conclude that this is too unpredictable and crazy to be of any use, turns away from the only place where the solutions it needs could possibly come from, and intensifies its limited quest to make a nourishing soup with water alone because the meat and vegetables are no longer on the menu.

Being repeatedly confronted with these "impossible" missions from the heart is what then causes the thought systems to start ignoring the heart's messages - and now, we are in very serious trouble indeed.

Now, we have people going through the motions without aim, without motivation, without passion or mission on the one hand, and on the other hand with endless questions as to, "What's the point at all? What am I doing here? What's going on?" that can never be answered.

It is then when entire civilisations and societies turn to thought-world substitutes to avoid going altogether mad or into depression and they make the false gods - cars, nice holidays, power over people, relationships with other people; strange construct concepts and twisted enlightenment theories that make no sense at all plus a whole lot of general busy work to keep the general sense of failure and emptiness at bay, preferably until we die.

Just as we need to make a willing point to hand over problems and questions to the other systems of our totality for resolution, we also need to make a willing point of **using the resulting moments of silence** as the thought loops stop to listen out for any messages coming in from the heart - what it wants, what it needs, indeed, what our hearts desire.

Just as we have to stop and no longer try to make conscious thought judgements on matters the thought systems are entirely unqualified to understand and deal with, we must also re-learn to not judge the desires of the heart as being wrong, impractical, bad or childish or any of the many, many other reasons the grown ups used to give us for just why we couldn't have what we wanted and needed, from a special toy to just a bit more attention or a new gown or story, it matters not.

All the thought system has to do in this case is to become a willing messenger who passes on the request from the heart to the other systems, without interfering or putting its own spin, judgements, problems, contortions or whatever on it. And that you could call is when the system begins to **flow** - no impediments, just passing through as the heart's desire is translated via the medium of thought and stepped across to make the next move on the conveyor belt and towards resolution and manifestation.

The very act of passing thought to the other processing systems causes a space and pull to bring the heart's desires into conscious awareness and helps those who have long ceased to pay attention to those unreasonable demands to once again, begin to get a notion and awareness of what it is the heart needs, wants, or even has to give to the entire flow and change as the energy system begins to grow and develop, as it was designed to, as it must do unless major stagnation and a huge amount of pain will result for the totality, in every sense of the word.

Congruency, the holy grail of personal development, is then in this model not an arrow linear alignment towards a certain goal and consists only of conscious/unconscious mind agreement on both means and ends; but indeed, it is the outcome of for once, experiencing a fast and complete flow through the entire totality system where each part contributes in turn to the wellness and functionality of every other.

Raw "heart power" rushing into the thought system with all the new information and all that energy added is exactly what the stale, exhausted thought systems need - this is motivation, this is flow, this is fascinating and fun, the very opposite of dreary, repetitive, boring tasks which are a constant drain on will power.

Will power, the outcome of the thought system processes, charges in turn the magical systems and as the system completes its cycle, the magic systems feed the heart very powerfully exactly with what the heart has always needed to be strong and a source of power, a central ruler and the true meeting point of all the levels and layers of the totality which, when it in turn sends its power to the thought systems, creates a will that can and will inscribe the fabric of time and space.

That's how it works.

That's how you make magic.

And that is how words such as self esteem, motivation, healing, self actualisation are rendered entirely obsolete in a perfection of flow that is simply, joy expressed and the awakening of the true human being, indeed.

System Clearing In Preparation For Flow

Now, that sounds straightforward enough and basically very simple, doesn't it.

The heart desires, the thought system passes this on to the higher processing systems and these see to the manifesting of the desire, having at its disposal both magical solutions as well as motivation and behaviour as these come together and act in accord to bring about new circumstances and new desires which follow from these.

In practice, this system is far from flowing yet and passing over the first few questions and judgements and such for further processing is only the beginning.

One of the problems with people I noticed a long time ago is what I then called "the unfulfilled needs reservoir" – all those heart's desires that were never fulfilled, were not even attempted to be fulfilled and just got stuck somewhere, were put on ice, rejected as impossible altogether or argued away as not being worth having, being too dangerous, to

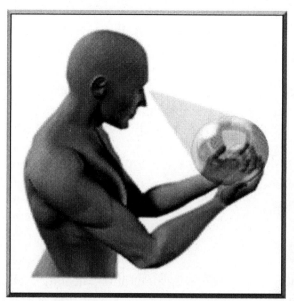

impossible and relegated to a shadow existence god knows where in the energy system.

As we have noted above, if the heart's desires are constantly rejected and never fulfilled, not even the very basic simple ones such as comfort, love, attention and happiness, the flow of these will cease, sooner or later, altogether.

As we begin to consider again, and from a very

different vantage point on this occasion, what our old unfulfilled heart's desires actually are, we find we are dealing with not a single thought or single emotion or memory, but indeed, these reservoirs containing so very much in every sense of the word. Desires, judgements about them, traumas, guiding stars, memories of all kinds – a lot of thoughtfields have become attached to the old desires, creating a veritable whirlpool of chaos on even the simplest of topics.

Still, they will all have to be handed over out of the thought systems and conscious memory systems to the higher operating and processing centres to make any headway at all, and for this I have found the Snow Globe technique very useful indeed. It seems natural to do this and is in actuality, a powerful experience.

Introducing The Snow Globe

Here, we allow the totality of a topic to gather together first before we "hand it over" to the higher systems by pouring all and everything connected to this into one thought form which I call the Snow Globe.

Quite difficult to describe and yet quite easy to do, here is a visual representation of creating a Snow Globe:

Simply pour out the entire thought group into your own open hands until you feel you have got most if not all of it out, then take the Snow Globe and pass it over your head, allowing it to fall down behind you in the basic Thought Flow manoeuvre to move to the higher processing systems for the sorting out that should have occurred a long time ago.

As usual, don't worry about overloading the higher processing systems. These are quantum based and can handle anything you might care to throw at them, even a lifetime's worth of contortions and memories, misery, happiness, huge emotions, a billion separate and conflicting thoughts - this is truly nothing to these systems and indeed, you could consider it simply food for these, fuel to have them come to life and run more powerfully, more clearly which in turn helps to kick-start the entire circuit of "processing to a higher level" which this represents.

The Snow Globe technique is a very powerful and extremely useful method that has more applications and practical advantages than you might guess at this point.

Snow Globe Do's & Don'ts

It really helps to use your whole body for this technique, i.e. not to do the whole thing with your eyes shut but to really and physically hold out your hands and pour the contents of your thoughts into your hands, allowing it to collect there and take on the density of the Snow Globe.

It will happen that with certain Snow Globes you will find a strong reluctance to "let it go" or even raise it up and over to initiate the handing over to the higher processing systems.

It is important to remember that you are not "letting go" as in, getting rid of or losing any of this.

Nothing is lost. Your memories will remain perfectly intact but what you are doing is returning these things to their rightful place in all ways.

It might also help you to consider that "What we don't have is what we hold on to."

A heart's desire blocked at the heart or thought level or stuck there (which it has to be by definition else you couldn't put it now into a Snow Globe!) blocks the manifesting of itself AND any further related applications. Holding on to an ancient love, for example, will not only prevent the processing into a state of bereavement resolution, gratitude and grace but will also effectively prevent any other love from coming and flowing.

Trauma too if not processed to its resolution will keep an individual stuck where they were back then, forcing them to exist partially always at that time, in that place and preventing the totality systems overall from organising themselves to a higher level.

It is true that sometimes, courage is needed and some faith in yourself and your life here to release the Snow Globe to the higher processing systems; it might further help for you to know that you holding a resource that really is needed elsewhere in your own totality to move forward, to develop and grow as you were designed to, and to help become what you always knew you should be moving towards.

Further, it might become important for you to know that the higher processing systems don't judge the absolute mess the thought systems have made of many of these things over time. Judgement ONLY exists in the thought system and nowhere else. The rest of your totality just functions and resolves as best as it is allowed to. Whether you are handing over moments of transpersonal glory which have kept you stuck in limbo or moments of utter and total failure and unconditional capitulation, or immense foolishness, cowardice, evil even, to the higher processing systems it is nothing but incoming data which it really needs to have something to do, have a purpose, and provide energy for all of your totality.

Likewise, the concept of "punishment" exists only in consciousness and in the thought system. If you feel you need to continue to punish yourself and this is a "reason" for holding on to something or other, let me just say that what the thought-systems consider to be reasonable is usually anything but and in the greater scheme of things, the concept of punishment is simply ridiculous and implodes in on itself as one of those classic limited thought-system misapprehensions, of which there are many.

Lastly, if you are concerned about "learning your lessons", I would say that they cannot have been learned if the higher processing systems were not involved and did not create a change of heart in response. So have some courage, hand over some things, find out for yourself what it feels like when you do.

Snow Globe Applications In Brief

There basically isn't a thing you cannot put into a Snow Globe and thus, pass it along to the higher processing systems. Here are just some ideas to get you started.

Heart's Desires

I think this might be one of the most important uses for this technique, namely to allow yourself to remember something you've always wanted, ached for, hungered for but never experienced.

This could be as simple as a special toy you wanted when you were a child, and as complex as "the perfect relationship" or "being loved unconditionally" - either way, once you take the breaks off and really allow yourself to remember all that pertains to this topic, the pain and hurt, the disappointment, the rationalisations, the memories, the judgements and the further pain and hurt that flowed from those, the decisions you made, the "realisations" you had - all of it is an interconnected whirlpool that can be let go of and collected in that thought-field of the Snow Globe in your hands.

People (including self constructs, identity issues, conflicting "selves" etc)

Places ("I left my heart in San Francisco")

Dreams

Goals & Magick

Trauma & "Issues"

Guiding Stars

Feelings & Their Corresponding Thoughts

Sanctuary Habitats (in their entirety)

Symbols and Representations

Fears & Representations/Manifestations Thereof

Questions, Conflicts, Dilemmas

In Conclusion

The Snow Globe technique has four main purposes, the first of which is to clear out some of the existing accumulated debris from the thought system fast by collecting whole large thought-groups and moving them through all at once.

The second purpose which follows from this is to make space for new "heart's messages" to come through and to get movement into the old stuck ones.

The third purpose is to actively feed the higher processing systems so that in turn, their output becomes more powerful to begin to charge and re-energise the entire developmental learning and processing systems of the totality.

The fourth purpose is to teach the thought-systems (or what we still think of as "us", "me", "I") the principles of both releasing and passing on things that it was never meant to work out by its lonesome self to our own higher authorities on the one hand, and on the other to listen to incoming information from the heart system.

Factor X

We all have grown up and lived in a world that is primarily if not exclusively constructed **by the thought system** working in isolation.

The thought system, that which creates our HUGE problems of identity and of course, the hugely bizarre way we live and conduct ourselves, is LINEAR in nature.

It works on cause and effect. It doesn't know anything about the future and can do very little to influence the present, for all it's machinations and attempts at trying to control, for example, the physical body. If that is too abstract, just think as to what happens to logic when a teenage girl falls in love and what good the "practical thought-systems" are under such conditions :-)

The thought-system needs cause-and-effect in a correctly linked, LINEAR FORWARD progression in order to learn what was right and what was wrong. It can't do anything else and that's what it's good for - to look at the past and make conclusions, theories and lessons for the future, always with an eye out for the EFFECT of the actions it set into motion.

But unfortunately, there are these tales of another world altogether.

Of a world where in order to become rich, you have to have FAITH first and BEFORE any proof has manifest.

Of a world where you manifest the proof by **KNOWING THAT IT IS SO - FIRST.**

This is a complete reversal of all the thought-systems know and have experienced to be true their entire existence worth, and not only theirs, but all of their ancestors, all role models, all loved ones.

The entire thought-system linear proof method is everywhere - you have to write a good exam FIRST and THEN you are given a certificate.

You have to prove that you are loveable FIRST, and THEN you are loved as a result.

It makes sense, doesn't it. How else could we possibly KNOW? We need PROOF in order to BELIEVE.

Ah. But then there's this annoying other world again.

Where you are told to believe first IN ORDER to manifest the proof AFTERWARDS.

Now, where's the SENSE in that???? Nonsense! Bu-humbug! We want PROOF FIRST!

Thus quoth the thought-system.

Who doesn't know any better.

Who cannot know any better and who is right in it's own context and in its own little encapsulated world that is less than a mere percentage of the real reality of things.

But consider this. On average, an author these days receives between 275 and 700 rejections before they are published.

That's a really good example. Even if you're not an author, consider the enormity of the weight of rejection for a moment. How on EARTH do they keep going? Why don't they stop? Why are they not taking the REALITY FEEDBACK which clearly tells them that they are no good, that they will never "be an author"?

And it's true. Many people don't collect that many rejections. They take their feedback and get a "real job" instead, in a paper mill or such.

But some keep on going and they end up as the authors of the next generation, those who are trotted out for the young students as "a great author".

What they needed to weather all the "reality feedback" was **the faith first that they were indeed, an author.**

That is and was the only way to "make it" as an author - and indeed, that's the way the world works in all truth and actuality.

You cannot say, for example, that "When I have won the Nobel prize, I know that I am a genius."

You have to believe that you are a genius FIRST in order to produce the goods that will in the end bring you the Nobel prize.

That is indeed, the core of magic and all reality creation - that the thought-systems belief in cause and effect are absolutely reversed.

When that happens, the so-called "impossible" becomes possible or even inevitable, if you will. The more manuscripts the author sends out, the higher the sheer statistical likelihood becomes that they will get published. But it's not about just good old thought-system cause-and-effect tenacity.

Magic and reality don't work that way at all.

They work in truly mysterious ways. The author's manuscript is chucked into the bin. The bin falls over. The manuscript slides under a desk. Here, it is found by a cleaner who loves it and carries it surreptitiously into the "approved manuscripts bin" on the other side of the building.

Synchronicity. The strangest and most unexpected manifestations of chains of improbabilities. All sorts of things can and do happen - when there is FAITH FIRST.

But faith and the reversed cause-and-effect of reality creation is an anathema to the thought-mind. It's too complicated for one thing and entirely outside of its reach for another.

Further, faith is not something you think up and then collect evidence to support it (which is the only thing the thought-mind is capable of doing!).

Faith is an overall totality state - heart, mind, all systems aligned in congruency, in that elusive Zen state where magic just happens, be it on a keyboard, in a sports field or a laboratory.

The thought-system CAN STRUCTURALLY not manifest faith or love, or trust, or ecstasy or any of these things associated with the "higher enlightenment states".

Those come into being when the totality works together in a system of which the thought-systems are but a small part, playing their important part, that is for sure, but where the world is very much larger than the thought-systems could ever allow it to be (for then it would become way too complex and it couldn't keep in control any longer).

Now, and to bring this back to the thought flow system and the question of results.

The very reason I have published this whole process and idea is because we need a way OUT of the endless loops our thought-system is running.

It cannot answer questions such as, "Why am I here?" based on previous evidence.

It cannot answer questions such as, "What is to come?" based on previous evidence.

And it absolutely cannot construct a self concept with all the conflicting information of past evidence that it has stored up - am "I" a genius or an idiot? I have evidence for both - what am I?????????

What we need is a way OUT of this.

I have spend an entire lifetime (and sometimes it seems, many more than one!!) observing people NOT being able to answer this using what passes for logic and reason by the encapsulated thought-systems that are doing the very best they can with their limited abilities, running themselves ragged and becoming self-destructive in the futile endeavour to make sense of it all.

Frankly, and if cause-and-effect is all we have, it simply doesn't make any sense at all. It can't make sense, and that understanding is a huge relief in and of itself.

Come on, guys.

Didn't we always know deep down that we needed help?

That we DIDN'T know the answers and had NO way of finding them?

That we were doing all sorts of things terribly wrong and wanting it to be better but not knowing how to get out of it?

That "we" is our thought-systems in desperation, overstretched by the truth of actual existing reality. By how things don't make sense in a cause-and-effect fashion.

It doesn't make sense if someone was really trying hard to be good all their lives getting dreadful diseases, little children suffering and dying "who didn't deserve it", love and attempts at love being stomped on and cruelty reigning supreme, insanity reigning supreme - in the cause-and-effect Universe it doesn't make any sense at all and it never will.

Thinking more and harder, being more "logical" in the thought-mind sense, is not and has never been the way out of it or forward, not ever.

ALL - and check this out, for it is true! - ALL progress in science, for example, is NOT the result of people being logical but time and time again, just an "accident" or some weirdo having a dream where they ride on a beam of light.

233

Some guy "forgetting" to put a dish away and "discovering" penicillin.

Some other guy seeing a spiral stair case and understanding how DNA works.

Who are the celebrated geniuses of humankind?

Madmen and madwomen to a man, not a single Spock amongst them.

I saw this, and noted it. Time and time again. All the thought-mind clerics come up with is to push the pieces of existing "effect" around and around on their puzzle boards. Forever, if necessary. Making nothing happen, no shifts, no breakthroughs to a higher level of organisation. Cluttering often the existing breakthrough insights with so much detail nonsense that the original break through ceases to work at all anymore (see hypnosis and Reiki for current examples).

So when the time came and I ran into my own "walls of logic" I stopped, and I said, this is not the way to do it.

"I" cannot think my way out of this.

To believe that "I" can is a total delusion and if I use my thought-system, based on simple observed cause and effect, the only answer "I" can come up with is that this system cannot ever produce the answer.

To be clear about this, like everyone else, I did not trust my own thought-system, for like all the rest of "us", "I" am just a fool, right?

I did my historical research and collect the data, and the data really is quite incontrovertible if one would care to really look at it.

The thought-mind does not have the answers.

Now, if I was a thought-mind alone, if indeed, I was Mr Spock, I would now simply say that **THERE IS NO ANSWER.**

But if one was to use one's thought-mind as it was designed to be, which actually collects ALL evidence for consideration, and does not shrink in fear to look at ALL available evidence, there is evidence to the contrary.

There is plenty of evidence to suggest that there may, indeed, be answer to be had.

Sometimes, somewhere, someone (and usually, some lunatic misfit) does something, dreams up something and then there is indeed some form of real noticeable shift. Vistas widen out. Possibilities emerge that simply weren't there before. New lines of enquiry arise - from nowhere.

From nowhere?

Not from nowhere.

From somewhere.

Let's be logical here - even cause-and-effect logically, why not. It's all we have, and we have it for a reason.

There is **something** available to humans which makes breakthrough insights possible.

Let's call it factor X as they sometimes do in mathematics when there's a constant that, if you insert it into an equation, will solve the unsolvable equation every time.

You don't need to know what factor X might be, you can deduct its properties from what happens when you insert it into the unsolvable equations.

And then you can run a scientific experiment, just like the thought-mind would like us to, and it can get to start computing as it should, and it can make connections when there weren't any before, and in the process of doing this, re-arrange the existing pieces on the puzzle table to come to whole new conclusions.

For a long time, I considered the so-called "unconscious mind" to be factor X.

It seems to fit the bill in a way, what with dreaming about riding on beams of light and such.

So I sought to test this assumption, and I made Project Sanctuary (note, the name - PROJECT Sanctuary) to use this as factor X in the equations.

Now, and it's true, the "unconscious mind" (whatever THAT may be!) is a most fascinating factor X indeed but it doesn't serve to solve the equations - at least not in and of itself.

However, it does something else which was indeed, essential to this entire investigation.

(Just to remind us, the investigation title of my long term project was, "What THE HELL is going on here????" - my response to life as it is :-)

During the Project Sanctuary experiments, it came to my attention what I had previously erroneously believed to be logic was no such thing, but indeed, a highly impoverished version that could handle only the tiniest proportion of the input, stimuli and environments we find ourselves in by virtue of being alive.

The thought-mind system responded to this with, "Wow! That's why I could never figure it out! Thank goodness! NOW, and with this added set of math-rules at hand, I can finally get to work and re-process the entire thing! Thank goodness!"

And once more, the poor old thought-system went to work with a vengeance.

And once again, it ran into those damned barriers beyond which it simply could not go.

Granted, they were further and wider than before, but it now really became clear that the sheer linearity of it was in and of itself the problem.

So, now where do you go to find a truly non-linear processing system?

One that actually results in changes, behavioural changes, observable changes? The good old cause-and-effect of the thought-mind still there, present and correct, as it cannot help but being.

And now, finally, the metaphor of "the human energy system" comes to the rescue.

Let's presume for a moment that we are designed quite structurally to simply develop and live as we should as totality beings in our incarnations here.

Let's presume for a moment that we are not some evolutionary death trap but that we have a right to be just as we are, just the same as a crocodile or a plant of some kind.

Let's leave all religion, delusion and nonsense out of it for a moment and simply consider our structure and what we are currently doing with it.

From the available evidence, humans as a species can do some things that are really quite extraordinary.

That whole thought-system thing, for one thing, is really extraordinary.

To use it, as we do in Sanctuary, to actually create worlds, have them be real, move in and live in them, in many, many worlds in a matter of a few short weeks, to learn lesson there that may be applied in hard, is quite something.

It is clearly an evolutionary advantage if we take survival for a measuring stick.

Then, there is our physicality.

The richness of it, the rightness of it. The resilience which is breathtaking. If you've ever watched someone die, living on a breath at a time in a body that you cannot believe could possibly still hold together, you will know what I mean when I saw that I am absolutely in awe of the power and total congruency of the physicality to survive.

Our neurology is a part of that awesome totality. The neurology that expresses itself in our thought-systems and also in the other aspects of it, such as the so-called "unconscious mind" and which lies asleep most of the time as cat-scans reveal so powerfully.

These systems are interwoven and a part of a totality - but there is a detachment, a breakage that has occurred and they are not working together as they should.

The unconscious mind, my previous factor X, turned out not to be that bridge.

There were further components at work.

Then, we were made consciously aware of a whole new dimension of the human totality - the so-called "energy system".

This had been talked about in one way or the other for many, many generations, right back into the mist of recorded history but was not being factored into any of our current equations as a whole; as it cannot be made visible or "proven" with the current mechanisms, it was and is excluded from the puzzle pieces in a great many thought-systems amongst the current billions who live on this planet.

When Roger Callahan started tapping on meridian points to make fears go away, he made a bridge over which those who were not too deeply enmeshed and entrained might travel and begin to factor the "energy system" into their own thought-mind equations as their very own missing factor X - because it is my assumption that all people are born to try and make sense of the world the best they can.

Now, I had encountered these "invisible realities" before I met EFT but what I had done with it was to keep it on a shelf, away from all the other data that had been assembled, because I simply didn't know just where to put it. It was so other, and also so "unproven" (!) that it didn't fit into the ongoing experiments and thought-mind constructs at the time.

Divisions.

Divisions are the hallmark of the thought-mind unlogic.

"A thing is one thing or another", said Aristotle and that "made sense" to thought-minds ever since.

Dividing our totality into a conscious mind, an unconscious mind, a physicality and an energy system and then studying the bits in isolation - that is classical thought-mind action in order to be able to keep in control, to simplify these incredibly complicated systems and to in actuality, **make** those puzzle pieces in the first place that we push around on our puzzle boards - endlessly.

Dividing the human race into males and females and dividing up resources between them that is exclusive to either and not available to each, so that no complete picture can ever emerge.

Dividing a human tribe into artists and farmers and warriors likewise, each faction holding their own pieces and not one being able to ever construct a full picture.

That's what the thought-systems have to do to keep the illusion of understanding and control alive - to divide up and reduce the overwhelming information density of the world to manageable proportions.

Now, and factoring in all the various puzzle pieces of my own in one great big overarching map, I started the other way around.

Let's start with a human totality.

A totality that is NOT divided but a system where everything flows, everything is exchanged, and where energy flow changes the system itself in direct response to the environment.

A system where physicality and energy body are one and the same.

Step one. Otherwise known as EmoTrance. And yes, it works a treat.

Now, step two. This is a system where thought and the rest of it are one and the same. No division.

Thoughts are created and they need to go somewhere - energy must flow, right?

That's the prime directive.

Where do they flow?

Well, it seems they loop for the most part round and round, feeding back upon themselves, irresolvable, unending, overheating the system, causing chaos in every sense and every part, from sanity to sickness.

They need to go **somewhere** - and that **somewhere** would by definition, need them in order to function at all, be fed by them and return, produce something of its own that is then passed on to somewhere else.

A new factor X.

A system that is not just willing and able to receive the "output" of the thought-system but is COMPLETELY AND STRUCTURALLY DESIGNED to do just that and RELIANT on the output from the thought-system for its own full and proper functioning.

After all, that's just how the rest of our totality seems to work - there's always flow and if we have even a simple linear chained system, the second system is reliant on the input of the first, else it has nothing to work with.

So I went back to my imaginary drawing board and used the new factor X, a processing system that actually "fed on conscious thought" and ran my imaginary Tesla machine to see what would happen if there was such a thing.

When I did, the problem equations resolved themselves most beautifully - and not just the one I had been working on, which was how to get out of the eternally looped thought-systems with its terrible contortions and hopeless overheating with no noticeable benefits to everyone concerned.

Do you know what the most successful weight loss system EVER is?

The one with the highest actual weight loss rates, and the one with the lowest "fall back" rate?

You might laugh, but it is "Slimming With Jesus".

Religious women get together and they pray to Jesus for strength, forgiveness and to help them with weight loss.

It works. It outperforms every single known behavioural modification technique in the Western world - and what's more, the participants on the programme are happy, delighted, relieved - they simply LOVE it.

I have known many very religious people who are really happy, and do you know what they do in a moment of real crisis?

They "hand it all over to Jesus".

They take their worries, their doubts and their unanswered questions and they simply "outsource" them - with the result of immediate relief, a huge sigh of relief and then, being able to get on with life in a much more pro-active fashion.

This "handing over of problems and questions" to a higher authority is a true hallmark of just about every human religion ever invented and I looked at that, the evidence across the ages, and I said to myself, "What if there was a system that every human is born with, something you can't see, a higher processing system that we all have and to which we can, indeed, outsource our thought-system derived contortions for resolution?"

"What if it was either on a similar strata of existence as these gods, dead prophets and saints we've heard so much about or just plain of the same realm?"

"What if there was such a system - factor X - that is absolutely a part of our own totality and to which we are **supposed to** hand over the question the thought-mind has come up with?"

It was certainly a most intriguing supposition and I decided to test this. I won't go into just how I came up with the idea of physically catching thoughts and putting them right over your head and "putting them behind you" rather than to pass them on and up straight to < or angel guardian deity, favourite>

Now, here we are.

YOU are a part of this test.

You, who are right here, right now, have become involved in highly experimental, quite untried set of experiments based on a theory I have made about the flow of information as energy through the totality of us.

In the past, a one such as me would have beavered away for a lifetime in my tower by the sea and you might or might not have one day become aware of the giant manuscript I left behind when I died.

All conclusions drawn, that's it, folks, that's the truth, now take it or be damned.

But we are in the present.

In a very strange place where I can sit here in my tower in England this afternoon and write down my ongoing thoughts and as I write them, you read them and you get to play at the same time as I and send me feedback on what happened when other people did this, what their reservations are, if it worked for them.

My thought-mind, used to "the old ways" by sheer entrainment finds that a very difficult proposition and concept indeed.

I'm supposed to write a big knowledgeable book and pretend to be an expert after years and years - but I'm not doing that. Instead I am presenting my findings on an ongoing basis as and when.

And it could well be so that I am entirely and totally wrong about everything!

Allow yourselves, each one, for a moment the sheer wonder of this.

There's never been anything like it as far as we know in all the times of humanity.

So, and with the disclaimers out of the way, here's the current state of play.

I posit that the thought-mind cannot create material changes to ourselves or our environment because it is always reliant on the past and what was always there in the past.

It cannot run behaviour, and it cannot run the body. It sure as hell as no control whatsoever over any form of higher realities and it can't figure out the very basic questions of identity, nor construct a "self image" that isn't a complete mess in every way possible.

Most of all, it cannot provide the real energy drivers so necessary to all human endeavour - energy states described in words such as faith and love, for example.

These come from somewhere else, namely from a processing centre metaphorically called "the heart".

I'm not happy with that word because we get it mixed up with the muscle of the same name in our chests but until I come up with something better, we might as well call it that.

The heart cannot generate these powerful energies without getting fed within the system, and I further posit that the food it needs is the end result of the higher processing systems; so we have a very simple 3 point spiral through which energy must travel:

The heart

The thought system

The higher processing systems (factor X)

As the energy travels through one to the other, it is changed **materially** and in interacting with these systems, the energy itself is also **changed materially**.

This is an evolutionary, developing system in process, always in flow.

A "change of heart" (i.e. a really sweeping re-organisation of the conclusions drawn from information) causes totality change directly - this is the system that controls the physicality and influences it directly.

It changes the neurology which is part of the physicality and so, thought changes as well.

As thought changes, new computations arise which in turn are handed over to the higher processing systems which in turn, produce new "changes of heart" - and so on in an ever-lasting flow that strengthens and develops all the systems involved, grows them all by design.

By structurally detaching the thought-system from this flow and making it solely responsible for everything, which is what we have done, not only are we starving the other two systems which rely on a flow through the thought-system for their functioning and survival, but we are also placing inordinate strain on the totality in every way and that includes our physicality.

We are also disabling our own magic if you will, and our own innate abilities to not just create reality with our thoughts and actions, but also to experience it in turn.

Now, and after all of that, back to the original question.

How can we proceed if we **are** at this point ONLY our thought-systems, and thus by the very design, NEED proof before we can "change our minds" or "believe" in something **wholeheartedly**?

Well that's the million dollar question, isn't it :-)

As I am fully aware that I am talking to thought-systems in preference here, in this very linear and slow, slow way of information exchange we have become so used to, I would smile and say, "Hey look at the practical evidence."

When you **do** the simply thought-flow technique, specially made by Silvia (PhD!) for all those looping thought-minds out there, you stop worrying!

That's a result, isn't it?

That's an effect, don't you **think**? :-)

And further, consider the evidence over time.

How many times have you tried to solve the problem, to your very best ability and then beyond the call of duty, but simply failed to do so?

That's evidence - just count it up. That question, that thought, that problem - how many computations across your time of life?

Doesn't it make sense to at least **try** a new avenue of exploration?

And it does, doesn't it :-)

Here's more evidence.

When you lay in bed or wherever you were, driving yourself crazy with worry about tomorrow, or about a loved one far away, or about your own self, what good did that ever do?

When did that actually **work** to bring about a change for yourself, to protect that loved one far away, give you a sense of control and destiny?

That's evidence alright if you allow yourself to consider it.

But there's a lot more.

A lot more.

How many times have you "changed your mind" only to find that nothing, but absolutely NOTHING had changed - for all your tears, willpower and endeavour, hard graft and desperation, day in and day out?

Are we ready yet to, in the light of such overwhelming statistical evidence, to begin to consider some other options, including the central one, namely that the thought-systems cannot get us out of the various corners our thought-systems (individually, combined, culturally, hereditarily!) have painted us into?

Now, I can't honestly promise any one of you that this simple 3 step system of information flow actually works to bring us back online as a functioning totality.

I certainly won't stand here and declare that when you factor **your own soul** into this energetic equation, your problems in body, mind and spirit will simply resolve themselves within the next few months and your lives will become completely unrecognisable from what they are today.

But come on - have you anything better to do than to give it a try?

If the thought-system had any idea of how to resolve any of your long standing problems, it would have done so by now. It is a serving part of the totality and truly will drive itself insane and rip itself to shreds than giving up on its single minded task to help the totality live and grow.

I was going to make a call to have some faith to motivate you to have a go, but that's really unfair because it's one of those things that is just way out of reach for our poor thought-systems to artificially manufacture, and so I won't.

Let's just be logical instead and run a truly scientific experiment each.

The Totality

Ever since I've started talking and writing and thinking about events and states that are happening in people over time in an interlinked, interactive and always completely logical fashion, I've been looking for a better word than "mind-body unit" or "mind-body-spirit system".

For starters, I did not then and do not now believe that we actually know about all the bits that comprise a human across their developmental stages.

Further, these distinctions are really dangerous in two ways.

One, you can't know or ever find out what a real frog is all about in every sense of the word by dissecting them and studying the bits left over, no matter how long and intensive and no matter what the magnification of your electron microscope.

To talk about the body in the absence of also talking about the mind is not practical and inefficient; as they are a system you can't ever get to the correct cause-and-effect computations if you study the systems in isolation. They simply then do not make any sense because centrally important data is missing altogether.

Then, the words themselves are highly problematic. What the hell is the "spirit" bit supposed to be? Where is it? Go look up definitions and you get really vague and unhelpful - and as one of the members pointed out so powerfully, totally conflicting and mutually exclusive information. What, exactly, is a mind? Where is the demarcation between mind, thought and neurology?

Duh.

You can tie yourself into knots for ever and a day and if you did, you would join the happy club of the billions who have gone before you and did the same. The big knot club in the sky. :-)

If something annoys me enough, I'll throw it right out of the window. Sometimes I don't even bother to check if it was open, either.

So I threw that away and used the concept of "the totality" instead and that is an overarching description that encompasses **everything** - even if we have no idea at this point what this everything may consist of in detail.

The instance I did this, I immediately understood something which I believe is the absolute key to making those higher forms of existence and experience we have heard so much about and including enlightenment and magic a possibility at last.

Namely that in order to develop as a human may, you can't leave bits behind - all of you has to go.

All of you, unconditionally, as a totality.

Imagine an adult with a head that stopped growing when they were 2 months old.

Not a pretty sight. Not natural. Not how it's supposed to be, right?

Trying to leave bits of the totality behind in any form of totality development is like attempting to enter a club but leaving your feet at the front door. Completely pointless and you'd really ask yourself what kind of lunatic would even believe this was a good idea.

Similarly, you can't develop as a human if you try to get rid of your body, for example. A lot of the old fashioned religions are famous for that, trying to drive people literally out of their bodies and into the "spirit world" whilst they were still alive with torture and deprivation regimes of all kinds.

The Long Suffering Physicality

Let's expand on this mistreatment of the human physicality aspects a little here.

Let's make a simile of a human family which is the totality. They need to work together to get something done and they need all the help they can get. They have two kids. One is declared to be "unworthy" and they spend 24-7 hating it, beating it, ignoring its demands, starving it, making it do all the dirty work, shouting abuse at it and telling it that if it wasn't there at all, they would be all be much happier.

Give that a few years and now, what do you have? Mum, dad and two strong and powerful young adults which is exactly what's needed to move that boulder and get into the promised land?

246

No. They have three people and an insane cripple if they're lucky. Either way, they are now under strength and can't move the boulder, not now and not ever. Game over, you fools.

This division into having parts of the totality be "holy" and other bits be "dirty and disgusting and evil" is a travesty and a total insult on the Creator's work. It is completely bizarre, completely insane and deserves every bit of the pain and suffering that indeed, folk are and have been experiencing who subscribe to this heinous notion.

By bringing the physicality back into the totality and making it an essential part of the entire structure, at least this one part is set to rights, at least this one insane injustice has been corrected and finally, the physicality gets to receive the same unconditional awe and admiration that is due to something as extraordinary as the totality.

Let's be completely clear about this, completely uncompromising - without the physicality there is no totality.

The physicality is not a sack, a mere hanger on, a bag of rotting bones or a corpse to be.

It is not a weakness at all in humans that the physicality has an *override system* to stop it from severe harm, such as a spy or tortured prophet recanting because they simply cannot stand the pain.

It is an essential device to keep the totality intact so that it may live to reach the next step in the enlightenment process another day.

Without the physicality, THERE CAN BE NO TOTALITY. Without physicality, there IS NO enlightenment process.

So, and with apologies to Pink Floyd - hey, religions, leave that bod alone!!!!

The physicality is the most horribly mistreated and most greatly suffering part of the totality, and if you have any intentions at all towards so called "enlightenment" processes, restitution will have to be made. You will have to have a big time change of heart in your ego relationship. You don't have to cry with shame and guilt, and you don't have to beg its forgiveness, for it will always and faithfully serve you the best it can to the very bitterest of ends. But you will need to welcome it back and learn to receive it, and to have the physicality take its rightful, and immensely holy place in the greater scheme of the totality if you wish to "develop further" as a human.

This has nothing whatsoever to do with turning into some health freak who goes round declaring that "their body is a temple". This has nothing to do with becoming vegetarian, starting to run down to the gym or giving up beer, for that matter. If there is a totality alignment, and the totality likes steak, then the physicality will also like steak and all is well in the totality. And that's all we're looking for here - a sympathetic, mutually supportive overall system with flow across everything and everything in it's rightful place, working together simply as it was always designed to be in the first place.

The Thought-Mind

Next in our line of totality abuse victims is the thought-mind system.

This long suffering part of the totality is not just constantly denigrated and brutally abused in the kinds of religions that seek to get rid of it in any way possible, from meditations via brain washing to brutal sun dance ceremonies. Even in the other religions of science, where it is put up to be the be all and end all of what it means to be human, where it is made responsible for every single aspect of the totality's functions, behaviours, needs and developments, the thought-mind is mistreated as it simply cannot fulfil these functions and just like the physicality, tears itself apart trying to do as it is asked in its fruitless quest to make sense of things, control things, understand things without being able to do any of that.

I would make the comment here that I no longer subscribe to the further division of the thought-mind systems into conscious and unconscious mind. I believe this is one system, forced into a seeming division by the use of unsuitable and limiting operating devices of "language and logic" but this indeed is by the by.

Exactly as with the physicality, we will have to make much more of an effort to learn to understand the needs of this system and how to run it as it was intended; in the context of this discussion on the totality I would note that once again, we need to fully and completely accept and invite this entire system in and correct our attitude and understanding of usage to help accomplish this.

248

The Thought Flow system is a first attempt to relieve some of the suffering and ongoing misuse of the thought-mind system.

The Energy Systems

There is a particularly nasty form of abuse in rearing human children which causes fundamental structural damage and extreme illness, even shut down and complete functions cessation - and this abuse form is neglect.

As far as the majority of the currently active humans is concerned, there isn't even any such thing as an energy system - the act of total ignorance.

You might think that the energy systems are lucky to have escaped our attention and have not been as profoundly victimised and mistreated as the other two totality aspects we have already discussed but you might think that neglect is even worse than mistreatment.

I would also draw your attention to the subject of human emotions, a manifestation directly from the energy systems, a device designed to draw attention to injuries, untenable conditions and malfunctions, disturbances, imbalances - but these cries for help are also ignored entirely.

This appalling lack of attention, lack of understanding of how this works and the following lack of any will or intention to alleviate the energy systems suffering and chaos is probably more damaging still than what is done to the physicality and to the thought-mind systems.

Babies die when no attention is given; in native villages people can be declared as being already dead and ghosts and when everyone in the group ignores them, they can indeed, fade away and die from this.

The energy systems suffer even more from the fact that this neglect has been going on for millennia. Even those who work with these systems are rarely enquiring as to this one particular totality's needs, and often entirely unsuitable remedies are presented - the misconceptions and misunderstandings about the human totality energy systems are legion.

Now, to one more aspect of the totality which puts the suffering by neglect of the energy systems into perspective as not being the worst it can get.

For the lack of a better word, I shall call it:

The Soul System

The general energy systems produce emotions as cries for help.

What cries for help does a "soul" produce?

It's an interesting question and before we go any further, I would like to clearly state that I understand the term of soul not as some weird spooky floaty something that may or may not be a fairy tale, but as an existing processing system of the totality, a functional and necessary part of the totality that is not at all some alien hanger-on that is detached and just waits around for us to die so it can be "set free".

As a functional, contributing, necessary part of the totality, it both takes and contributes to the overall flow of the system and is an essential aspect of, but no "better than" any other parts of the system.

As so very little is actually known about this system, beyond the wildest possible forms of speculation and old wife's tales of the worst kind, I propose we go to work and design some ideas and experiments to find out more.

The following things **may be possible** about this system, pending further investigation.

1. As a part of the totality and in interaction with the totality, each one system becomes structurally unique to that one human from the moment of conception onwards.

2. As the general energy systems suggest, these systems are a-temporal or para temporal.

3. This system might either continue to exist after the dissolution of the totality in a para temporal space or it might be able to encode itself into a more general existing para-temporal structure, thus in effect "inscribing a totality" and making it and all its experiences to all intents and purposes, immortal.

4. This system may also have para-local aspects to it which may be resonance contact to other systems of the same nature - in a para-temporal, para-local forum which allows a flow of energy between all which reside there.

250

Lastly, and this is highly speculative but a fun idea:

5. This system may either be in and of itself a further developmental stage of the totality, or a metamorphosis state or seed in the development of the totality.

As a fun metaphor, I have once described this system in the context of the totality as "being pregnant with the angel child".

This is fun and you shouldn't take it any more serious than that; it is important to note that when I talk about a "soul system", by pre-supposition this means it has a real, absolute and practically measurable **function** and provides **many benefits** for the totality, is absolutely necessary and not something you have to drag around and wear yourself out trying to develop or appease in some strange way. It is here to **serve** the totality (or YOU, in other words, in the true sense of the word YOU!) as a functional aspect, no more and no less.

With the available evidence and even including anecdotal evidence, the existence of this system as a part of the developing totality fits a great many bills and solves a great many equations which otherwise would make little sense or none at all and I offer you this highly speculative theory for your own personal consideration and evidence procedure testing in all ways.

Saving The Totality

I can't know if you remember ever having someone you trusted and respected looking you straight in the eye and saying, quite conversationally, "You have an immortal soul, did you know?"

I am rather sorry to say that in all my travels on this planet and wherever I have been, no-one ever said that to me or even proposed the idea in any shape or form that would make any sense to me.

I have never been particularly religious and I'm sure no-one was more surprised than I when the idea came up to have an explanation for some of the strange occurrences in our totalities across the ages.

My brief notes on what appalling conditions exist for the totality and the aspects of the totality I have discussed (and which may not be either complete or exclusive) also shows us what needs to be done to redress the situation.

It really doesn't matter if one might want to do this motivated by real compassion with these sub-systems or simply because it is truly appallingly inefficient and downright foolish to try and operate even a simple factory conveyor belt by ignoring the vast majority of the robots on the assembly line and pretending they don't even exist, overheating one part and misusing another and generally speaking completely failing to **pay attention** to the most simple acts of maintenance and input-output.

You might be motivated to do something about this because you have always sought "enlightenment" or like myself, simply thought, "Oh for God's sake, this is just ridiculous! There MUST be a better way than THIS!"

Either way, to start considering **ourselves** not just as a construct ego-worm but as a full totality of which "we" are at this moment only the spokespeople, and that whatever we may think about ourselves, we are indeed speaking and acting on behalf of a huge, incredibly impressive and absolutely awe-inspiring work of art (signed, The Creative Force Of The Universe, Itself) that is nowhere near complete yet in its ongoing development, changes a good many things.

From this vantage, it is quite impossible to continue whining on about "how ugly I am" or "how I don't deserve to be loved".

Clearly, it is only right and just that the thought-mind should believe this but there's a whole lot more to the totality than just the thought-mind.

As an aside, one of the great surprises about the Thought Flow system was to me how non-existent the resistance of the thought-mind was to release control and hand over to the other totality systems whatever it could not cope with.

I had expected there to be a lot of struggling but there wasn't - in the contrary. Great big relief all the way around and eager co-operation was the experience of the users.

To me, this is a small but important indicator of how useful it is to consider everything as a totality and not just as a thought-mind, or just a body, or just a "spiritual being" - all the bits and **including the soul** by themselves are nothing like the sum of the parts, the entire totality aligned and switched on, at last.

That is ONE powerful entity indeed.

It is **perfectly** equipped to deal with everything, but absolutely everything "reality" or "the hard" could throw at it - even insane, self constructed, bizarre and nonsensical environments.

The totality is something that absolutely will flow through challenges that would leave the greatest, smartest, strongest heroes gasping with fear at the impossibility of any hope of succeeding.

It has access by design to help beyond its own self in many different ways and guises and at the very least the possibility of indeed being inscribed in the very fabric of the Universe.

To be in the presence of this entity (you) would be a real experience indeed, something worth having in all ways.

Now, and in conclusion, I would say that of course, this is hypothetical. Of course, it is a very rough sketch indeed and just a theory at this point.

But in truth, it is one of the most sensible, most compassionate and also, most **hopeful** theories I have heard for a very long time, if ever.

Even if some of it is wrong, I really cannot see the harm in beginning to treat the various aspects that we really and absolutely comprise of with attention and with some respect, at last.

Only good come out of widening the concept of "I" way beyond the thought-mind constructs, which are clearly so faulty, entirely inefficient and bizarre as they should not and never have been derived by the thought-mind in isolation.

Just the simple will and decision to learn more about the totalities we are and to pay more attention, have a bit more respect for the work of the creative forces of the Universe and to make the most basic of reparations where this may be necessary for each totality, for each of us, will most likely turn out to have been a very, very good idea indeed.

Reversing Reversals (Focal Time Movement)

Focussing on the future is a very useful device to be helping us out energetically at this point of transition. Points. Loads more flowing by even as I'm typing this ...:-)

Here's why.

Thinking about the past puts your energy system into reversal.

Whether this is about past mistakes or past glories, it matters not really. It's all in the past and should be stored out of harm's reach in the energy matrix anyway, cleansed and filed, and not be spooking around in our brains and conscious awareness unless we seek to call it forth - and THEN we are only calling forth the information content, not the requisite states of misery and heartache which inevitably go with "brain stored" material.

So, any thoughts about the past, immediately down the old nadi (see Thought Flow Process) and attention placed with **volition** on future projects, preferably delightful ones that help move you forward towards them.[8]

We look forward and not at the now.

Why not the Now? Aren't we always told we're supposed to be "in the now, in our bodies, fully associated"???

Yes sure. But we're neither in our bodies yet nor fully associated, that's something we are all working on.

At the moment it's mostly and mainly consciousness and brain doing its brain thing - so if you are looking at the Now, all we do is **judge the now** (which unless the now is really cool ends up leading to depression mostly and wanting to be even MORE out of your body and NOT in the now as a direct result!) plus:

We endlessly re-create the Now if we keep staring at it.

---

[8] Little note - if you have nasty depressing swirlyslime-mountain events on your future timeline which make you want to stay in bed and never get up again, and no matter what they might be, best to eradicate them, take them out and explode them with a Quantum X grenade or put them into the nadi as well. You can also phone up and actually physically cancel them sometimes. I just did that version to clear some forward looking space :-)

Just as you endlessly re-create the past by staring at it.

Same principle.

Where you place your attention, the next step stone appears - it's like we really have the capacity to walk in this space where there is nothing, and wherever you turn your head, the road will appear THAT way as a direct response.

So if you keep staring at the Now, that's it. No step stones. Only judgements about the Now and it gets endlessly re-created, no forward movement.

So for now and until we've worked out how to be in our bodies and work as totalities once more, the best trick, energywise as well as statewise, is to focus our conscious attention on a pleasurable future to stop reversals, downward spirals into very draining and miserable energy states, and to remind us of the whole Flow principle of life whilst we're at it.

This keeps the "now" energy state light and buoyant as a direct result, even if the Now is not exactly conducive to such a thing.

Example - being stuck at a Supermarket checkout with a ton of stuff, kids screaming, total pressure to pack it all away, bags piling up, backache, hot and bothered, flustered → **NOW STRESS.**

Deep breath, focus on lying on the couch AFTER the shopping has been put away, with an ice-cream or such. This will happen inevitably and that energy state is available right here, in the Supermarket Hell Now, to provide the energy to actually **get thru it** and get **out of there** without doing long lasting damage to oneself :-)

As this works a treat and is further, highly pleasurable and effective, very non-controversial and simple to do, you get to remember to do it more and more often and in more and more situations. It really does work for just about everything.

I'd make the note that directly related thoughts of a future nature are the most efficient and the easiest to learn to have.

For example, I could focus on retirement in the Supermarket but I don't, I focus on just **beyond the current situation** instead.

When I have work related thoughts, I focus on the future projects and products, not on retirement or lying on a couch.

When I have thoughts of past miseries with people coming up, I focus forward on **future joyful experiences** with different people.

If I have nothing on the timeline, I use a Project Sanctuary habitat to simply create something attractive to think about instead that is relevant.

You can experiment also with what kind of "focal lengths" work best with what. For example, you can focus on very close-up future nows - five minutes from now or even less, all the way out to "on my death bed" which is as far as that goes; if need be, you can even go out into "the light" or the after death states.

Of course, there's a whole range in between.

The past run "focal lengths" are also interesting and can absolutely do with some basic practice because unless you take charge of this, you get drawn (contents-specific) into the same old things time and time again. With each repetition it gets easier - ooh ...

Whilst you're at it, you are ...

- learning LOADS about how you treat time, neurologically as well as energetically;
- your relationships with present, now and future;
- your preferred focal lengths;
- where and how bugging memories turn up;
- how you shift from now states into past states via memory anchors and triggers;
- and you really get to expand the flexibility and power of your conscious attention, how it works, what you can use it for,
- how your energy system and your physical states respond to this "attention led" energy movement;

and a whole heap besides - including ...

- outmoded goal-entities that were never removed or rescinded,
- things you just wouldn't want in your future any more,
- things that have been put into your future by others and you didn't even know you had them in there (nasty, nasty ...)

- how you actually FEEL about events in your future and how that affects such evergreen topics as procrastination, joy of life, identity et al;

... to mention but a very, very few benefits of doing this.

But aside from all of this good fun, the main deal once more, here is to

- take the focus of conscious attention firmly away from the past (total waste of time and very energy destroying)[9]

- AND from the Now (as it doesn't do anything and even if the Now should be wonderfully pleasant, put your attention on it and - boom, the experience is gone anyway. If you don't know what I mean by that, remember the last time you "woke up" in the middle of an experience, such as sex, and went, "Wow! I'm having a great experience!" - oh dear oh dear ...:-)

... and place it for now and until we're a bit more sorted out in all ways, into and towards pleasant and attractive future event to help us stabilise our states in the Now, get out of our own ways for once, and get used to that all important FORWARD movement of going with the Even Flow.

Try it. It is handy and it helps.

Calling up deliberately a time of the past to **work** with it and to **restore, heal, repair** it or simply to send it off to be rightfully processed and cleansed for storage in the energy matrix is a very, very different energetic move and perfectly ok to do at any time you feel like it.

This is also the same for the NOW. Calling this up deliberately or putting attention there deliberately can be necessary and useful. What is not useful is to stare at the now, fall into the now and *use* the now to re-affirm the now itself - states of poverty, discontent, non-success (thus far!) details derangement, "not being where I want to be", "not doing what I want to do", "not living in the house I want to live in", "not having the car I really want", "being all alone again" etc and et al.

---

[9] If you are choosing to **do** therapy or healing the past, this is a different proposition from drifting off into a downward spiral of depression as you remember all those past failures, pains, injuries, voices, miseries ..... from which THEN there was no hope of ever escaping, which leads to a no hope state NOW ... going down and down... blearch...

Innocent Energy & Perfect Personal Healing

Here is a truly wonderful "technique" that happened quite spontaneously in a hotel room in Germany - and it is so perfect and amazingly relaxing, I'm delighted to share this with you. It is also a very, very easy way for even beginners with EmoTrance to get some really good results all over, and to practise and experience energy flow and the evocation of Innocent Energy for clearing, calming and refreshing all the core systems "with a little help from a friend". It is a wonderful experience - as I can testify most personally and I highly recommend it!

Innocent Energy & Perfect Personal Healing

This was the evening on the third day of the conference, and just after I had returned to the hotel, still buzzing after a superb first day of the EmoTrance practitioner training and dinner with some of the participants - and of course, we'd been doing, thinking, breathing and then eating ET all day!

So all of that was very much still on my mind as I stepped under the shower on that night.

Now, at home, I prefer to take baths so that's probably why this particular move had never occurred to me, but as soon as the water began to fall down on me, I couldn't help but giggle and think of the "innocent energy" falling through your energy system.

Well, here was the "hard thing" happening and how easy did THAT make adding the energetic dimension at the same time, letting the innocent energy rush through my wider field to clear it after that whole day, all those experiences, all those re-alignments I had personally undertaken?

I'm really good with energy work but even so, it was delightful to be "supported by the actual physical presence of the water" in order to support the process - I spent the first delightful moments of this "totality experience" simply letting the water fall as it would on all planes, all levels, accepting and supporting the process and noting with increasing gratitude just how that made me feel overall - very nice indeed.

So and feeling far more connected all around and as though I had just woken up, I took the shower head off and without thought, my right hand immediately directed the fast stream of hot water to an erea on my left shoulder, near the neck, where a stress tension-knot revealed itself as soon as I followed with my attention.

It really was quite fascinating; I felt much **closer** somehow to the energetic happenings at that point than I normally do, possibly because of the preceding "innocent energy" experience and the water actually bringing the energy levels and the physicality together in the same place in consciousness; my hands moved automatically and my intention found it incredibly easy to "soften and flow" that knot, that energy blockage, the hot water being absolutely perfect to "stroke down its channel" as it went, softening more and more along its path down my back.

It was a really wonderful energy shift and I couldn't help but think that simply by the fact that no clothing was in the way and the entire path was being "stroked" directly and so that I could also feel it physically and energetically at the same time, it represented a kind of lesson in energy, physicality and intention all aligned for any human "child" such as myself trying to re-learn the ways of the totality.

There were other ereas of which I was absolutely aware even as I was soothing and flowing the first with the wonderfully welcome help of the warm water's gentle pressure on my skin; and I did those too, beautifully gentle releases each, so easy, so natural, feeling so very good.

I really didn't want to stop and then became aware of a pressure in my throat; when I directed the water there I found a sadness and a gratitude for "being cared for", something I guess I don't have a whole lot of experience with; when that blockage was released, I felt extremely serene and knew EXACTLY what I wanted to do next.

I directed the water and with it, my conscious attention to my feet and said, "Thank you so much for carrying me today, I really appreciate it on every level, and I'm sorry about those tight shoes, you deserve better than that. Let this water and the energy it represents clear all memories of hardship and pain away now, and that I thank you and love you immensely."

Thus, I went on all the way through every aspect of my body, stroking each part and thanking each part in consciousness, until I had arrived at my head and fixed the showerhead back to the holder. One last overall benediction from the innocent energy and the process was entirely complete.

It had taken altogether just under 15 minutes.

I don't think I've ever felt so light and serene in my life as I did when I stepped from the shower and to be honest, I was both moved and quite overcome by the experience.

I've tried and done a very great many things on the topic of self healing, self acceptance, self "therapy" and so forth in my time, but this thing which happened there quite spontaneously and so very naturally was - I can only say, of a different order altogether to anything at all I've ever experienced, by myself or with another.

It was really profound and so very, very simple in the concept; all it had taken on my part was the decision to let the process begin by consciously bringing in the concept of the innocent energy at the start, and what was normally a physical process only with the conscious thoughts being on other matters somewhere else already, had brought on a full totality experience of such love and caring, I've never experienced anything like it.

I truly hope you try this for yourself; even if you only catch a glimpse of what this does to your totality in the way of re-connection, re-alignment and mutual coming together from all sides in real caring and understanding, it will be worth more than many hours in therapy.

Finding The One

It is true that most people go through life with a nagging sense that there's something wrong. That they're missing out on something important. That no matter where they are, they are far from home; and that by themselves, they are simply NOT ENOUGH to make it through all the challenges of life. This is so very global that the time has come to look at this more seriously and ask ourselves, "What if that was actually true?" If you haven't found THE ONE yet, read on ...

This topic keeps coming up in private conversations and I do like this so very much, I thought I'd make a brief note on this.

One of the core surprises of my investigations over the past few months were the HEROS (higher energetic reality operating systems) which included the energy heart, energy mind and the factor X system I eventually decided to call the soul. Might as well. This system does NOT have a physiological equivalent and actually is the one which ties or bridges us as totalities into these very different, very OTHER realms.

There are so many aspects of this theory which are way beyond cool, it's difficult to know where to start sometimes.

One of the very most wonderful things about this is, if correct, that we were actually RIGHT all along when, trapped in the construct of the conscious mind and functionally detached from the rest of the totality which includes the HEROS system, we used to think things like:

I am not enough.

There's something missing in me/my life.

I can't take care of myself.

I can't work this out, it's too complicated.

Life is too overwhelming.

I don't have what it takes to succeed.

When I die there's nothing left.

I can't make it on my own, I need help!

I wish someone would tell me what to do/think/be!

How am I supposed to make a decision? I can't compute all the variables!

I must turn to someone smarter, wiser, more insightful for guidance!

I am lonely, alone and need someone else to help me out.

... and so on and so forth.

Previously classed as "signs of low self esteem", under the Triad theory they are actually nothing more than perfectly correct assessments of an untenable situation!

I also actually really like that under this theory, it is not only correct but basically a structural necessity of the construct encaged conscious mind to seek out leaders, gurus, kings, generals and such - because that would be the function of the conscious mind, not decision making in its own right, but simply to ask for further clarification and assistance from the Triad.

If a construct mind doesn't KNOW there's such a thing of which it is supposed to be an integral part, it will make these feedback connections NATURALLY with someone OUTSIDE of themselves when such a thing is offered. It's a vast relief to me actually to have a system where people are then not incredibly stupid idiots that follow every quack and smooth talker who comes their way because they're so incompetent, but that they indeed do this because it is structurally built in and a natural thing to be wanting to do.

One of the other and very first things I saw right away was that when people are looking for an "external soul mate", what they're looking for is of course their own HEROS.

And here we come to something that really quite blew me away - and what is I do believe the deep structural foundation of what we call here "Constructville" - the construct societies across the ages of men where all these disabled and helpless constructs come together to try and make things work somehow.

I believe at the core of the problem lies the "One Delusion".

It goes something like that. Construct men and women have the various available resources for a construct split up between them. So men get to be strong, honourable, powerful and logical; and women get to be weak, martyr-suffering, emotionally unstable and intuitive.

Of course, these halflings haven't got the resources to be doing anything very much by themselves in the Hard; and in order to make up for their shortcomings, they get put together into these teams to try and make a functioning whole out of the two crippled halves.

Most if not every single activity in Constructville, from dressing a newborn baby girl in frilly pinks to owning a HUGE yacht, is all designed to attract "the ONE" - that one other human who will make EVERYTHING all right.

Who will protect us, love us, cherish us, support us, feed all our needs, understand us, give us all those things we've ever been conditioned to value and dream about and then some.

It is really quite extraordinary to muse how all the various gender and also class behaviours and rules and regulations children get submitted to is ALL AND EXCLUSIVELY to that end - parents don't want their girls to be sweet, beautiful, with perfect teeth and every so prettily turned out for THEM or society, but actually, to give the lass a chance to "find the one" who will make it all alright. Same with the boys - all the exhortations to be perfect and clever and rich and strong is basically nothing more to create a nice strutting peacock with the requisite shiny feathers to which the hens will flock, so he can pick the best of the bunch, you know, THE ONE who will make him happy ... and with whom he will "live happily ever after ..."

It is indeed fantastic to muse on how in spite of the fact that it has just NEVER worked like that, not in 12,000 years of recorded human history, to get to have "everything made all right" by the finding of the ONE this has never changed at all, regardless of all the generations upon generations of men and women across the tribes who fell in love, thought that was the ONE, got married, found that they DIDN'T AND COULDN'T make it "all alright" and lived the proverbial lives of quiet desperation then.

"Well," thinks defeated mummy and daddy, "Well it didn't work for me, but I wish for better for my children. At least THEY'LL have a chance at finding their ONE. Let's enrol them in extra ballet-lessons, buy a couple of more cows for a better dowry and add three more tattoos, that way, they'll have a BETTER chance than I did ..."

I reckon that the reason this "the ONE delusion" has persisted so perfectly persistently across the ages and all knowable cultures in some form or the other (and it's always interesting to note how even the cultures with the most rabid mating controls STILL have fairy tales, music, songs and plays ala Romeo & Juliet in them!) is that the quest for one's own true self is such a profound driver, you can't not do that as a human being!

Only, being totally misplaced on the ONE "soul mate" (that term really drives me crazy! Come ON! We're ALL soul mates when we have access to our OWN souls!! There ain't just two of 'em - that is just so ludicrous, words fail me!!) what happens again that all these billions are going in the wrong direction, and in their earnest efforts to "get things right" for themselves and their tribes, groups, families et al, they are spending entire lifetimes grooming and preening, competing and fighting, working and earning, and ALL of it is completely pointless and deeply counter-productive if the end result is to really find "THE ONE" who will make you basically invulnerable, endlessly beloved and entirely immortal.

What I also found immeasurably interesting is the aspect of this whereby we've been trying to "bring things INTO the existing conscious constructs" in order to have them work better.

Dragging in resources or at least, trying to do that, which would structurally serve to - mimic the REAL effects of having access to the HEROS systems!

Thing is, you absolutely cannot drag the energy mind, the lionheart and the immortal soul into a self construct.

It just doesn't work AT ALL - and here we are again with one of those strange truths and drivers to human behaviours which are actually completely correct in all ways, but because they're so very misdirected, are entirely doomed to failure.

The construct must **go to the HEROS** and not the other way around!

Indeed, the efforts and acts to get the construct BACK to these systems and to re-connect it, could be termed a "hero's journey" - LOL! Or perhaps you could call it "the search for the philosopher's stone" or "the holy grail" instead, which if found, will make you immortal and lets you transmute lead into gold. And then some!

The self construct is already way, way too full with all sorts of things that don't belong there at all, but should have been passed over to the HEROS systems for processing, for resolution and most especially, for long term storage.

There's a lot to this but I would briefly mention that **memories held in the conscious mind** are what is disturbing the entire energy matrix, causes abreactions and reversals, nightmares, all sorts of problems, because they are really only supposed to be passing through on their way to storage in the energy matrix itself. From there, they are immediately retrievable but have that special quality that one finds with memories which have been treated with energy therapies sometimes - they are of brilliant clarity, incredible depth of information and richness, AND they cause NO pain AT ALL when they are recalled.

Anyway, back to the whole "soul quest" deal, the ONE delusion (when wrongfully directed to another human, or even in the truly strange "bride of Christ" versions which abound!) and what we can do here to do our own hero's journeys BACK to self.

Let's briefly go over how NOT to do this.

Sitting somewhere in a dusty cave and getting ever more lost in the construct, and then beginning to *hallucinate* angels and such from the sheer stress and desperation is blatantly not very effective. (For evidence procedure, please see Hermits Across The Ages. Bunch of raving lunatics! Poor guys!)

Rolling from one holy site to the other either horizontally or vertically.

Sitting in front of blank walls for 30 years and/or until your legs drop off.

Any version of stumbling through forests, deserts, up mountain sides for any length of time, with or without a company of elves and gnomes in attendance;

Hanging yourself up by your nipples for three days and having others beat you with sticks during this time;

Taking vast quantities of hallucinogenic drugs (which have a tendency to lend inordinate breadth and depth to one's own experiences of further illusions INSIDE the construct);

Trying to get rid of the conscious mind and to dissolve it altogether. Often attempted, of course doomed to inevitable struggle and failure as it's the conscious mind that's being used to try and get rid of itself - LOL!

Hanging yourself in a small plastic box from a crane without any food for 44 days and 44 nights.

Praying for getting this done miraculously to the blue fairy, or other potentially non-existent source which usually doesn't answer back.

Now that we've covered as to how NOT to achieve the homecoming of the construct/consciousness to the rest of the totality, we may consider what we can do instead.

I believe to have the right focus of attention is of the essence.

For example, directing heartfelt pleadings straight up and to the starry skies above tends to direct such messages straight outside one's own energy system - the HEROS watch it go by and shrug and say, "Ah well, that's not for us then ..."

With many things in consciousness and construct-city, it is often just simply to express a will or readiness for something to happen is all that's required - only the construct doesn't know this.

At an ET training, there was this gentleman who had had a heavy pain in his chest for about 12 years, on and off. It caused him much fear, sleeplessness, stress and all sorts and I have no doubt that when he came to the training, we were on the very verge of the breakthrough of this into his physicality.

Anyway, in true ET fashion, he was asked to put his healing hands on the place and to flow it away.

It did so most readily and the gentleman was really astonished as well as somewhat disconcerted. He said, "But if that's so easy, WHY hasn't it resolved before????"

I remember responding with, "Because you've never put your hand there before and asked it to do so."

That's the deal with the consciousness - that's its actual JOB in the greater scheme of things, to turn all these computations that have run through the entire system INTO ACTION. It's the red button that unless it is pressed, sod all else can happen.

Which is why it is counter-productive to try and meditate it away, berate it or undermine it in any way. We need it. It needs to be *in it's rightful place, doing what it was designed to do* and in conjunction with all the rest of the totality, with full support, guidance, help, co-operation and communication of the HEROS.

Personally, I haven't found anything better or faster yet than Thought Flow and Heart Healing to begin this communication process and to start looking in the right direction for "those who will make it all alright" and where "we" (construct selves) will finally be at home, come home in a hero's welcome and get all those things we always knew we needed and deserved. And THOSE things won't be plastic surgery vouchers or diamond rings, of that I'm pretty sure ;->

What one needs to do is then now not to even TRY to "integrate or discover one's female side" or to "enhance one's creativity" or such. All of that is really not in the brief of the construct, and when such things are undertaken *within the construct*, they tend to be only illusions anyway - projected into the walls of the construct to give that feeling something has been achieved, and yet one kind of knows deep down that it was only a game, it wasn't *real*.

Real is when it's a full body experience, physicality responding, vision going much clearer, hearing getting sharper, energy rushing and whole new realms of insights arrive at our fingertips.

So and to conclude, the very act of taking whatever VOWs were made at some point about the mistaken nature of "THE ONE", misleading ideas and ideals, all that stuff about what YOUR construct has to be like to get saved and loved etc. and to either snow-globe the lot once and for all, or to simply re-direct all of that in the light of the new information to start questing for one's own lionheart, energy mind and soul, is a very good start indeed.

The same would hold true to past and present VOWs, help calls and promises etc. to external "power sources" in whatever shape or form; dissolve or redirect them or simply pass them over so a space is created within the construct for guidance to emerge as to how exactly that re-unification process is to continue forward in each particular case.

A general statement of purpose and intent, spoken traditionally aloud and with one's hand on one's own heart, such as, "I now seek to re-join the totality." is also always very useful. If you don't ask, it doesn't get given ...

And just in case you're now thinking, oh no! Silvia's taken the romance right out of my life! Hope of romance! Oh no oh no!! please let me say this.

Two halfling constructs rolling around uncomfortably together have never really been anything other than a huge disappointment for all concerned.

Now, imagine if you will, if you were to put two humans together who are fairly switched on and integrated in their totality. What you get then is what they call "more than the sum of its parts" - and I am pretty congruent that A LOT MORE fun and romance on a level we might not even be able to conceive of as yet, can and will be had.

The Laws Of The Universe

There are two kinds of laws in the universe.

One set are the real laws of reality and the creative order.

The second kind are laws which people have made up.

The first set is useful, practical and knowing about these laws will make a person happy, effective and flowing.

The second set is not worth the mental paper they're stored on because they are simply wrong.

Example:

Universal Law: All things must evolve.

People Law: Healing means returning a body to the state it was in BEFORE the accident ever happened.

Apart from one set of laws being always right, and the other being mostly and usually completely wrong, there is another major distinction between them and therein lies some hope for any one who wishes to take matters more decisively into their own and very human hands.

This major distinction is that the human made laws may be changed at will, any time you should choose to do so, simply because you're also a human and thereby have the exact same right to make up your own laws, just the same as the next human (and regardless of how many velvet robes they pile upon themselves, gold rings or pieces of parchment to pretend to be a "better class of human" than your lowly self).

Human laws are only theatre, after all, there's nothing really particularly real about them - only people do tend to forget this, to their peril and their pain.

We forget this, to our own peril and our pain.

In the very last ever episode of Buffy the Vampire slayer, she changes the laws of her universe. She says that instead of one slayer, there should be many - indeed, anyone who wants to can become one from now on. So instantly, reality has changed and now there is hope and a whole new world has emerged.

One may think that fictional rule changing is not the same as "reality" rule changing but it must always, always be remembered that HUMAN LAWS ARE NOT REALITY but only theatre, created by humans for humans, and have absolutely nothing to do at the end of the day with the truth and the laws of the universe at all.

We further need not concern ourselves with other people's laws at all, but just our own for now and what laws we have each made which constrict and define our own universes.

"It is impossible for a poor black man to succeed."

"Women can't manage staff successfully, they're not ruthless enough. I'm a woman and therefore ..."

"In order to have a top ten hit, you have to be 14 and anorexic and sing meaningless shit, badly. I am not and I like to sing well about important topics so therefore ..."

"You can't make your own rules. You have to follow the rules of your forefathers. The forefathers said that pigs are dirty creatures, therefore pigs are dirty creatures."

Human rules are just nonsense - that means that they do NOT make any sense logically and of course, they don't. So in order to protect a law, once it has been arrived at, we have to delete things contrary to that law.

That would be the scientist who has a research project he well knows will give him a Nobel prize - IF it wasn't for that unfortunate spike in the middle of the chart. One single incident ... it could be erased altogether in one single stroke of the key, and no-one would ever know ... think of all that money, all that fame ...

This throws up another difference between divine or universal laws and human laws.

Divine laws HAVE NO EXCEPTIONS.

Human laws do, and in doing so, they demonstrate that they're not actually laws at all but just guesses that are clearly off the mark:

"In order to have a top ten record, you have to be 14, anorexic and sing shit material, badly. Hmm ... well except ... that guy who did the Smurf song ... and Bohemian Rhapsody ... and ..."

But the law's still good, generally, right? Those are just "exceptions which prove the point even further still"?

Oh come on! Baloney to that.

Divine laws have no exceptions. Emergent stars do not plead for mitigating circumstances. Population dynamics don't miraculously do wild things without explanation.

The simple rule of thumb - if it has an exception, it ain't a law but just some clearly wrong thing that HAS NOT TAKEN ALL THE RELEVANT FACTORS INTO CONSIDERATION.

"Women only marry men with big dicks. Well. Except for Peter. I saw him in the shower once and boy he has a small one. And he's married ..."

If it has an exception, it isn't a law and should not or ever BE TREATED AS A LAW.

Laws are immutable. Everything else is MUTABLE, up for discussion, up for grabs, up for revision, up for redecoration, up for a major re-write in the light of new experiences at least.

But do THAT long enough and you find out that as far as these human laws are concerned, there is no right or wrong and you make your own, and as you do, you set the laws for your reality, exactly how your reality functions, interactively, a computer game with rules designed by you for you to play for as long as you're alive.

If your dick is small, why not make a rule that "Women may have one-night stands with big dicked men if they're drunk enough, but will truly ever be able to really love and appreciate small dicked men"? Or vice versa, should that appeal more? Or one today that way, and tomorrow, another, depending on the circumstances ...

You make that a rule, or a people law in YOUR universe, and it will be proven to be true, just for you if nowhere else and that's a good small place to be starting.

Now you might think that if there are MANY people involved in these laws, such as the Hollywood law of the anorexic 14 year old which is splattered all over everything we know and see around us, it is harder or impossible to change a law.

But that's not true at all, because the law is really only for one person at a time. If one person should decided in a law fashion that the time is right for a really fat superstar who is 60 years of age and indeed, that's what is the truth about the universe in all ways (which is how people get human and universal laws confused in the first place!), then just watch it unfold. This guy'll be on Opera before long. Nothing can stand in their way. Buying in to other people's laws has never gotten Einstein a Theory of Relativity, nor Bohemian Rhapsody to No. 1 in the British charts.

Making new laws that are as POWERFUL as the old perceived "truths about the universe" were is a little challenging, but not that hard.

The very first law of course which needs to be changed is that "changing laws is difficult, challenging or impossible."

There are very many various entrainments which used to support that notion, right to the idea that such things are so deeply embedded in the unconscious mind and gaining access to re-writing them is a life long pursuit doomed to failure.

Of course, now we know that it is simply a question of understanding (or having a law to that effect - LOL!) that the unconscious mind is an energetic matrix which is seeking procedural guidance from the conscious mind, and will perfectly happily accept ANY law the conscious mind decides upon - even if they should be mutually exclusive, no matter how many there are, the poor old mind of energy will try to follow and plot courses for all these laws. It will do so even if they lead to self destruction and to tearing yourself into multiple personality pieces, at that.

For this to work, I do believe that a good communications system between the conscious and the energy mind are of the essence; and that it has to be addressed directly.

That might be just one of my laws though. A step-stone law if you will to allow more gradual change or to manage a gradual growing into the immense responsibility and power, and yes, joy of getting to write your own laws absolutely in the end.

Your own laws as regards the people theatre, that is of course. Not God's laws. They are not the issue here.

But, and if that should be an issue for you, make sure to make a law that states clearly, "People and that includes me are perfectly equipped to understand the universal laws."

That is a useful thing to have.

But other than that, and all things human made, are, as I said, entirely up for grabs.

What laws would you like to change today?

What laws have made YOUR life a misery and now, that you're at the helm, they can be abandoned, rephrased, enlarged, enlightened or simply rescinded altogether?

We have many, and as these laws are the deep structure to what is possible and what is not, and absolutely form the boundaries of what can be achieved and what is "outside of the law of probabilities", it makes sense that a good set of targeted investigations in that area would produce some interesting and VERY fruitful results.

Reclaiming The Power Of Words

This is the scenario.

I say, "God has given me this body."

X says, "Don't use the word God. I have convulsions over it."

I say, "I use that word. **I have A RIGHT TO THAT WORD**. I will NOT let those lying bastards take the right from me to know what I mean by that, and make it dirty and disgusting, and then teach everyone else that it is."

X says, "You're right. I have given "them" the power to mess up that word for me. I also know what I want it to mean. So it shall mean what *I* want it to mean."

X sighed deeply and started to smile to himself.

"You know," he said, "It is extraordinary how much better that feels."

This instance marked a true turning point in my personal use of the powers I have over my autogenic universe - namely the **POWER TO NAME THINGS AND TO KNOW WHAT I MEAN BY THAT.**

I took the term "woman" and ripped it away from the claws of convention, shook it and flamed it through until it was clear, clean and shiny once more, and then it was mine.

I am a woman and this is my word for a state of being that "their" usage couldn't even begin to encompass.

Like my friend X, as soon as I did it, I experienced an inordinate sense of relief, as though a great war that had been raging within me forever had simply ceased to be.

I tried the term again, tried it on to describe an aspect of me, being a woman and for the first time in my life, there was no longer any rage and anger, disappointment, hatred and sadness but simply peace.

The process was so simple, and so profoundly healing, that we continued to take words and re-claim them, re-shape them to the meaning that made sense to us, how we understood them, taking them back and the true power they represented.

Words such as, love.

I know what I mean by that, and against THAT, I have no argument - to want it, to need it, to actively seek it, and to accept it when it is offered to me.

My problems were in THEIR usage of that word, which had muddied the waters and made a beautiful and pure concept into a travesty, a monstrosity full of pain and suffering, when it is nothing of the kind.

So, ladies and gentlemen all, take your words and re-claim them, re-write your own existence in your own image and that of the creative order itself.

It comes very naturally and with it, there comes immediate peace and the absolute cessation of conflict that needed never to have been there - if we had only known just how powerful the magic of words really is, and their meanings.

I don't need a hundred years in therapy to reconcile me to being a woman any longer - for what THEY mean by that, I could NEVER reconcile myself towards. To my own understanding on the other hand, no reconciliation is necessary and the resolution is INSTANTANEOUS.

Further, by reclaiming the essence of such a word as "woman" in this very personal and powerful fashion, you are detaching yourself absolutely from the disturbed powerfields of the ages, that resonate with women victims, women animals, women suffering and women disempowerment.

None of that has anything to do with me any longer, because I am just not THAT kind of woman. I am my own woman, if you will.

From this follows more.

I also claimed as a word, I am a man. And I am human. As well as, I am a child, and each time simply replacing what THEY had meant this to mean, with my very own in-depth understanding of the truth of the essence of that, desirable, beloved and entirely holy.

So whether you wish to apply this to attributes such as beauty or power, to what it means to be white or black, man or woman, sick or healthy, good or evil or whatever "words" have caused you problems with their distortions and their meanings, please go right ahead.

It can only be for the best.

And what a truly magical, adult thing it is to do to re-claim the words and meanings for our own.

Art Solutions

Now of course, there's as many definitions of what art is or an artist is as there are reasons why the president can't actually do anything about poverty and discrimination, but that is bye the bye.

I'd like to talk instead about my personal observations about art and artists, and my propositions to do something different for a change.

Ever noticed that most successful artists have a major screw loose?

Sure you have.

When DO you turn to writing poetry, mostly?

In moments of severe emotional stress, when the "good behaviour" rules have broken down and there's a bit of honesty and connection for once. Then something of power and impact pours out onto the paper - like the "The Scream" painting, for example.

But in pouring it all out, and although this provides a temporary pressure valve relief, NOTHING MATERIAL CHANGES about the reasons or causes for that pain.

Nothing at all.

You can pour this bile onto parchment, and onto canvasses, and into twisted sculptures, and into screeching, moaning music until the cows have become evolutionary dead ends and NOTHING GETS ANY BETTER - indeed, if you survive that long because **the repeated accessing of intense states of emotional disturbances and pure anguish WITHOUT changing them into something else or RESOLVING THEM eventually, will KILL YOU.**

Just ask Jim Morrison. Or Janis Joplin. Or Van Gogh. Or Beethoven. Or any of the many others who gave their energy, spirit, life and sanity in that fruitless quest for pain cessation via art.

Unfortunately, these "pain performances" do get rewarded not just internally because they feel so REAL AND TRUE (when everything else feels like nothing or just so horribly wrong somehow ...) but also by the paying public who is just as hungry for something REAL AND TRUE and will encourage the artist from their end to keep dipping into those pain states, go deeper, we want more, more, more truth, more real...

Not knowing that **REAL does NOT mean pain alone**, and having ONLY pain as the access door to these realms of truth and reality, the artists go diving deeper for ever more pain and destroy themselves in the process.

As though this wasn't bad enough, they ALSO leave behind what can only be termed A LEGACY OF PAIN AND INSANITY for everyone else.

A Legacy Of Pain

Their energy of pain and true misery is caught and bottled in the works of art and people cry just as heartbrokenly successfully today over the Adagio in G minor as the artist did who wrote the goddamned thing in the 15th century - a legacy of tears, talk about "Cry me a river ..."!

How many tears is that good man responsible for, just in those last 500 years alone, just with A SINGLE PIECE OF MUSIC?

Just how many poster-reproductions of the "The Scream" painting are hanging on suicidal student's bedroom walls right now, making things worse than they already are, sapping those youngster's will to live even further still?

If YOU are an artist, is THAT the legacy you want to leave the World?

Sadly, mostly that would be, no.

Most artists don't wish their own suffering onto anyone else at all, not even on their worst enemies. In spite of everything, they retain a sense of rightness and wrongness, and, having suffered themselves so profoundly at the hands of the "general wrongness of being a human here under these untenable conditions", would rather destroy their own works of art than contributing even further by pouring even more desperation, misery and bile into the churning rivers of humanity.

However, the problem for me always lay in the observation that presenting someone who is ALSO suffering with a happy bunny picture of bliss and harmony is more likely to MAKE THEM WORSE rather than to do any good whatsoever.

People are DRAWN to the screams and adagios in G minor (of all things!) BECAUSE they feel a resonance to that truth of misery and forsakenness, of anger and desperation - it reflects and MATCHES their own experiences, and even though they may be well aware just before they put that "child abuse special" record on for the 14,880th time that it WILL make them feel even worse, they have to proceed because - what else is there?

What else IS THERE?

WHO ELSE understands their pain or how they are suffering?

Offering such a person in a moment of crisis a copy of "We are going on a summer holiday ..." will cause more harm in every sense - but if the rapport of the "suffering artist" is ALSO causing more harm in every sense as the misery is being deepened, endlessly affirmed and constantly re-experienced and focussed upon, what else is there left to do?

The Power Of The Solution

Well, the answer came to me most surprisingly and quite unexpectedly one night.

After having looked through an old poetry book of mine, which truly was a revelling in, a regurgitation of, and a serious attempt at deepening the "oldest wounds", pages and pages and pages after pages of it, it occurred to me that this truth and art might be used in a different and more pro-active way.

Rather than just "telling about the pain" (and thereby, reliving it and re-experiencing it every time, time and time again!) why not **use art to provide THE SOLUTION TO THE PAIN?**

All that is needed to achieve this is to make what was previously a one step process - namely pouring out the misery AS IT IS CURRENTLY EXPERIENCED - into a two step process, namely:

1. Becoming aware of the pain or problem

2. Asking directly for a solution.

And this is as simple as sitting down in front of a blank canvass, piece of paper or unshaped bit of clay, a piano or with a guitar in one's hand and thinking for a while upon the problem, getting right down into the middle of it, cry out for help, and then **letting the artwork BECOME THE ANSWER AND THE SOLUTION.**

Everyone and anyone who has ever engaged in ANY form of artistic endeavour will find this remarkably easy - you literally just let your pencil or brush paint the solution for you, in whatever medium you choose to work (rather than just "express yourself" - are we oranges or what?!).

"I am lonely and lovesick - give me a cure for my malady! Show me a way out, a star of hope, give me an inspiration! A colour, a note, a shape, SOMETHING that will HELP ME, make this easier to bear, something that is just right FOR ME!"

Images and sounds begin to stream, energy flows IN A WHOLE NEW WAY and in a TOTALLY DIFFERENT DIRECTION - and what you get as a result is ...

- NOT A DENIAL AT ALL of the things which caused the pain;

- NOT A LYING CHEATING HAPPY BUNNY ILLUSION in any sense;

- NOT SOMETHING FLAT AND LIFELESS at all;

... but indeed something that is so rich, complex, magical and superb it will take your breath away, literally.

Even a beginner's very first attempts to turn around from suffering to FORWARD MOMENTUM has immediate effects - on their states of being, on their levels of clarity and it does more, far more than that.

Immediately, and instead of "painting the same picture over and over again" as the old "pain expression" would have produced, we have ...

- o   new directions opening up;
- o   new doorways presenting themselves;
- o   at the very least a SENSE of the vastness that is out there and entirely unexplored;
- o   a sense of dawning excitement and most importantly,
- o   that immediate switch into STRONG FORWARD MOMENTUM ...

... as the artist discovers new forms, new ideas, new approaches and also, a different sense of what energies there are.

NOT ONLY pain produces that sense of truth and reality, magic and really being in contact with something profound.

THAT does but so do all sorts of other states of being, which people in society do NOT experience EITHER.

When societies are constructed to make sure the sitting room is never ever too hot, nor ever too cold, but "always just right" it is not just the experience of hot and cold that goes astray, but a whole lot more - the seasons, the many different sensations of wind across your bare body, in your hair; the smell of autumn as opposed to spring; the crispness of a winter morning and the pure power of a thunderstorm - so much is lost, so very much, and only the TINIEST PROPORTION of that is pain, anguish and misery.

And here's another thing.

Maintaining The Crucial Rapport To The Original Question

Artwork produced AS THE SOLUTION to a problem does retain the rapport and understanding to the CURRENT SUFFERERS OF THE PROBLEM - the "I'm not alone and someone understands me" factor that caused the poor people to put on the sad records and hang "The Scream" on their dormitory walls is STILL IN ACTION - only this time, they're not left with simply a "Highlights of Misery" TV report, but with **A DIRECT PATH TOWARDS A POSSIBLE SOLUTION INSTEAD.**

Just pause for a moment and contemplate what that would be like, if a person in a "The Scream" state was to come across something - a song, a poem, a sculpture, a TV play, etc. etc - which he or she would immediately CONNECT WITH, recognise and - WHICH WOULD HELP THEM TRANSGRESS their darkness and begin their journey to the stars instead!

Wow.

Art as a perfect solution.

Role Modelling The QUEST For Solutions

Now, a person looking at someone else's picture, or listing to THEIR songs, would not have exactly the same response and they might well not be healed by that second hand experience - but they would have a role model of a VERY DIFFERENT KIND as we have been used to.

A Janis Joplin who DID NOT kill themselves, but went on to become a superb artist who could touch and tell MUCH MUCH DEEPER, STRONGER, MORE POWERFUL TRUTHS about being a human being, and inspire others to find their own.

Would that be worth something?

To a single individual person?

To a single individual artist?

To their fan club of thousands?

To society as a whole?

To humanity?

Well, I leave that up to you to decide or wonder about; in the meantime, I'd like to close with the suggestion and idea that you might owe it to yourself to at least try this.

To at least attempt to create an artistic solution to a problem of your own. To monitor your thoughts and **your energy shifts** as you work your way through the process, and to learn something from this, even if you are only doing a doodle on a scratch-pad or a few notes on a piano - focussing on YOUR SOLUTIONS instead of re-iterating about your (already well known!) problems in the creation of artistic materials.

It is truly extraordinary what that can do for you, and I don't think there's a limit as to how far one may take that principle in all one seeks to do.

And let us not forget that in this format of seeking solutions, not only do you get your HEROS to speak to you in a way they otherwise never could, but also that you end up with a magical object, song, sculpture which has both YOUR WILL TOWARDS SOLUTIONS as well as the ENERGY OF SOLUTION.

Sing it, listen to it, read it, touch it and just notice how this serves to:

- remind you of solutions and magic in a moment of crisis;

- energise your environment, your person;

- notice the effect it has on others who may know nothing of art, or of your problems.

This is one of the oldest and most truly wonderful and precious ways of working with messages from our HEROS, and creating solutions for ourselves, from within ourselves.

Even if you thought you were "not artistic", just think again. Get a pen and put on a paper and allow your own hand to draw a doodle as you are asking for a solution to a problem.

Resolve your blockages to this and let your hand do the drawing, simply don't get in the way.

Then keep your magical symbol close by – and just watch what happens next!

NB: This principle was discovered in the creation of, "For You, A Star", in mid-winter of 03/04.

Heart Healing

The "heart of energy" is the centre of our energy body and the true ruler of how we experience life, what we think, and what we do. All major human emotions are "cries from the heart" - joy, love, ecstasy just as well as sorrow, pain, anger and fear. For 12,000 years or more, human beings have unsuccessfully tried to run their worlds via the mind and it has not worked to bring about a true emergence of Even Flow - a harmony of all in mind, body and spirit. Here is a very simple yet very profound technique for "Healing The Heart", a powerful tool for all who seek healing or are actively involved in human actualisation.

The Importance Of The Heart Of Energy

In ancient text, the "heart" is held to be the king of the energy system - the ruler.

Although I do not consider the energy systems a hierarchy, but view them as an interactive ecology, I also believe the energetic heart to be of central importance.

In my simple pyramid model of the human energy system, it is clearly the heart system which sets the experiences of a person - or in other words, if they feel pain, fear and sadness with all the corresponding effects on thoughts, beliefs, choices and actions; and let us not forget the toll this takes on the body directly and in second hand fashion through poisonous addictions and behaviours.

The heart system also provides the other kinds of emotional energies which likewise produce the opposite effect - joy, love, ecstasy, happiness, feeling at home and light, effortless, balanced.

Most importantly, the feedback from the heart systems sets the mental states for people. Simply put, if you are happy in yourself, you think positive, loving thoughts; you see opportunities everywhere and you have the enthusiasm and energy to do something with them.

The Importance Of SELF Healing

To me, it is of utmost importance to take the healing of our hearts **into our own hands**.

Let me explain just why I consider this so important.

You might well be familiar with the wonderful feeling of "being in love". The entire world looks as though it has been freshly washed and polished for you; rain clouds smile at you; gravity is much reduced, or so it seems.

You find a smile for every tramp, for every beggar and all your tasks seem so easy all of a sudden.

Being in love is indeed, a wonderful feeling.

Unfortunately, it is really easy to mistakenly attribute this state of being to **another person** or even, another entity, such as a prophet or spirit.

Because this particular person triggered the state of being in love, it seems logical that it was THEIR love which caused this wonderful feeling and being, but consider this.

How many rich people, for example, have been simply targeted by a ruthless trickster who didn't love them at all, but just pretended that they did?

And believed it, and as a result of this, danced off joyously, entirely happy, entirely in love?

No real love was ever given at all, and all that joy and happiness was entirely generated WITHIN the person themselves - the state of being in love was always theirs, and theirs alone.

It is such a shame that people don't know this, or if they do, don't really appreciate what that means. If they did, they could no longer be blackmailed by false gurus, tricksters and con men and women into having to pay for being allowed to feel loved. If they did, they would no longer be terrified that "this one person" might leave them one day, and with them, all that love would disappear, leaving them lost and broken, all alone.

Having a go at healing your own heart, as best as you can, sets you free from second parties and their attempts to manipulate you on the one hand, and on the other hand, makes sure that your heart receives true love at last, which is what it really needs to heal.

Although the false love of a trickster can make a person feel better for a time, or while they are under the spell of the trickster, as soon as the spell goes, the good feelings go as well.

When you address your own heart directly and give it your own love, you will be giving true healing love which is what your heart needed all along and you will be twice empowered by being both the giver as well as the receiver.

What Little I Have ...

I have said many times that our energy systems are not working as well as they could. The energy of "love" is something which is generated by the heart; so if someone's heart is broken, they will not be able to generate this energy as powerfully as would otherwise be the case.

Many people feel because of this that their healing might not be good enough or it might not work; or that they have to seek out a great healer so that these might do the work for them.

However, in the realms of energy it is not the quantity that counts, or the so called purity, or power, or anything like that. A prophet once said that the tears of a prostitute, honestly shed, were worth her salvation when the bowl of gold from a rich man was nowhere near enough.

I sometimes use the simile of a learning disabled child who after years and years of trying their heart out says their first word. It's just a single syllable, nothing more and yet in energetic terms it is worth more than a mind bogglingly clever speech a bored university educated artist might spout forth at any time.

To give ALL you have to give is the key to heart healing. Whatever it is, however little or however much, whatever you have, if you give it freely and willingly and with all your heart, it will be powerful and it will begin the healing process in that instant.

If your heart is "broken" and ALL you have is 15%, then that ALL is ALL and as powerful as it could possibly be.

That is why your healing will be so effective and so powerful; and although as more of your heart's systems come on line, are restored, refreshed and re-energised your healing will become more powerful, it will always only be as effective as your will to give your all.

The Benefits Of Healing The Heart

Even if one was to consider the energy system of the heart in a strictly technical sense as the nuclear reactor at the very centre of our energy body, it would be immediately obvious that just about everything else depends on the state of function and the output of this reactor.

Personally, I believe that all the major human emotions are "cries from the heart" - joyful and terrified both, it matters not.

What does matter however is the power of human emotions to drive endeavour, totally control thought, absolutely impact the body and of course, entirely control behaviour.

For thousands of years, people have tried to control emotions, not to have them at all and to run the world and our affairs through the thought system.

It has blatantly failed, because the thought system is and was always only the "general" the true "king" - the heart.

It is the heart which gives the orders and the mind which tries to carry them out, and really it is as simple as that. Emotion overrides logic, every time and to try and cut out your heart leads to nothing but nonsense, misery, and enormous suffering in mind, body and spirit.

Heal the heart and the mind MUST follow suit. It cannot do any other. It is structurally impossible to feel vibrantly happy and to think suicide; to feel love and think hatred or revenge; to be joyous and think sad thoughts. Intelligence, insight and creativity are all at their very peak when there are mental states of clarity and connectedness, when everything flows cleanly and a person is absolutely grounded in their own selves, and in the here and now.

Dismantling The Self Constructs

Lastly, I would draw your attention to a further benefit of concentrating on the heart that I consider to be of supreme importance and impact on the quality of a persons life.

People "think" the most bizarre things about themselves. Whether they are having delusions of grandeur, or delusions of misery or whether they are wildly fluctuating between the two matters little; all of these delusions are thought-constructs and worth - nothing.

Yet, their churning and conflicting messages and motivations cause THE most intense problems to people on a long term basis; some settle with one kind of construct or another and this will functionally become their very own cage from which they will never be able to escape; others drive themselves insane vacillating between this and that from day to day, always at the mercy of a stranger's look or comment to send them into a spiral of misery, or on a brief and just as ill-fated journey of delight.

- **All these different self-constructs are nothing but fragile thought forms at the energetic level, and none of them actually have a true heart - only the REAL energy body has that.**

By focussing on the one and only real heart, a stabilisation of the true self begins to occur. It becomes clearer and clearer and ever more powerfully apparent what is really the self - the true totality - and what was nothing but a half formed thought form, created from pain or confusion, as an accident, as a shield from fear or pain or simply because it was pushed on an individual from the outside.

By focussing on simply healing our hearts, we begin the process of getting to know ourselves again, to find out who we really are. What our true heart's desires are. What is real and what was always just an illusion.

Your Own Hands, Your Own Heart

So, I would offer you the simple heart healing meditation to try for yourself and find out for yourself what it can do for you. It takes no time at all and can be done for its own sake; indeed I would encourage you strongly to consider giving some attention to your heart of energy in the same way that you would remember to brush your teeth. Hearts go on when teeth have long become history, trust me, it is really worth it on so many levels, for so many reasons.

You can also use this very, very simple healing technique at any time you are sad, or frightened, and when you feel lonely.

It really doesn't matter why you feel the way you do, who it was that broke your heart or what happened in the past. When your heart is really healed, there will be no more history. You will be you and you will be new. In this spirit, this technique does not require any investigation and hardly any thought - just the will to healing and the gesture is quite enough.

Should you ever find yourself in a place where you cannot place your hands on your heart, it is equally effective to imagine the healing hands on your heart of energy, allowing your own energy system, who knows you the best and most intimately in all the world, do what must be done to help restore the Even Flow.

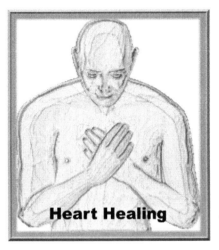

Heart Healing

The Heart Healing Prayer

Simply follow the instructions given in the evocation below. You might like to repeat the evocation as you place your hands on your own heart of energy in the very centre of your chest to help you focus your mind on healing the heart, and to get into the right attitude and state of being. Hold the posture for as long as you want, or just a minute or two; when you are done for now, take a deep breath in and out and come back to ordinary awareness. Please do not be deceived by the apparent simplicity of this method.

The most powerfully effective principles in this world have a habit of being extremely simple, and the theory and practice of Heart Healing are an example of this.

Heart Healing

I place my own

healing hands

on my own

broken heart

with the gentleness

and with exquisite care

the care

you would afford

a tiny frozen bird

you found

there on your doorstep.

With your gentle

healing hands

I speak in my touch

of warmth and love

of my desire

to make whole

what once was broken,

of my desire and my will

to right what once was wronged.

Whisper softly,

I will do

what I can

for you,

my little love.

Fear not.

I am here for you.

For sure, I am no angel

but what I have to give,

I give to you.

The words of the Heart Healing prayer are an example of something to say.

You can replace them with your own words and your own prayers and as a way to contact the totality firstly, and through the totality, realms and forces beyond as well.

The Heart Healing posture is inordinately powerful and extremely helpful, for example:

- Starting and finishing any energy healing endeavour;
- Communicating with the HEROS;
- To stabilise/anchor yourself in a moment of crisis;
- To state intents, evocations, affirmations;
- To begin meditations or other exercises;
- To ask your totality for help.

Make it your own and use it every day; it is one of the very easiest and most powerful "energy exercises" you can undertake.

ADDENDUM 3 - FURTHER INFORMATION

Glossary Of Terms

2 Minute Stress Clearer - Also known as the Marlene animation. Facial points only, used as a "quick demo" to get people to try EFT. http://1-EFT.com

360' Field Clearer - Energy clearing pattern. Oceans Of Energy ET 1, Tachyon-EmoTrance Special

7 Lessons In Web Magic - 7 Project Sanctuary events-lessons for magical webmasters. Web Magic

Addiction MET Protocols - Complete set of professional MET patterns for treating high end addictions and using a wide frame of reference in the definition of Addiction beyond substances. MET Practitioner Course Advanced Patterns of EFT

Advanced Aspects - Also Sequential & Simultaneous Aspects, Aspect Mapping. Advanced Patterns of EFT

Animal EFT - EFT Emotional Freedom Techniques for animals.

ASBD - Attention Seeking Behaviour Disorders. See also Harmony Programme.

A-State - Amphetamine like "fast energy state" induced by breathing technique.

Asha - Word/label used for a particular human quality of going on after defeat, without hope of the situation ever improving and in spite of constant suffering. Named in honour of an African mother who brought up her 6 children by herself in spite of being in agonising pain from a degenerative disease which precluded her from sleeping.

Attachments – Ereas in the wider energy field which were not generated or derived from the individual whose field it is. See also Evil CDs.

Autogenic Relationships - Key pattern for advanced Project Sanctuary players dealing with ... autogenic relationships. Project Sanctuary Advanced.

Body Protocol EFT - The basic EmoTrance protocol, backward-engineered so EFT users can also gain at least some of the benefits. Advanced Patterns of EFT

Black Space Of Thought - See Unspoken Realms. Energy Healing For Animals, Project Sanctuary Advanced

Bridging - Actively creating energetic pathways and connections in healing and repair work. See also Rainbow Bridge. Energy Healing For Animals.

Channel Clearing Protocol EFT - Advanced Patterns of EFT

Channelling - Term used to have information free flow from any aspect of the totality to the conscious awareness, such as from the physicality, or from the energy mind. Project Energy

Chaos Literature - see Melville Pattern

Chay! - Humorous phrase used instead of Hallelujah! or Jaya! etc. because it is non-denominational. A bit like, "Praise be!".

Chay Catena - One of the three central characters from In Serein.

Celebration - Track 03 on HD2 Heart Healing. An invitation to join life. HypnoDreams

CH Device - Structural device inherent in human neurology which creates false memories. The Story Teller

Child, The - Track 08 on HD2, Heart Healing. HypnoDreams

Class Of Self - Meta pattern to understand global features about the self across time which never change. Project Sanctuary

Client Avidity - 3rd alternative to client resistance and client compliance which is necessary for energy work. Advanced Patterns Of EFT

Conjunction - Refers to the drivers created when traumas and guiding stars are aligned to push someone from both ends in a singular direction. When this happens in a person, they become pretty unstoppable and are often regarded as unusual, either as serial killers or as geniuses. From "Goal Setting The Hard Way" essay.

Construct - Also Crystalline Construct. Artificial reality created directly by conscious thought. Most notably, these are time bound and not flowing, thereby being quite by design and naturally always wrong, untrue and never useful. Living Energy ET 2

Corn Story, The - Teaching story about nurture vs. nature debate. The Story Teller

C-P-M Triad - Creator-Project-Market as a single interactive system through which an exchange of information, nourishment and energy flows, feeding their respective needs and balancing them all, growing them all in the process. Project Energy

Creator's Block - When people have one particular highly charged experience of creating a "breakthrough" work of art or invention or such, but then go on to never do anything like it again or of that same quality, being then driven to "repeat the old" forevermore and suffering greatly in the process. Project Energy

CrimeLine - Resolution/Absolution pattern, timeline based, but focussing on the crimes someone has committed. Also see Quantum CrimeLine. Originally from In Serein. Advanced Patterns of EFT

Diamond Transformation - The act of changing by allowing major events to change the energy matrix. Oceans Of Energy ET 1

Displaced Time Chunks - Reference to thoughtfields which are not stored and out of time and sequence. These cause wide ranging disturbances. Energy Healing For Animals.

Dive To Diamond - Tack 02 on HD1, The Wisdom Of The Water. Opens extra-sensory acuity. HypnoDreams

Dancing Pixies - (Tanzende Gartenwerge!) Humorous term given for an attempted metaphoric descriptions of existing energetic realities that seem to make absolutely no sense whatsoever if one was to judge them by 2 dimensional logic or by previous experiences in The Hard and which happens quite naturally when someone seeks to describe an erea that *doesn't have* ANY equivalency in the Hard whatsoever in the first place!. The Story Teller

Dark Energy Systems - Energy Healing For Animals

Darling - Revolutionary and controversial evocation. Track 07 from HD1 The Wisdom of The Water. HypnoDreams

Dream Lover - See Autogenic Relationships.

EFT As A Ritual - EFT Article. http://1-EFT.com/main/

EFT Stress Bunny - Very funny animation from http://1-EFT.com/main/

EHA - Energy Healing For Animals - Multi-ordinate pure energy healing course.

EI Scale - Emotional Intensity Scale. Open-ended alternative to SUDS & VOC which can be used in "layered tracks" to track multi-systemic emotional interactions and responses in advanced MET treatments. MET Practitioner Course

EmoTrance - Revolutionary energy worlds exploration system that is prejudice free, physiology led and entirely experiential. http://EmoTrance.com , Oceans Of Energy ET 1

EmoTrance Introduction - First introduction to EmoTrance.

EmoTrance Hypnosis Release Induction - Hypnotic induction (for hypnotherapists) to induce and support the EmoTrance release process. Contains all the main wordings used by ETPs also.

EmoTrance Self Help Protocol - http://emotrance.com

Energetic Relationships Patterns - Invisible strings binding individual energy systems to others and also, binding artificial thoughtfields and constructs to and within each other. Advanced Patterns of EFT

Energetic Bereavement Resolutions - See also Immortal Beloved, Energy Healing For Animals, Advanced Patterns of EFT

Energy Dancing - (1) Physically moving ereas and interacting with them directly. (2) Actually dancing with energy. Oceans Of Energy ET 1

Energy Mind - One of the three HEROS. Previously known as the "unconscious mind", the energy mind is to the brain as the energy heart is to the heart. Living Energy ET 2

Energy Nutrition – Thinking of energy flowing as the equivalent of nutrients flowing into, through and out the physical systems and, in their passing and interaction with those systems, bringing the building blocks for existence, growth, repair and energy for all living functions. Oceans Of Energy ET 1

Energy Of Learning, The - Learning via the energy matrix which becomes *inscribed* with experiences. Living Energy ET 2

Energy Vampire - This is a pattern which deals NOT with how to protect oneself from those, but how to become one. It is said to contribute greatly to longevity, sex appeal, personal power and classical good looks ... Oceans Of Energy ET 1

Erea - Existing energetic reality, i.e. something that's really there and is energetic in origin. A more useful term than many metaphors (such as "spirit attachment") which only frighten people and seriously confuse the issues. Oceans Of Energy ET 1

ET - EmoTrance

Ethical Pledge - Rather than promising cures or any form of change or symptom cessation, the ethical pledge is for the healer to say, "I will do the very best I can for you." Energy Healing For Animals

ETP - EmoTrance Practitioner Oceans Of Energy ET 1

Even Flow - When everything works exactly as it was designed to work by the creator. Oceans Of Energy ET 1, Energy Healing For Animals, HypnoDreams

Evil CD Pattern - Refers to thought fields and other ereas which have become "stuck" inside someone's energy body, and once they're inside, it seems as though they are self generated and belong there, causing inordinate chaos. Advanced Patterns of EFT, Living Energy ET 2

Evocation – The act of raising and shaping energy by intention.

Extra-Sensory Acuity - Learning to pay attention to realities beyond sight, sound and touch. See also Night Eyes. Project Sanctuary Advanced, Living Energy ET 2

Fairy Dust - Humorous description for small energetic building blocks used in causal plane work as it appears weightless and sparkly; also because construct constructs which don't have this magical component are flat, lifeless and lack "sparkle". Living Energy ET 2

Fairy Wish - EmoTrance pattern for making wishes. Oceans Of Energy ET 1

Fault Lines - Damaged ereas which always show totality stress first and hence confuse ordinary "cause-and-effect" approaches. Oceans Of Energy ET 1

Fault Lines Patterns EFT - Advanced Patterns of EFT

Feeding & Care Of The Energy Body - Refreshing ET pattern originated from the MM project.

First Guitar - Metaphorical reference for someone whose higher energy systems are functioning and thus are creating a resonance effect in others, awakening their higher energy systems in return. Comes from the analogy of one guitar striking a note creating a resonance sound on a second, dusty guitar which has not been touched in years. Living Energy ET 2

Focal Time Movement Patterns - Living Energy ET 2

Forgiveness Patterns EFT - Advanced Patterns of EFT

Fractal Imagination - see Melville Pattern

Generative Gift - See also The Gift. More advanced version of The Gift which triggers incremental change. Energy Healing For Animals.

Gift, The - See also Generative Gift. Very popular and easy quantum energy healing pattern with many uses; perfect for beginners and children, powerful advanced applications. Living Energy ET 2, Project Sanctuary, Energy Healing For Animals , The Story Teller

Golden Horse, The - Original Fairy Tale by Silvia Hartmann.

Good & Evil - Essay on how people decide which team they want to play on.

Greeting The Day, Greeting The Night - Basic and important "energy awareness practice pattern", originally from Energy Healing For Animals. Oceans Of Energy ET 1

Guiding Stars - Moments of glory (numinous experiences) that shape someone's life eternally in their image because of the high impact and charge; see also The Higher Taste Pattern. Originally released as a special report Guiding Stars 2000/2, now only availably in Advanced Patterns of EFT

Habitat - Cohesive environment, landscape, event environment for a particular Project Sanctuary story or occurrence. Project Sanctuary

Hands Of Ghost - Non-physical versions of the Healing Hands. Also sometimes called ghosthands. Originally from In Serein. Oceans Of Energy ET 1

Hard - The Hard. Term used for physical reality as being less than, but part of, the entirety of REALITY which also encompasses the energetic levels, up and down. This term is used in order to not have to use the term reality in the limiting form because so many say reality and they really mean "the Hard", thus missing the most important points about real reality which is more by far. Also used in versions of "the hard table" as to make a distinction between a metaphor used for an energetic reality, or for a physical manifestation. Originally from In Serein

Harmony Programme - Hierarchical systems cause unnecessary conflicts and chaos, and can NEVER support or live within the Even Flow. The Harmony Programme replaces entrained hierarchical responses with a flow based methodology. First developed to high end Attention Seeking Behaviour Disorders in social mammals. Free download at http://a1harmony.com from Energy Healing For Animals

Healer Model EFT - Advanced Patterns of EFT , EFT & NLP

Healing Servitor - Functional erea with response capabilities. Energy Healing For Animals. Project Sanctuary Advanced.

Healing Star - Energetic occurrence between healer and client whereby the client's own healing systems are actualised or awoken. Energy Healing For Animals.

Heart Healing - (1) HypnoDreams track from HD2 "Heart Healing". HypnoDreams (2) Title of HD2 CD Heart Healing and title of accompanying E-Book. (3) Very simple stand-alone stabilisation and healing technique which also serves as a state anchor. Living Energy ET 2

Heirloom Stories - Powerfield metaphors which get passed down in tribes, groups, races, and families to maintain a cohesive construct and "racial identity". The Story Teller

HEROS - Abbreviation for Higher Energetic Reality Organising Systems and referring to the energy mind, the energy heart and the soul. Living Energy ET 2

Herosphere - Object from Varillian.

High Energy Morphogenetic Systems - Energy Healing For Animals

Higher Taste Pattern - Neurological organisation pattern normal and wired in people whereby the "best taste so far" becomes the new goal and target and overwrites the previous higher tastes. See also "Guiding Stars". Living Energy ET 2

HoloDreams - Also see HypnoDreams. Sanctuary State energy hypnosis with the vocal track deleted to allow the user to "flow into" the space left behind for even more personalised expression and experiences. http://hypnodreams.org

HypnoDreams - Also see HoloDreams. Sanctuary State energy hypnosis. Groundbreaking energy states work.

Ice River - Track 05 on HD1, The Wisdom of The Water. Reconnects in safety to the magical realms and/or parts of the energy system. HypnoDreams - http://hypnodreams.org

IEFT Instant EFT Practice Patterns - Instead of physical tapping, a single anchor or trigger sets a flash fire sequence automatically in motion to accomplish the meridian re-balancing. Advanced Patterns of EFT

Immortal Beloved Pattern - From "Energetic Bereavements Resolution Sets". Energy Healing For Animals, Advanced Patterns of EFT

Inner Child Healing Spiral EFT - An energy therapies re-parenting pattern for neglected, abused and unloved past children, adjusted for EFT. Advanced Patterns of EFT

Innocent Energy - A natural energy form like water which simply falls and clears, and doesn't judge. Unlike "the light", this is accepted and received by the entire energy system, whether or not they were labelled "of the dark" or "evil" and regardless of whether they are undeserving or not, hence by-passing a great many shields and layers of defences which often keep healing energy away from many parts and aspects of the energy body. Originally from In Serein, Oceans Of Energy ET 1

Innocent Energy & Perfect Personal Healing - Article/pattern for EmoTrance self help.

In Serein - Fantasy Fiction Trilogy by Silvia Hartmann. Book 1, Sorcerer & Apprentice, Book 2, The Cage, Book 3, End Of Dreams. http://InSerein.com

Instant Past Life Regression - No trance method to elicit past lives. Also used in character creation for fiction authors, PS games and therapy. The Story Teller

Isca - One of the three central fiction characters from In Serein.

Listen To The Land Pattern - Geopathic stress diagnostic exercise. Energy Healing For Animals

Lord Lucian Tremain - One of the three central characters from In Serein.

LoveLine - Timeline based pattern for discovering how much love someone has received in their lives and what they have done with it. Project Sanctuary

Magic Moment - Refers to a lightning strike instant actualisation of previously inexperienced energy body systems; usually the genesis of a Guiding Star. Energy Healing For Animals

Matrix Globe - Erea created and used for the transfer of information to the HEROS. Unlike Snow Globes, Matrix Globes contain pure data so there is no need to access pictures, sounds or feelings during creation and transfer. Living Energy ET 2

Moment Of Perfect Clarity - A totality state when something has been truly understood, learned, decided and there is congruency in mind, body and energy system. Energy Healing For Animals.

Moment Of Stillness - Crucial incident during the Thought Flow technique to allow consciousness a chance to set a new direction. Living Energy ET 2

Morning Light - Track 06 from HD2, Heart Healing. HypnoDreams

Mountain Part II, The - Teaching story about ecology and outcomes in personal development. The Story Teller

Melville Pattern - One of the Zoom patterns. Changes perceptual position infinitely and teaches smooth movement through infinite logical levels. Also handy self help pattern to change state and creativity enhancer. Project Sanctuary Advanced.

Metaphoric Abstraction Levels - Using consciously a range of abstractions to describe different kind of energetic occurrences across the planes. The more abstract, the further away from the Hard. Project Energy - Project Sanctuary Advanced.

Metaphoric Fluidity - One of the key principles of metaphor work, i.e. that a metaphor is something which is meant to develop and flow (prince turns to frog, frog turns to leaf, leaf turns to grassy landscape etc) as it seeks to translate and describe the ever flowing energetic reality behind it. The Story Teller

MindWalk - Experiencing a sequence of events in mind rather than in physicality. Advanced Patterns of EFT

MTP Multi-Tasking Personality Pattern - Learning to use and place "aspects of self" (parts) at the right time and in the right environment. Practice pattern from Project Sanctuary.

Natural Healing While You Sleep - Project Sanctuary related autogenic protocol to deliberately create soothing and healing energetic environments and states before going to sleep. Helps also with insomnia. Project Sanctuary.

Needs & Wants Protocol EFT - Advanced Patterns of EFT

Neverland Pattern - Training pattern from Project Sanctuary III to explain how damaging it is to try and create Sanctuary structures and habitats mistakenly in the Hard. Project Sanctuary

Night Eyes - The metaphorical eyes through which humans perceive the energetic realms and realities. Also see extra-sensory acuity. Project Sanctuary Advanced, Living Energy ET 2

Nothing Principle, The - States that a nothing is nothing and cannot be improved upon. In order to have anything other than nothing, one needs to start with an anything - which then may be shaped or improved upon to become a suitable something. Project Sanctuary

Oceans Of Energy - (1) Evocation Dedication originally written for Energy Healing For Animals (2) Track 01 on HD1, Wisdom Of The Water, HypnoDreams. (3) Title of EmoTrance Volume 1 Book. Oceans Of Energy ET 1

Ocean Wood - Track 04 on HD2, Heart Healing. Deep rest and absolution. HypnoDreams

Organic DHE - One of the many nicknames for the processes of Project Sanctuary

Organising Plane - Higher energetic level plane where ideas first form into being. Living Energy ET 2

Pertineri Market – Inter-dimensional meeting place external to any one given individual. Project Sanctuary Advanced.

Planes - Different levels of existence or so it seems to the consciousness as it travels between them, inhabiting only one at the time and thus thinking they are very different and possibly even unrelated.

Planes Confusion - Trying to do something on one plane that should be done on another instead and thus causing chaos and conflict. Project Sanctuary, Living Energy ET 2

PowerField - Thoughtfield made up out of many contributions from many individuals over a long time. PowerFields Paper 2000. Energy Healing For Animals.

Prayer Prescription - Basically wrapping up a custom made energy cocktail in words so that another can repeat the words at home to raise the requisite energies. Energy Healing For Animals.

Precious - Track 07 on HD2, Heart Healing. HypnoDreams

Presenting EFT To The Public - Advanced Patterns of EFT

Project Energy - Energy magic techniques set which begins with aligning the energy of a project (or product) before action is taken in the hard. Living Energy ET 2, MindMillion Intensive

Project Sanctuary - Quantum logic training manual which is both fun to do as well as being capable of generating endless, totally individualised healing and learning experiences for the player. Also known as the wellspring.

Proxy Tapping EFT - Advanced Patterns of EFT

Quantum CrimeLine Movement - States that the punishment for the past and current crimes was the original causative event/s and once this is understood, absolution has resulted. See also CrimeLine. Originally from In Serein.

Quantum X Grenade - Useful device to blow up thoughtfields and all other forms of ereas and a part of the energetic 2nd level origination plane and goal patterns. Living Energy ET 2

Redemption Patterns - Advanced Patterns of EFT

Reversing Reversals (Focal Time Movement) - Using attention to direct global flow directions in the energy system. Living Energy ET 2

Rainbow Connection - A method for bridging ereas to encourage information flow between them which will change them in the process. Fields Of Stars

Rainbow Bridge - Complex metaphor for quantum solutions & quantum thinking - Energy Healing For Animals.

Raising Your Metabolism With EFT - Hypnosis technique cross-engineered for use with EFT.

Receiving The Colours - Energy alignment set to enable active receiving of a wide range of universal energies. This is Track 02 on HD 2 Heart Healing HypnoDreams and originated in Web Magic.

Red Bicycle Pattern, The - The impossibility of physically healing a past need injury by fulfilling it in the Now, by for example a Grandfather buying the red bicycle THEY never had for the grandchild who never wanted it, or by buying a sports car when you're 90 when you needed it when you were 17. Project Sanctuary

Resonance Connection - (1) Track 05 on HD2, Heart Healing. (2) Also phrase used to describe the connection between souls, standing communication field. HypnoDreams

Sanctuary State - A particular range of totality states where all of the self is present - energy mind, energy body, physicality and consciousness. Technically placed at the Alpha/Theta overlap, with Beta and Delta traces brought right up. HypnoDreams

SBSFF - Humorous reference to "Silvia's BSFF". Unreleased.

Sereyah's Song - Fairy tale story for child abuse survivors and others.

Shadow Emotions EFT - Emotions/experiences around which entire lives have been constructed to avoid ever having to have them again. Also Holographic Emotions. Advanced Patterns of EFT

Shields - Energy barriers erected for protection consciously which now impede the Even Flow. Oceans Of Energy ET 1.

S-L-O-W EFT - Advanced Patterns of EFT

Snow Globes - Ereas created for the purpose of transferring materials and thoughtfields to the higher processing systems or HEROS. See also Matrix Globes. Living Energy ET 2

Solus Device - Holographic place holder for use when a component, puzzle piece or picture is not yet known, or to replace unwanted aspects without having to know what might replace them. The Story Teller

Soul - One of the three HEROS. Actually existing system in the energy body which is functionally immortal and survives physical death. Living Energy ET 2

Soul Quest - Re-orientating internal devices to be searching for one's own soul, making contact with it, and learning communication with it. Like "soul searching" only we really do search for the soul! Living Energy ET 2

Sylvia Plath Pattern - Creativity without performance pressure pattern to establish communications flow, and also general energy flow. For use in all energy work but also as a creativity enhancer for artists. The Story Teller.

StarFall - Track 04 on HD1, The Wisdom of The Water. Endless peace and rest for recharging before change is undertaken. Originally from In Serein HypnoDreams

StarFields - Metaphor/picture for all souls in resonance connection. Living Energy ET 2

StarFields Group - Silvia Hartmann's newsgroup. http://StarFields-Group.com

Star Seed - A version of the "Generative Gift". Energy Healing For Animals. Project Sanctuary

Storm Drains – Specific major channels designed to be capable of handling the strongest and fastest energy situations – if there is no damage to these channels or blockages in those channels and if they have developed properly as they should and have not become atrophied. Oceans Of Energy ET 1

Story Healing - Interactive and explorative process between conscious and energy mind to create a healing solution. Energy Healing For Animals, Project Sanctuary Advanced.

Tesla Machine (Organic) - Constructing something that will run by itself and in so doing, show up the flaws in its original design over time, giving the creator an opportunity to correct this before running it again. When it is perfect, it gets build in the Hard. Project Sanctuary, Project Sanctuary Advanced

Therapeutic Tapping Pattern - Advanced Patterns of EFT

ThoughtField - An erea which comes into being by someone making it via conscious thought. ThoughtFields can become very real if they are fed with a great deal of intention. See also PowerFields. Living Energy ET 2

Thought Flow Pattern - Self help pattern to break out of repetitive thought loops by passing on specific thoughts and irresolvable questions, paradox, desires etc. to the HEROS (higher energetic reality operating systems).

Threshold Model - Systemic model for charting interactive events which all together make up a presenting problem (as opposed to single cause-single effect manifestations). Energy Healing For Animals MET Practitioner Course

Totality - All and everything which comprises a human being, known as well as unknown, all levels, all layers, all dimensions, all times. Living Energy ET 2

Totality Chakra Protocol - Energy systems clearer from the MindMillion project. MindMillion Intensive

Totality Mirror Pattern - Physical mirrors only show the physicality. To see the totality self, one would use a totality mirror. Project Sanctuary Advanced

Touch & Heal - Internal & external mind maps for use with METs - Advanced Patterns of EFT

Touching The Creative - Becoming aware of "the great web of life". Also sometimes called a "numinous experience" (Jung's word choice for the same experience). The Story Teller

Treasures & Riches - Track 06 on HD1, The Wisdom of The Water. This is not about money. HypnoDreams

Unspoken Realms - Also Unseen Realms. A state where the mind no longer processes in thoughts, sounds or pictures but interacts with the energy matrices directly. See also Black Space Of Thought. Energy Healing For Animals, Project Sanctuary Advanced.

Unchanging You - What came into being at the moment of conception and has never changed, will never change. The very foundational (and immortal) core of any one given individual. Also known as the Immortal Beloved. Original PowerFields Paper, Energy Healing For Animals.

Varillian - Novel by Silvia Hartmann. http://varillian.com

Vortex Pattern - Shamanic type "merging with the problem" energy movement to discover an Even Flow resolution. Energy Healing For Animals, Originally from In Serein

VOW - "Very Overriding Warrant". Conscious decision made in conjunction with highly charged states that unless rescinded or fulfilled, can run an entire incarnation. Vows override values.

Web Magic - Free 7 lesson course on ... web magic. http://sidereus.org/web-magic/

What Every Person Needs - Evocation/dedication for the totality. HypnoDreams, Advanced Patterns of EFT

Whining Your Way To Happiness, Health & Prosperity With EFT - Using EFT to clear daily annoyances rather than super traumas.

Wisdom Of The Water, The - (1) Title of HD1. (2) Track 03 on HD1. Used for recharging and re-balancing energy systems and often used in EmoTrance trainings. HypnoDreams

World Seed - See also Seeds. Developing a world or habitat from a single object, thought, colour, emotion et al.. Project Sanctuary

Zodiac Cage Induction - A short meditation/PS experience to both break down prejudices acquired as a result of "Zodiac predictions" from the past, as well as teaching one of the essential zoom movements from Project Sanctuary.

References

The Energy Of Learning

First published 22. 10. 2002 The Sidereus Foundation, http://sidereus.org

Innocent Energy & Perfect Personal Healing

First Published 15. 09. 2003, http://EmoTrance.com

Heart Healing

Poem © April 2003; Heart Healing Article first published 29. 5. 2003, http://EmoTrance.com

Thought Flow – Breaking Out Of Thought Loops

First Published March 2003, http://EmoTrance.com

Thought Flow - Snow Globes

First Published April 2003, The Sidereus Foundation, http://sidereus.org

Factor X

First Published April 2003, The Sidereus Foundation, http://sidereus.org

The Totality

First Published April 2003, The Sidereus Foundation, http://sidereus.org

Focal Time Movement Pattern

First Published To The StarFields Group, http://starfields-group.com

Finding The One

First Published September 2003, The Sidereus Foundation, http://sidereus.org

Micro-EmoTrance

First Published January 2004, The StarFields Group.

About The Author

Silvia Hartmann PhD is a highly qualified and experienced trainer of Hypnosis, Hypnotherapy, Energy Therapies and Neuro-Linguistic Programming, author, international lecturer and motivational speaker. She is the Co-Founder and Director of The Association For Meridian & Energy Therapies and founder of the oldest established MET internet newsgroup, Meridiantherapy, as well as being a Contributing Editor to Gary Craig's EmoFree List.

With an extensive record in trainings design, she is well known for her outstanding ability to create trainings that allow the participants to understand and integrate even highly complex materials and making it easy to learn, easy to do and easy to replicate.

She is the author of numerous highly acclaimed original works in the field, including "Project Sanctuary" and "Guiding Stars 2002".

Silvia Hartmann's best-selling EFT Training Manual "Adventures In EFT" has to date been translated into four languages and is acknowledged to be "The Best Book on EFT".

After studying and re-searching Energy Psychology & Meridian Energy Therapies approaches in-depth for four years, Silvia Hartmann created EmoTrance™, a truly groundbreaking and entirely innovative approach to working with the human energy system for mental and physical health.

For Further Information about Silvia's Work please visit:

http://sidereus.org - News & Library Portal Of The Sidereus Foundation

http://silviahartmann.com - Complete Online Catalogue of Manuals & Trainings

http://dragonrising.com - Books, Courses, Events, CDs etc.

http://emotrance.com - The EmoTrance™ News & Library Portal

Also By The Author

Oceans of Energy: The Patterns & Techniques of EmoTrance, Vol 1

EmoTrance is a new system for handling the human energy body. 'Oceans of Energy' gives a thorough grounding in the underlying principles of EmoTrance™ for self help and use with others and introduces the uses of the system, namely self healing, healing others, goal setting, and state management, especially of new and previously un-experienced enlightenment states. Includes discussion of the developmental history of the system, stories from practitioners and first person reports of EmoTrance™ in the field.

Oceans of Energy

The Patterns & Techniques of

EmoTrance, Volume 1

by Silvia Hartmann, PhD

ISBN 1 873483 73 2

Available from

http://DragonRising.com - +44(0) 1323 729 666

and all good bookshops.

Adventures In EFT is the World's best selling guide for beginners to Gary Craig's Emotional Freedom Techniques EFT.

Now in its sixth revised edition, Adventures does not require any previous knowledge of healing, counselling, psychology or human health or changework at all – anyone who can read can pick up this book and start to make their lives feel a whole lot better, right away.

Yet, in spite of Adventures' easy to read, friendly and informative style, all the base patterns of EFT are here – modelled on Gary Craig himself and with additional modelling from the leading EFT therapists in the World, Adventures is also a fine handbook for any healer or counsellor wishing to begin to make use of the extraordinary powers of EFT to make profound changes in people's lives.

Sparkling with ideas, enthusiasm and lively suggestions for how to take the Classic EFT protocols and make them come to life for you.

Adventures In EFT

The Essential Field Guide To

Emotional Freedom Techniques

by Silvia Hartmann, PhD

ISBN 1 873483 63 5

Available from

http://DragonRising.com - +44(0) 1323 729 666

and all good bookshops.

The Advanced Patterns Of EFT

Primarily for professional therapists, psychologists and students and researchers in the field of Meridian & Energy Therapies, The Advanced Patterns of EFT by Silvia Hartmann, PhD, re-writes the limits of what used to be.

The first part of this advanced manual concentrates on the EFT treatment flow and describes essential patterns, techniques and variations on the Classic EFT process which move an EFT treatment into the realms of true quantum healing.

The second part consists of the advanced patterns themselves – treatment guides, techniques and approaches for guilt, bereavement, high end addictions, parts healing, shamanic applications and the original Guiding Stars patterns, released for the first time.

The Advanced Patterns Of EFT is an outstanding, original contribution to the emergent field of Meridian & Energy Therapies and an invaluable resource to any serious student, practitioner and researcher in the field.

The Advanced Patterns Of EFT

by Silvia Hartmann, PhD

ISBN 1 873483 68 6

Available from

http://DragonRising.com - +44(0) 1323 729 666

and all good bookshops.

Project Sanctuary

So now, we are working with the energy body, with thoughtfields, with meridians and energy shields and in the Quantum spaces where what we have learned about time, gravity, distance and more is no longer applicable. If we go into those spaces with our limited four-dimensional thinking, formed by the cause-and-effects of the physicality and after a lifetime of conditioning in the Hard, we will never be able to be at home here, never be able to actually understand and never mind affect these spaces and their processes as we should and as we can.

What is required is to learn a whole new way of thinking.

A logic based on entirely different principles, on entirely different laws of nature – quantum logic. Project Sanctuary is probably the first training manual ever written in the history of humanity to be a self help guide and device to teach quantum logic and to make it easy for anyone who wishes to learn.

Fascinating from the start, utilising immediately what we have remaining by the way of connection to our intuition, creativity, magic and the wider realms of the universe, Project Sanctuary is easy.

Indeed, it is surprisingly easy and what so many find so much more surprising still is the fact that this is not head-hurting school learning at all but exciting, fun, stimulating, sexy, funny, breath-takingly amazing and on occasion frighteningly exciting, too.

And that IS our first lesson in quantum logic – FORGET about learning being difficult or painful. FORGET THAT. That was learning the hard way and you can't learn hard amidst the flowing, glowing vibrant Oceans of Energy from which we came, and to which we will return in glory and delight, a homecoming of such wonder and awe, it will take your breath away.

For anyone seriously interested in getting really serious about learning, it's time to seriously lighten up and start learning for yourself, by yourself, in yourself – a one-on-one tuition between you and the universe itself. Project Sanctuary is your manual, handbook and tour guide - if you want it.

Project Sanctuary v3 by Silvia Hartmann, PhD

ISBN 1 873483 98 8

Available from: http://DragonRising.com +44(0) 1323 729 666

and all good bookshops

HypnoDreams 1: The Wisdom of The Water - Audio CD

 Developed in parallel with the breakthrough techniques of Energy Flow of EmoTrance, 'The Wisdom of the Water' is a fantastic collection of healing dreams, each one evoking a rich tapestry of healing energies, of states and of experiences.

You can simply allow yourself to relax and feel or you can actively use the journeys in conjunction with EmoTrance to run the energies being evoked smoothly and powerfully.

From the simply wonderful energy clearing and recharging experience that is 'The Wisdom Of The Water', used around the world by practitioners and teachers of EmoTrance with their clients and students, to the powerful and truly amazing 'Darling', this full length audio CD is a truly stunning experience.

Silvia Hartmann's masterful evocation of energies, subtle and extremely powerful, multi-layered and multi-ordinate is raised and supported by Ananga Sivyer's original music, using traditional healing instruments from shamanic cultures across the World. Additional background vocals by Pia complete the extraordinary depth and richness of texture as three master healers align to prepare your energy system, your body and your mind for deep healing and for transformation.

The Wisdom of The Water - Audio CD

Audio Self Healing Guide On CD

by Silvia Hartmann, Ananga Sivyer & Pia

ISBN 1 873483 08 2

Available from

http://DragonRising.com - +44(0) 1323 729 666

and all good bookshops

HypnoDreams 2: Heart Healing - Audio CD

A superbly healing energy experience awaits you. Three master healers, one intent - to help you heal your heart, contact your soul and to celebrate your uniqueness and the precious gift you are.

Use these powerful healing evocations to balance you, to lift you, to support you or simply as the perfect holiday in mind, body and spirit.

7 + 1 unique dreams of healing, 7 + 1 absolutely personal experiences of re-alignment and expansion. From the pure power of 'Heart Healing' to the celebration of 'The Child', we are immensely proud to present 'Heart Healing' with and by Silvia Hartmann, Ananga Sivyer and Pia.

On this fantastic CD for you: Eight wonderful healing dreams, to engage with and experience time and time again - and each time afresh:

Heart Healing, Receiving The Colours, Celebration, Ocean Wood, Resonance Connection, Morning Light, Precious, The Child

This extraordinary collection of mystical healing dreams was especially written for those who wish to both release the injuries of the past and to prepare for the new dawn of a different way of feeling, being and doing. Evoking powerful energies and images, sensations and emotions, 'Heart Healing' calls to your heart, your mind and to your soul and guides you towards reconnecting within yourself, and with yourself to the Universe around us.

Incredible experiences - as often as you need them, and fresh and different each time you embark on the healing dream. Each healing dream is an absolutely unique energy field restorer in its own right and for its own purposes. All eight sessions together make up a healing journey like you have never experienced - gentle, loving, and yet powerfully moving as master healers Pia, Ananga Sivyer and Silvia Hartmann combine their intent to raise you, restore and empower you, their unique words, visions, music and vibrations becoming the powerful wind beneath your wings.

Align YOUR heart, YOUR mind and YOUR soul in a whole new way. Pure Energy Healing, Pure Energy Magic - The Heart Healing Journey Complete.

Heart Healing Audio CD by Silvia Hartmann, Ananga Sivyer & Pia

Audio Self Healing Guide On CD - ISBN 1873483 09 0

Available from: http://DragonRising.com +44(0) 1323 729 666

and all good bookshops

For You, A Star: Essential Magic For Every Day

- 55 Positive, Magical Essences
- 55 Psychoenergetic Remedies For Every Day use!
- No work to do - just pick your Essence, look at the image, read the poem and take a deep breath
- and move away from every day stress, from trouble and strife -
- and instead contact the calm and healing energy of your Essence of choice!

For You, A Star: Essential Magic For Every Day

by Silvia Hartmann

ISBN 1873483 57 0

Available from

http://DragonRising.com - +44(0) 1323 729 666

About Dragon Rising

Dragon Rising is an International Publisher of high quality books, courses, events, audio CDs & trainings in the fields of EmoTrance, Emotional Freedom Techniques (EFT), Ayurveda, Creativity and Magic.

Working with cutting-edge authors and presenters at the forefront of our fields, Dragon Rising has helped thousands of people around the world to learn more about these 21st century modalities and therapeutic techniques.

To find out more about us, please visit our website:

http://DragonRising.com

You'll find our latest news, reviews, product samples free to download, information for affiliates & resellers and our online shop.

We love to hear from our customers so if you have any reviews, opinions, criticisms, praise & suggestions then we'd love to hear from you.

If you haven't got access to a computer and still want to stay in touch then we have an offline mailing list & news letter. To add yourself, write to the following address requesting to be included:

Dragon Rising
18 Marlow Avenue
Eastbourne
East Sussex
BN22 8SJ
United Kingdom

Tel: +44 (0)1323 729 666